PURE LAND IN THE MAKING

Pure Land in the Making

VIETNAMESE BUDDHISM IN THE US GULF SOUTH

Allison J. Truitt

UNIVERSITY OF WASHINGTON PRESS

Seattle

Composed in Warnock Pro, typeface designed by Robert Slimbach

25   24   23   22   21   5   4   3   2   1

Printed and bound in the United States of America

UNIVERSITY OF WASHINGTON PRESS
uwapress.uw.edu

LIBRARY OF CONGRESS CATALOGING-IN-PUBLICATION DATA
Names: Truitt, Allison, author.
Title: Pure Land in the making : Vietnamese Buddhism in the
   US Gulf South / Allison J. Truitt.
Description: Seattle : University of Washington Press, 2021. | Includes
   bibliographical references and index.
Identifiers: LCCN 2020043714 (print) | LCCN 2020043715 (ebook) |
   ISBN 9780295748467 (hardcover) | ISBN 9780295748474 (paperback) |
   ISBN 9780295748481 (ebook)
Subjects: LCSH: Pure Land Buddhism—Gulf States. | Vietnamese Americans—
   Religious life—Gulf States. | United States—Emigration and immigration—
   Religious aspects—Buddhism. | United States—Civilization—Pure Land
   influences.
Classification: LCC BQ8502.U72 G8587 2021 (print) | LCC BQ8502.U72 (ebook) |
   DDC 294.3/9260976—dc23
LC record available at https://lccn.loc.gov/2020043714
LC ebook record available at https://lccn.loc.gov/2020043715

The paper used in this publication is acid free and meets the minimum requirements of American National Standard for Information Sciences—Permanence of Paper for Printed Library Materials, ANSI Z39.48–1984.∞

To all those who contributed to making Buddhism in its many forms along the US Gulf Coast

CONTENTS

PREFACE

This book about Vietnamese Buddhism emerged out of a confluence of my academic interests, family relations, and a hurricane. In July 2005, I arrived as a new professor in New Orleans. I settled into my new job, but my husband, a Vietnamese national, was not authorized to work. He spent his days exploring the edges of the city—its easternmost neighborhood and the west bank of the Mississippi River—where Vietnamese refugees and immigrants had resettled after 1975. I joined him one Sunday at a Buddhist temple for Vu Lan, popularly known as Vietnamese Mother's Day, which is celebrated during the seventh lunar month and whose ritual significance resides in liberating souls trapped in the lower regions of hell. The connections we made there proved fortuitous. Later that week, Hurricane Katrina made landfall in Florida and then entered the Gulf of Mexico, where it rapidly intensified. Its projected path headed straight to New Orleans. One of the lay leaders of the temple called and urged us to leave the city. My husband, our eleven-month-old daughter, and I left for Houston the next day, with only the Louisiana driver's license my husband had recently obtained as identification to prove our status as New Orleans residents.

In Houston, we found solace with people we had met at the temple who were also adrift. We took shelter with friends of my husband's family. They guided us around the city, helping us figure out the vast array of state and social services available for Katrina evacuees. While we were not refugees, we were now participants in a system that refugees had learned to navigate on their road to becoming citizens.[1] After a month, we moved into an apartment provided by Boat People SOS, an organization that transformed itself from resettling Southeast Asian refugees to aiding people displaced by Hurricane Katrina. When we returned to New Orleans at the end of 2005, grateful for the companionship and support we had received during our stay in Houston, we continued to attend services at the Buddhist temple.

Not everyone we met that August returned. The resident monk left for Atlanta, Georgia. Many of the members relocated from New Orleans and the lower parishes along the Mississippi River to cities in other states. Not surprisingly, the temple did not garner the media attention that the prominent Catholic church nearby did for mobilizing Vietnamese parishioners to rebuild their neighborhood infrastructure. The temple's story was less about resilience than impermanence, less about the guiding hand of spiritual leaders than institutional instability. Eventually, with the hard work of its members and a generous insurance payout for wind damage during the hurricane, the temple was not just repaired but was transformed by the construction of a prominent worship hall.

Gradually, I came to understand how the lack of media attention was not merely a matter of reporting in post-Katrina New Orleans, but a question of how Buddhism was portrayed in the United States. In the years after 2005, I taught a seminar, "Global Vietnam," and would occasionally take a few interested college students at Tulane University for a regular Sunday service held at one of the four temples in New Orleans. The service consisted of chanting in Vietnamese, bowing, and listening to a talk by a monk in Vietnamese for thirty or so minutes. These services tried the students' patience. One said that if they had only meditated, she would have enjoyed the experience. On another occasion, I brought several students to a different temple, where a Vietnamese monk who had received a PhD in India and taught at one of the leading Buddhist universities in Vietnam would be speaking. The monk first led the group in reciting an English translation of the Heart Sutra, one of the most frequently recited Mahayana texts, and he then lectured on the sutra's most famous but perplexing lines: "Form is emptiness; emptiness is form." I later asked the students if they had learned about the Heart Sutra in their college class on Buddhism; they had not. I realized then that Vietnamese Buddhists were overlooked in multiple ways. First, the focus on the post-Katrina recovery of the Vietnamese community centered on the Catholic Church's initiatives, and, second, Buddhism as taught to US students emphasized the ancient past, not the actual practices of contemporary Buddhist communities just a thirty-minute drive away. This book began then as a path toward addressing those omissions.

As an anthropologist, I was trained in Asian studies, not Asian American studies. My first project focused on money, not religion. My entry point to pagodas in southern Vietnam was on the eve of the lunar New Year, when people collected *lộc*, a gift blessed by Buddha. One year, I visited a pagoda just off one of the major boulevards in Ho Chi Minh City, Vietnam's largest city. Its ornate and lavish façade was hidden from view, unless one stood back against the wall and looked straight up. A monk distributed red envelopes, each containing a hundred-dong note with a typewritten Buddhist saying taped to its face. In 2002, inflation and currency devaluations had eroded the value of the money so much that vendors refused to accept those notes. What brought people to the temple was not the sayings, and certainly not the economic value represented by those notes, but rather the promise of good fortune in the coming year.

I describe these sorts of practices in my book *Dreaming of Money in Ho Chi Minh City* to show how people in southern Vietnam used money as a symbolic token for fashioning themselves within a rapidly expanding marketplace. They handled not one but several currencies—gold ingots bearing the stamp of the Saigon Jewelry Company, US dollars, and the state-issued Vietnamese dong—all held together by the abstraction of money. People incorporated money into their ritual life, both as votive offerings to the dead and as money that would return as blessings, like the hundred-dong notes that the monk had passed out. But they also expressed concerns over the source of value of these money-objects, often scrutinizing them as if to discern how the material objects could sustain the value they purportedly represented. Much of what people saw in money reflected their recent experiences with currency reforms, hyperinflation, and devaluation. Cash in Vietnam, I learned, was not at all transparent, but an object that conveyed social and moral values, binding individuals into a community through its circulation. People exchanged bills, despite their suspicions that what they handled might be counterfeit.

Similar concerns spurred my interest in Buddhism. While many Vietnamese regard Buddhism as a source of tradition and a conveyor of cultural values, they also see the making of temples as contentious and open to debate. As in Vietnam, people expressed their devotion by engaging in ritual activities, but they also gossiped. They questioned the flows of money, expressed skepticism over spiritual authority, and even abandoned monks and temples, exposing what I argue in this book are the politics of Buddhism's transmission to the Gulf South. Spirituality, like money, accrues meaning from people's circumstances, relations, and ideals.

Yet not all Vietnamese in the Gulf South who identify as Buddhist participate in temple activities. Some are drawn to Tibetan Buddhism or Soka Gakkai. Others are in contact with not one but multiple faith-based communities. My goal is not to provide a representative ethnographic portrayal of Vietnamese temples on the Gulf Coast but to show how, through making Buddhism, participants also make sense of their collective place in the world. I do so by drawing attention to "compatriot Buddhists," fellow Vietnamese who do not regularly attend services or even identify as Buddhist but come to the temple on occasion to enjoy its convivial atmosphere. Temples are part of the material infrastructure of diasporic formation, and these diasporic subjects are, in turn, part of how Buddhism has become grounded in the Gulf South.

The temples at the heart of this study are located in an area ranging from southwestern Louisiana to the Florida Panhandle, no more than a day's drive from New Orleans on Interstate 10. Although I had visited these temples numerous times in the aftermath of Katrina, my study of Vietnamese Buddhism began in earnest in 2013. I selected the temples not because they represented particular sects or lineages but because they were the ones through which my husband and I had prior connections to the community. I knew the monks and some of the lay members, and they patiently listened to my questions, explained the history of the temples, and welcomed me into their homes. Thus, as with any ethnographic project, what I came to know was contingent on the conversations I had, the places I visited, the people I met. I did not include any Buddhist temples in Houston, home to one of the largest Vietnamese populations in the United States. As one of the most ethnically and racially diverse cities in the United States, its economic growth has eclipsed that of New Orleans, Biloxi, and Mobile, the port cities of the region I cover in this book. Houston instead marked an end point of sorts to this study: a point of arrival for many Buddhist monks from Vietnam and a destination for those who sought to establish new temples. I also did not include Magnolia Grove, a monastery in Batesville, Mississippi, established by Zen master Thích Nhất Hạnh, located about a five-hour drive from New Orleans and thus just beyond the geographic scope of my study. His teachings, nevertheless, have shaped the practice of some of the monks and lay practitioners described in this book.

Between 2013 and 2017, I attended more than fifty events in addition to Sunday services. On occasion, I served as a translator for monks who held retreats for English and Vietnamese speakers, or I transcribed their dharma talks. I publicized events, and during large celebrations, I prepped vegetables and washed out pots as I came to learn that kitchens are both the hearts and the hot spots of these communities. Afternoons setting up and taking down rows upon rows of folding chairs made me appreciate the labor required for large-scale celebrations.

I also collected twenty life histories. Some people had come to the United States in the 1970s, and others in the 1990s; thus, their life histories often included reflections on the differences in how they practiced

Buddhism in Vietnam and the United States. Some were middle-class professionals such as teachers and accountants, and men and women were roughly equally represented. I conducted interviews in Vietnamese and English. While I transcribed and translated the interviews, I also relied on native Vietnamese speakers for interpretation. The language of Buddhism, as any student can attest, draws on a vocabulary that seems familiar but conveys ideas that can be difficult to grasp. I have endeavored not to rely on Buddhist terms but to render discussions in everyday language.

My family was integral to the study. My husband and our two children often accompanied me. For those temples at a distance, my family and I would arrive the night before and sleep in a room or hut designated for retreatants. On a few occasions, when the event attracted many people, we would sleep on the floor of the worship hall. It was often at moments away from my formal research questions and from the sacred space that I learned the most, as I washed dishes or carried plates of food from the kitchen to the worship hall.

It was not only through my family's participation but also through their reluctance to participate that I came to understand the vicissitudes of support for the temples. At various times, our two children, my husband's parents, his siblings visiting from Vietnam, and even his nieces, who attended a local private high school, came with me. This unwieldy group turned out to be instructive as I gained insight into the tensions that flared over people's financial contributions and involvement, the aversion of teenagers to listen to dharma talks or attend lengthy ceremonies, and even the preferences of elderly Vietnamese regarding what they considered proper comportment on the part of monks. I also came to understand the shifting forms of participation. My father-in-law often hung back, politely demurring whenever a monk asked him to fill in the name of a deceased family member to be blessed during a formal service. His hesitation was not that he was not Buddhist, but that he was a different sort of Buddhist, trained in an esoteric form known as Ngũ Trí Như Lai, or the Five Wisdom Buddhas. He read the Lotus Sutra and chased away invisible spirits from our front porch. In Vietnam, he had blessed amulets that people carried with them when they escaped the country by boat. He was also an architect, and upon his retirement, he designed several temples, including one in India. His biography belied the divisions between the popular and the cosmopolitan, divisions that practitioners must bridge as they make Buddhism along the Gulf Coast.

My husband, Quang Huynh, was a crucial contributor to the project, and during the research he became a dedicated student of Buddhism. In the car, he listened to recorded dharma talks, and at home, he sat up late to chant passages from a Vietnamese-language version of the Lotus Sutra, underlining terms that he found perplexing with our son's colored pencils. During one trip to a monastery in Florida, my family took part in a ceremony known as "taking refuge in the Three Jewels," in which one declares the intention to become Buddhist by taking refuge in Buddha, the Dharma, and the Sangha and adhering to five precepts. The monk who performed the ceremony gave each of us dharma names and a "Buddhist passport" to the Pure Land. Still, his dedication to his practice reminded me that my faith was not as a disciple of Buddha but to the discipline of anthropology. Although I spoke Vietnamese and had kin connections by marriage, I was still an outsider, a foreigner, or *người ngoại quốc*, a term I saw used on calendars to designate retreats offered for English-speaking, non-Vietnamese participants. This term thus does political work by inverting the dynamics of belonging in which the refugee, immigrant, and Asian are seen as foreign. Ultimately, my presence as an interested outsider shaped what I saw and where I directed my attention. I hope that, within these limitations, this study will contribute to understanding the politics of making Buddhism in the Gulf South.

ACKNOWLEDGMENTS

A book may carry the name of a single author, but it is produced by the work of numerous people. I first want to express my gratitude for those people who welcomed me into their spaces of worship and homes, indulged my children during retreats and formal services, patiently answered my questions, and packed to-go boxes of food when my family and I headed back to New Orleans. I especially want to thank Thích Tịnh Từ, Thích Nữ Thanh Diệu Giác, Thích Thiện Trí, Thích Nguyên Tâm, Thích Giới Minh, Thích Nữ Thanh Diệu Mai, and Thích Nữ Thanh Trang for sharing the dharma with me for several years. Thích Nữ Thanh Diệu Giác has been an influential teacher, especially for my two children, and for holding a monthly retreat in English that drew people from New Orleans. Thích Thiện Trí offered retreats and classes and spoke to my students. In addition, I wish to thank Bác Thông, Cô Thanh, John-Hoa Nguyễn, Chị Yến, Chú Phước, Bác Sáu Long, Cô Huệ Hiền, Cô Bi Ngọc, Bi Quý, and Diệu Nguyệt, who have supported my journey. I also want to express my appreciation to Denise Graves, Angela King, Kelly LaCrosse, and Wendy Gaugin, who partook in some of the activities and transformed the lessons in order to bring them to communities who never stepped into the spaces described in this book.

Tulane University provided funding from a Marshall Grant from the Center for the Gulf South and a Glick Fellowship through the School of Liberal Arts to pay for a research assistant and cover some travel costs. Vy Dao, now at Columbus State University, assisted me with this project in its early stages, drawing on her in-depth ethnographic work across the Gulf South. Adam Beauchamp, now at Florida State University, diligently tracked down sources. My colleagues Adeline Masquelier, Kathy Carlin, and Michele White read early drafts of some of the chapters and provided insightful guidance. I also benefited from the collective work of colleagues working on similar issues, including Mark VanLandingham, Mai Do, Jana

Lipman, Carl Bankston, Bill Balee, Nick Spitzer, Sabia McCoy, Claudia Chávez Argüelles, and Andy McDowell, as well as colleagues outside Tulane, especially Maida Owens, Nina Hien, Ivan Small, Doreen Lee, Hung Cam Thai, Janet Hoskins, Thien-Huong T. Ninh, Dat Nguyen, and Erick White. Tara Dankel applied her keen editorial eye to shape a later draft of the introduction. This project emerged in part through discussions with my students, and I want to thank Jenny Ly and Loc Nguyen and especially my doctoral student Shao-Yun Chang, who read a draft of the manuscript.

Over the past five years, I had the opportunity to present this work to different audiences. Janet Hoskins encouraged me to think beyond the Gulf South to the transpacific at a University of Southern California conference. Petra Kuppinger included me in a panel, "Religion in the City," at the American Anthropological Association meetings and helped me to locate my argument more firmly in the city. At Tulane, my colleague Jana Lipman and I had the pleasure of hosting Yến Lê Espiritu, who read an early draft of the introduction and provided substantial critiques of my framework. She raised provocative questions about the work of Buddhist monks and practitioners at refugee camps, questions only touched upon in this book.

Some of the work presented in this book has been previously published, and I gratefully acknowledge the work of the editors, anonymous reviewers, and production staff who were instrumental in publishing material that appears in this book. Chapters 1 and 5 contain some material that was previously published as "Offerings to Kings and Buddha: Vietnamese Ritual Activities at Chua Bo De, Louisiana" (Louisiana Division of the Arts, Department of Culture, Recreation, and Tourism, Baton Rouge, 2006). Chapter 3 contains material previously published as "Bringing Buddha to the City," *City and Society* 31, no. 1 (2019): 17–33. Chapter 4 is based on previously published essays, "Not a Day but a Vu Lan Season: Celebrating Filial Piety in the Vietnamese Diaspora," *Journal of Asian American Studies* 18, no. 3 (2015): 289–311, and "Quán Thế Âm of the Transpacific," *Journal of Vietnamese Studies* 12, no. 2 (2017): 83–107.

For several years, Lorri Hagman of the University of Washington Press expressed steadfast interest in this project. She recruited two readers, who provided early substantive and critical feedback, and I hope those readers and Lorri see their hand in reshaping the book's arguments and presentation. I owe a special thanks to one of those readers, who generously read two more versions of this manuscript. Finally, I also want to acknowledge Margaret Sullivan and the rest of the production staff at the University of Washington Press, who moved this book into production so that it could reach a wider audience, as well as Jane Lichty, whose meticulous copyediting smoothed over my sentences and nudged me to clarify my meaning.

As this book makes clear, the family is a cornerstone of spiritual practices, even if they never attend formal religious services. My parents and sisters gave me their wholehearted support. My partner, Quang Huynh, opened many doors through his sheer friendliness and healing hands. His parents offered insight into their own experiences and the role of Buddhism within the family. Finally, our children, Kim Nhật and Quang Minh, accompanied us on retreats, to festivals, and during ordinary services. They carried flowers, dressed as baby Buddha, and chanted mantras. I began this project with the hope harbored by many parents, that our children would come to understand the sensibilities and ethical perspectives shaping how their extended family saw the world. It takes numerous people to build these institutions, and it is to their sincere efforts that I dedicate this book with the hope that it may be worthy of their gifts. All shortcomings and errors are mine.

PURE LAND IN THE MAKING

Introduction

Making Vietnamese Buddhism

I N 1974, a young monk from Vietnam arrived in the United States. Thích Tịnh Từ's destination was "Gold Mountain," as Asian migrants often called the part of Northern California that drew them with promises of fortune. His first stop, however, was Los Angeles, where he rented a small room in the International Buddhist Meditation Center, an institution founded in 1970 by the Venerable Thích Thiên-Ân, a well-known Buddhist studies scholar and Zen master from Vietnam.[1] The young monk studied during the day and washed dishes at a restaurant at night to earn money. Soon the long hours of study and work took their toll, and, forced to choose between the two, he soon stopped studying to work full-time as a dishwasher. Little did he know that events in Vietnam would quickly draw him back into the fold to guide his fellow Vietnamese Buddhists under unimaginable conditions.

In spring 1975, the Republic of Vietnam, also known as South Vietnam, collapsed under pressure from communist forces. Fearing for their safety under the new regime, 130,000 men, women, and children fled Vietnam and Cambodia.[2] These refugees were processed on the US territories of Guam and Wake Island before being housed on military bases in the United States. In early May, Thích Thiên-Ân summoned the young dishwashing monk to offer him a new job—he and another student would be dispatched to Fort Chaffee, Arkansas, where more than fifty thousand refugees would be housed as they awaited sponsors so they could be resettled elsewhere in the United States.[3] The monks were to provide spiritual guidance for their fellow Vietnamese. The two monks traveled to Fort Chaffee, carrying with them Buddhist images and ritual items that were not available in Arkansas.[4] On the military base, Thích Tịnh Từ worked as a Buddhist chaplain and stayed in a small room above a makeshift area for practicing Buddhism that the US Army had repurposed out of an old movie theater.[5] Over the next several months, Thích Tịnh Từ instructed people in the dharma, taught meditation, and conducted initiation rites in which participants declare their intention to be Buddhists by taking refuge (*quy y*) in the Three Jewels—the Buddha, the Dharma, and the Sangha.[6] By the end of 1975, Thích Tịnh Từ later recalled, ten thousand people had departed the camp as "official Buddhists" (*Phật tử chính thức*).[7]

In December 1975, as the last refugees prepared to leave Fort Chaffee, Thích Tịnh Từ published an essay titled "Seize the Opportunity" in the camp's bilingual newsletter.[8] He urged his fellow Vietnamese not to be beholden to the past but to look toward the future: "The miraculous door has been flung wide open. Let's boldly look into the future and to the long road that lies in front of us."[9] He knew that Vietnamese refugees faced an uncertain future. The camps outfitted with a Buddhist center and a monk employed by the US government were just a point of entry for the refugees' new life in the United States. Beyond the barbed fences of the military base, they faced the task of realizing their collective dignity in a landscape long encoded as white and Christian and where they would be expected to adopt American cultural values and models of personhood.[10] In the face of this cultural negotiation, he urged his fellow Vietnamese to focus on taking refuge within themselves.[11] While their sponsors—church groups, ordinary citizens, even US veterans—would meet their material needs with clothing, food, and shelter, his fellow Buddhists would also need to attend to their spiritual life to "perfect their dignity."[12]

Forty years later, Vietnamese Buddhist temples in North America number in the hundreds, from lay associations to home temples to elaborate monastic complexes on spacious grounds. Despite their numbers, these institutions are rarely featured in mainstream depictions of Buddhism in the United States, where the practice is widely associated with meditation and its secular variant, mindfulness. Pure Land, although widely practiced in China, Vietnam, and Japan, and many diasporic communities, is relatively unknown, often sidelined in favor of Zen.[13] Indeed, the two most widely known Vietnamese monks, Thích Nhất Hạnh and Thích Thiên-Ân, are associated with Zen, a "more elite, cosmopolitan strain of Vietnamese Buddhism that is quite distinct from the way Buddhism is understood and practiced by most Vietnamese."[14] Vietnamese Buddhists characterize their tradition of practice as a "union" of Zen–Pure Land, although multiple streams have influenced people's practices.[15] In the communities of practice that form the core of my research, these streams, often kept artificially separated for analytical reasons, become entangled in complex ways.

Temples are not only formal spaces of worship. They are also sites of sociability and memory where practitioners make sense of their place in history and reclaim their dignity as they reckon with the legacies of the Cold War and racial segregation. They are also sites where practitioners demonstrate fidelity to US ideals, in how they sometimes invoke "freedom" in ways more akin to gratitude for having escaped oppression at the hands of a communist government and for having adapted to US market-based liberalism, than to Buddhist ideals of liberation. But people also ritually enact the liberation of those who died in war and in their flight from Vietnam, making these temples political sites for representing the unsettled past of what Americans call the Vietnam War. And through their call to compatriot Buddhists (*đồng hương Phật tử*)—an identity framed in terms of common descent, geographic origins, and religious affiliation—they counter the dynamics of exclusion and social invisibility encoded by the color line in the US South. Vietnamese Buddhist temples in the Gulf South are key sites for troubling the concept of freedom as it relates to both American forms of liberalism and Buddhist ideals of liberation. Practitioners actively decenter neoliberal qualities of personhood by harnessing intergenerational debt (*nghiệp*), merit (*phước*), unseen beings (*cô hồn*), and repentance (*sám hối*) as part of how they fashion themselves not in ethnic but in ethical ways.[16] *Pure Land in the Making* resituates these temples within these broader political and historical contexts, underscoring not just the modernity of Vietnamese Buddhism but also the politics of its making in the Gulf South, in order to highlight the ethical considerations at play.

VIETNAMESE BUDDHISM IN THE GULF SOUTH

The US Gulf Coast is a region seldom associated with transpacific networks. Before the 1970s, Buddhism made few inroads to this region; consequently, Southeast Asian refugees and migrants built collective spaces of worship from the ground up. Region matters, especially in the US South, where formalized lineages peter out and hybrid forms appear to be emerging.[17] In a temple in Virginia, for example, people carry out practices associated with multiple lineages under one roof, expressing plasticity in what it means to practice Buddhism in a pluralistic society. Even among Vietnamese practitioners, distinctions among Buddhist centers (*trung tâm Phật giáo*), ashrams (*đạo tràng*), pagodas (*chùa*), and monasteries (*tu viện*) are collapsed into a single category, temple. In Vietnam, people distinguish between "temples" (*đền*), where local deities are served, and Buddhist pagodas (*chùa*), but the use of the English word *temple* speaks to the challenges in maintaining institutional distinctions in the Gulf South, where few Vietnamese identify as Buddhist.

Scholarly interest in Vietnamese resettlement in the region has focused instead on Vietnamese Catholics, and with good reason.[18] After 1975, New Orleans became a symbolic hub for Catholic refugees in large part because of the support provided by the Associated Catholic Charities (ACC) of New Orleans. Secondary migration patterns soon transformed the metropolitan region into one of the densest urban areas for Vietnamese resettlement. Even today, Vietnamese Buddhists are a minority within the larger Vietnamese population, a dynamic that contrasts with estimates of religious affiliation in Vietnam, where the number of people who identify as Buddhist is nearly double that of those who identify as Christian.[19] By overlooking religious pluralism and difference within the Vietnamese diaspora, we lose sight of how people practice their faith not only as private expressions of their belief but also as a mode of living relationally through ethics, culture, and even politics.[20]

Practicing Buddhism is one strategy for "staying Vietnamese."[21] At once a "collective issue of community-building and place-making," staying Vietnamese must also contend "not only with race and racialization, but also with the past."[22] Twenty years ago, religious scholars Cuong Tu Nguyen and A. W. Barber described Vietnamese Buddhism as a "nostalgic version," which would eventually be "reduced to an insignificant relic, a fossil of a vanished time, relevant only for a small number of people isolated within an ethnic ghetto."[23] To see Vietnamese Buddhism as a relic or fossil is to miss the broader dynamics by which participants craft their collective identity in response to the aftermath of war, racial subjugation, and marginalization. When participants voice those historical narratives that America prefers to silence, they make visible the entanglements of religion, politics, selfhood, and history in these spaces. Thus Buddhist temples are sites in which refugees and immigrants make sense of their place in time and space through practices of "dwelling," or home-making.[24] For these reasons, living relationally cannot be explained by Buddhist liturgical traditions or the formal spaces of worship alone, nor can its meanings be traced in a straight line to the presumed geographic homeland. As Vietnamese Buddhists in the Gulf Coast contend with the legacies of war and displacement as well as their aspirations for recognition, these conditions shape the dynamics of how Buddhism is being made. These temples are sites of sociability and belonging that contain both liturgical and political truths for the lives of their practitioners and reveal more significant processes of change in the religious landscape in the United States.

VIETNAMESE BUDDHISM AS A MODERN PROJECT

Vietnamese Buddhism is more than a shorthand designation for those temples and monasteries where Vietnamese is the primary language of both liturgy and everyday conversation. It is a collective project that reflects a more prolonged struggle of how spiritual practices are mobilized in renegotiating collective identities. Vietnamese Buddhism today is shaped as much by historical encounters with modernity, the Cold War, and US modes of citizenship as it is by the teachings of Buddha. It is a term that conveys how monks and laypeople have invoked Buddhist ideals to express modern aspirations, nationalist desires, and anticommunist views, both in Vietnam and in the Gulf South.

Buddhism has, of course, a long history in Vietnam. The two major traditions are Zen (Thiền) and Pure Land (Tịnh Độ). On the surface, the two streams could not be more different. Zen Buddhism emphasizes an "internal locus of control" or "self-power" in which individuals are responsible for modifying their own experiences through techniques for concentration, or purifying the mind. Pure Land, by contrast, emphasizes an "external locus" or "other-power" in which practitioners invoke numerous buddhas and bodhisattvas, above all, Amitābha Buddha, to ask for their help in the attainment of enlightenment. Pure Land depicts a cosmic realm overseen by Amitābha Buddha, and practitioners engage in Buddha name-recitation (*niệm Phật*), a practice sometimes said to produce a specific state of mind but sometimes disparaged as being an "easy path" toward enlightenment.[25] The two schools also differ in their emphasis placed on the importance of historical transmission. Zen emphasizes the historical Buddha (Shakyamuni) and Bodhidharma, who brought Zen (Chinese: Chan) from South Asia to China in the fifth or sixth century. Buddhist practices in Vietnam harnessed both of these schools, a "union" in spite of their differences, or, as Vietnamese often say, "Zen and Pure Land are parallel practices" (Thiền Tịnh song tu).[26]

Both Zen and Pure Land are part of Mahayana Buddhism, a branch that developed about two thousand years ago over debates about the nature of enlightenment and over practical questions such as who should hold spiritual authority.[27] Along with the Buddha and the Dharma, the Sangha is one of the Three Jewels wherein people take refuge. Historically, the sangha refers to those followers who first gathered around the historical Buddha as he traveled across the Indian subcontinent. Eventually, as the sangha grew, the Buddha established precepts or rules of training and discipline, later codified into Vinaya, that monks must follow. Today the split between Mahayana and Theravada Buddhism is not only doctrinal but political. Mahayana and Theravada align with modern nation-states, reflecting patterns of conquest but also differences in how the monastic sangha legitimates governing orders in those countries where Theravada Buddhism prevails, especially Thailand and Myanmar (also known as Burma).[28] In contrast to Theravada Buddhism, which emphasizes the largely male monastic sangha and individual attainment of enlightenment, Mahayana teachings promote a universalistic approach to salvation through direct contact with buddhas and bodhisattvas and other living beings who vow to defer enlightenment to remain among the living. The sangha, moreover, includes male and female monks and male and female lay followers who take bodhisattva vows. Consequently, an essential virtue of Mahayana Buddhism is compassion, envisioned as transcending bounded identities and affiliations. In Vietnam, the monastic sangha has not been as organized or influential as elsewhere in Southeast Asia where the Theravada tradition prevails. Ironically, it is the autonomy of monks and the influence of lay practitioners that have propelled Vietnamese Buddhism across the US Gulf South.

Despite evidence of Buddhism's long-standing influence, Vietnamese Buddhism as a self-conscious project has surprisingly modern roots. It was only in the late nineteenth and early twentieth centuries that European and Indigenous scholars endeavored to accord Buddhism the status of religion, as a response to both colonialism and its promotion of Christianity.[29] They distinguished Buddhism proper from those spiritual practices they saw as superstitious, such as blessing amulets and merit-transference ceremonies. They also rebuked monks for accepting payment for chanting prayers and chided lay Buddhists for chanting sutras they did not understand.[30]

Buddhist monks throughout Asia, however, sought to strengthen the monastic order as a bulwark against colonialism by reinforcing the ties between Buddhism and nationalism and by participating in internationalized circuits of exchange such as world congresses.[31] Mostly, Buddhist monks in Vietnam wanted to demonstrate to the West that their religion had a rational, and therefore modern, foundation, and thus they sought to purify it of its seemingly magical beliefs. The construction of a coherent, "rational" Buddhism, however, ultimately proved impossible, and the struggles over how to understand Buddhism in the modern world fractured into diverse movements. Some monks attempted to consolidate Buddhism by advocating for stricter standards, translating sutras and texts from Chinese into Vietnamese, and developing lay instruction.[32] Vietnamese intellectuals participated in new syncretic religions, such as Caodaism and the Hòa Hảo movement.[33] These divisions, although rooted in colonial encounters, still inform how people evaluate and assess practices in Buddhist temples along the Gulf Coast today.

Ultimately, the difficulty in unifying the elite, cosmopolitan versions with the vernacular practices reignited an age-old union between the two different strains, Zen and Pure Land. In southern Vietnam, small books and pamphlets with Buddhist texts and images widened the appeal of the bodhisattva Quán Thế Âm (Chinese: Guanyin; Sanskrit: Avalokiteśvara) as a central supernatural figure who responds to the suffering of women in particular.[34] People chanted fragments of sutras and recited syllabic prayers or mantras for protection, calling on Quan Âm and praying to be reborn in the Pure Land or Western Paradise, a celestial realm where no one suffered.[35] While monks were ordained in Zen traditions, they also practiced Pure Land methods, thus linking the formal transmission of Buddhism handed down from master to disciple with those vernacular practices that gained popularity in the twentieth century. As cosmopolitan monks attempted to distill Buddhism to its essence, free from superstition and magic, lay Buddhists spread miracle tales, endowing liturgies with supernatural potency, revealing the "double and indissociable legacy of the Buddha."[36] While it seems counterintuitive, both practices—both the here and now and what lies beyond human comprehension—are necessary to ensure the durability of the dharma. Its legacy has been preserved not only through the monastic sangha but also by ordinary people who recount miracle tales, carry amulets, and recite mantras believed to have protective powers. And both strands—the spiritual and the political, other-power and self-power, Pure Land and Zen—shape Vietnamese Buddhism in the Gulf South.

TRANSMITTING BUDDHISM TO AMERICA

Buddhism in the United States has been part of the religious landscape since the nineteenth century, yet scholars have struggled with classifying its diverse institutions and practices.[37] In the 1970s, scholars glossed the observed differences in congregations of immigrants and their US-born descendants as "ethnic" or "heritage" Buddhism; the practices of those people (e.g., predominantly but not exclusively white) who stood outside these traditions were designated as "American" or convert Buddhism.

These two concepts, sometimes marked as "Buddhism *in* America" as opposed to "American Buddhism," came to be known as the two-Buddhism model.[38]

In the 1990s, this model became the subject of debate, provoking practitioners to reflect not just on the variety of Buddhisms in the United States but also on issues around racial diversity and the long-standing marginalization of Asian Americans in the United States. By designating spiritual practices as "ethnic" or "heritage," scholars marginalize participants by measuring their practices against the practices of predominantly college-educated white middle-class Americans.[39] Buddhism in the United States is often described as "one dharma," a blend of Zen, Tibetan Buddhism, and Vipassanā, or insight meditation.[40] What this hybrid form excludes, however, is the tradition of practices associated with the Pure Land, thus revealing how Western Buddhism itself reflects the cultural preoccupations around the interior self.[41]

Some scholars suggest the Pure Land may be too much like Christianity to attract much academic or popular attention.[42] Participants draw on "external awakening," or what psychologists call an external locus of control, as they call upon buddhas and bodhisattvas. Even the cosmology of Pure Land Buddhism resembles Christianity: the Western Paradise is conflated with Heaven, and rebirth with salvation. Amitābha Buddha, who presides over the Pure Land, is a godlike figure, while Quan Âm resembles the Virgin Mary. By contrast, Zen, Tibetan Buddhism, and Vipassanā are more amenable to the "religio-therapeutic culture," in which adherents are concerned with issues of personal adjustment and turn to meditation as an internal and individualized solution for their stressors.[43]

The absence of Pure Land from Western Buddhism is not merely a matter of its resemblance to Christianity or its deviance from dominant cultural models of personhood. Its absence is also political, which is evident when we consider the conditions that shaped the lives of those Chinese and Japanese migrants who carried out similar practices in the nineteenth century. In the 1880s, the US Congress imposed restrictions on Chinese migrants, justifying those limits in terms of labor competition, but channeling the racialized anxieties of an Anglo-Protestant nation. The Chinese Exclusion Act of 1882 barred the entry of Chinese laborers for ten years, and the 1924 Immigration Act effectively closed the door on further Asian immigration.[44] The exclusion acts culminated with the incarceration of Japanese and Japanese Americans as enemies of the state after the bombing of Pearl Harbor in December 1941. US government officials rounded up Buddhist and Shinto priests drawn from lists that identified those spiritual leaders as threats to domestic security.[45] As the country prepared for war, even American-born Japanese with tenuous ties to their ancestral homeland were seen as aliens. Somewhere between 110,000 and 120,000 people of Japanese ancestry were forcibly relocated and interned in camps such as Camp Livingston in Louisiana and Fort Chaffee in Arkansas. Gradually, people in these camps built makeshift altars and listened to dharma talks as they sacralized the grounds of the camps in Buddhist terms. For Japanese and Japanese American Buddhists, the internment camps were laboratories where they adapted their practices so Buddhism could "ground itself more securely in the American religious landscape."[46] In doing so, they demonstrated their worthiness as Buddhists by claiming equal standing with Christians, in the process Americanizing Buddhism. Hence people's investment of resources—time, labor, money, and aspirations—in making Buddhism is not an ethnic story that can be told apart from US empire. Even heritage, often reduced to material artifacts or specific beliefs, is better understood as a form of "conscious culture," a compensatory claim in the face of broader shifts in economic and political power as relatively disempowered groups confront more powerful others.[47]

Buddhism in the United States has also been shaped by religious pluralism, even among Asian diasporas and relationships among compatriots. Scholars of Korean American religions, for example, note that religions "are not simply transplanted from one place to another; they are transformed in the process."[48] One such transformation involves forging a sense of identity in contrast to conationals who have adopted new spiritual orientations. Taiwanese Buddhists, for example, confront new meanings of what it is to practice Buddhism as they contend with the strong evangelical Christian presence within the Taiwanese community in Southern California.[49] Buddhism, an embedded religion in everyday life in Taiwan, has become an explicit religion in which participants see temples as places for learning, not socializing as the ethnic or heritage Buddhism model suggests. For many Vietnamese Americans, however, religious pluralism has been subsumed under "freedom," a key concept along with anticommunism.

In the US Gulf South, a symbol that is displayed on many temples is the Vietnamese Freedom and Heritage Flag, but it would never grace a pagoda or temple in the Socialist Republic of Vietnam. This flag was the official flag of the Republic of Vietnam, rendered defunct by the communist takeover in 1975. Today in the Gulf South, this flag is displayed alongside the five-color Buddhist flag and the American flag at some but not all temples, underscoring how some Vietnamese Buddhists have consecrated collective spaces of worship by displaying their fidelity to the United States through

At a temple in Biloxi, Mississippi, are two notable features. The statue of the bodhisattva Quán Thế Âm faces toward the street to greet people who approach. Displayed above the gate are three flags—the Vietnamese Freedom and Heritage Flag, the Buddhist flag, and the US flag. Photo by the author.

their continued commitment to an anticommunist identity (figure I.1).[50] That this gesture is approved by their host country can be seen in a spate of laws that designate the Freedom and Heritage Flag as Vietnam's official flag. For instance, in 2003, the Louisiana legislature passed State Bill 839, which declares that the only flag representing Vietnam is the flag of the former Republic of Vietnam. The bill is noteworthy for its anticommunist language:

> The people of the former Republic of Vietnam, also known as South Vietnam, were valiant in their resistance to the aggression of the communist North Vietnam. The legislature further finds that refugees from the former Republic of Vietnam who emigrated to the United States of America and settled in the state of Louisiana should be honored and remembered for their sacrifices.[51]

Spiritual leaders of different religious associations attend community-wide events to celebrate the lunar New Year or to mark April 30, the fall of Saigon in 1975. These efforts at containing difference have engendered an explicit discourse around "compatriot Buddhists" (*đồng hương Phật tử*), whose commitments are quite different from those of people who identify themselves as disciples (*đệ tử*) of a particular monk. The call to compatriot Buddhists widens the social field by welcoming people who may not regularly support the temple or even consider identifying as Buddhists (figure I.2). *Đồng hương* invokes common descent (*đồng bào*) and place-based origins (*quê hương*), designating a diasporic identity that is realized through the activities of these temples but exceeding the space of formal worship halls. Both disciples and compatriots are crucial to the support and maintenance of these institutions or the making of Vietnamese Buddhism in the United States.[52]

The flag thus is a complex symbol, one that frames the presence of Vietnamese in Louisiana within the Cold War by commemorating their sacrifices and honoring the Republic of Vietnam. Yet Vietnamese in the United States and Vietnam also seek to identify common features among these temples in Vietnam and the United States. In an online essay, "Vietnamese

I.2   Banner welcoming compatriot Buddhists (*đồng hương Phật tử*). Celebrations for the lunar New Year (Tet), Buddha's birthday (Vesak or Phật Đản), and Ullambana (Vu Lan) often attract large numbers of participants, evident in how the temple grounds are used to accommodate the greater number of parked cars. Photo by the author.

Buddhist Temples in America—the New Tourist Destination," Võ Văn Tường, the author of several books on ancient and present-day pagodas in Vietnam, describes a trip across the United States in which he visited "hundreds of Vietnamese Buddhist temples."[53] Wherever one finds Vietnamese people, he happily proclaims, one finds a Buddhist temple.[54] He points out that while each temple may be different, from a distance these spaces are recognizably Vietnamese, both because of the Buddhist flags and because of the open-air statues of the bodhisattva Quán Thế Âm. What is left unremarked is the display of this flag at some but not all temples. Its display should be regarded not as aberrant but rather as a symbol attesting to the history that separates and divides, even though it may be disregarded in public culture, even among Vietnamese observers.

As a symbol, the flag also exposes how Vietnamese Buddhism cannot be explained by the category of ethnicity but should instead be framed in terms of racialization. The categories of race and ethnicity are used interchangeably to designate Asian Americans, but these categories mark different orders in American political life.[55] By designating people's investment in the life of these temples as merely "ethnic," we misrecognize other dynamics at play. These dynamics like hoisting the Freedom and Heritage Flag mark race insofar as this term encodes histories of subjugation, including "legacies of conquest, enslavement, and non-national status that disturb the national peace, whose narrative must thus be silenced within public culture, or hived off from the national story into separate worlds of their own."[56] Within these temples, people invoke legacies otherwise silenced in public culture, reframing these narratives within a Buddhist idiom and helping residents navigate their historical experiences, present marginalization, and uncertain futures through their spiritual commitments. Displaying the flag is not merely nostalgic but is a ritual activity that alerts us to the fact that while most Americans assume the Cold War ended in 1989, it is not over for many Vietnamese.

FREEDOM, LIBERALISM, AND LIBERATION

The making of Vietnamese Buddhism in the US Gulf South is political—a vehicle of modern nationalism but also a beneficiary of US liberalism that masks the persistence of race by acknowledging religious pluralism and multiculturalism. After World War II, as the United States expanded into Asia to ward off the threat of communism, it set the stage for a new iteration of US empire, the Cold War. Americans understood the containment of communism as the protection of liberty around the globe, but US policy makers had to contend with the country's legacy of racial violence, especially against Asians. Because United States–Asia integration was a foundational concept in the Cold War, new ways of representing Asia began to circulate, the limitations of which can be seen in the figure of the "Oriental Monk."[57] Cold War Orientalism spurred reform of US immigration and naturalization laws, dismantling policies that had excluded Asians from becoming naturalized citizens.[58] Once-suspect Chinese and Japanese Americans were revalued as the good immigrants who assimilated into US society, and by rewarding the political loyalties of these immigrants (e.g., Republican Chinese, South Koreans, and citizens of a reconstructed Japan), the United States promoted new norms of desirability based on educational level, skill, and familial ties to Americans.[59] In 1965, the United States passed the Hart-Celler Immigration Act, which replaced the system of national origins with a system of quotas that applied to all countries, irrespective of size. It also introduced preferences for immediate family members, including parents, spouses, and unmarried minor children, who could enter as nonquota immigrants and, in turn, produce new chains of migration.[60]

Also in 1965, American combat troops were sent to protect a regime that US officials viewed as vital to its national security, the Republic of Vietnam, better known as South Vietnam. The Vietnam War is paradigmatic of the "other cold war," a term that unlike Cold War Orientalism draws attention to the devastating impacts in Asia by insisting that the geopolitical struggle involved real violence and death, not simply US and Soviet posturing and political maneuvers and their respective cultural representations of Asia.[61] If, as literary scholar Viet Thanh Nguyen insists, wars are always fought a second time in memory, how societies come to terms with the remains of the Cold War's extraordinary violence and mass death is vital for how those societies remember war itself.[62] Buddhist temples may not be seen as strategic memory projects, but they are sites in which practitioners seek to liberate the souls of those people who died in war, thus making visible otherwise unrepresented elements of the past.[63]

In 1954, Vietnam was split into two mutually hostile postcolonial states—the Democratic Republic and the Republic of Vietnam—and each regime invoked religion as a critical factor in its nation-building projects.[64] In the Democratic Republic, or North Vietnam, leaders saw religion as out of step with a revolutionary society, and so pagodas were largely deserted.[65] However, in the Republic of Vietnam, both Catholic and Buddhist leaders portrayed their respective religions as a force against communism.[66] US officials effectively weaponized religion by tapping the monastic sangha in Southeast Asia as a possible anticommunist force.[67] By channeling financial support through private organizations like the Asia Foundation, the United States funded Buddhist education in Thailand, underscoring how internationalizing Buddhism went hand in hand with geopolitical strategies. While these efforts were successful in Thailand, US officials failed to recognize the growing tensions between Buddhists and Catholics in southern Vietnam. By the early 1960s, those tensions erupted in what came to be known as the "Buddhist crisis."[68] From that point forward, Buddhism and Catholicism vied as competing guardians of Vietnamese nationalism.[69] After the countless deaths of soldiers and civilians, the United States withdrew its troops in 1973, leaving the Army of the Republic of Vietnam exposed to communist forces. The Republic of Vietnam fell in April 1975, spurring the mass evacuation of 130,000 people, the vast majority of whom resettled in the United States. The dividing line in Vietnam would henceforth be no longer between North and South, or even between Buddhists and Catholics, but between the Vietnamese state and its diasporas.

Today Vietnamese in the United States number nearly two million, but not every individual arrived as a refugee. Some people came via sponsorship from family members already in the United States, others are US-born, and still others are transmigrants who live in both Vietnam and the United States. For these people, the term *refugee* may seem a misnomer.[70] The term, however, is more than a legal-juridical category; it has been a dominant model for representing Vietnamese in the mainstream media and academic scholarship.[71] Vietnamese community leaders also describe their journey to the United States as one of "freedom," invoking the moral vocabulary of the Cold War in which freedom designates anticommunism, liberal democracy, and even religious pluralism.

Scholars of the Cold War era argue that US commitments to racial liberalism and cultural pluralism were only strategic approaches to containing communism and US domestic racial conflicts.[72] Even the political category "refugee" privileged "freedom fighters," people who had fled oppressive communist regimes for the geopolitical West, in contrast to international law that emphasized human rights. As the communist government assumed control of southern Vietnam, thousands of Vietnamese evacuated the country, seeking refuge in the United States and elsewhere. In Vietnam, officials quickly imposed restrictions on religious activities, clergy, and organizations; seized the landholdings of Buddhist monasteries and Catholic churches; and threatened spiritual leaders with arrest. The revolutionary government set up a group, the Unification of Buddhist Organizations, and even though arrests and detainment of monks did not cease, people grew mistrustful as monks were perceived as allied with the socialist regime. Leading monks fled the country under harrowing circumstances as refugees in the late 1970s and early 1980s. Consequently, the slogans of freedom of religion and anticommunism would shape how people fashioned themselves in the United States through their spiritual practices as refugee identity became an important element for constituting Vietnamese communities in diaspora.

Discourses of freedom have imposed costs as refugees are obligated to become good US citizens by performing gratitude for having been rescued.[73] Freedom requires forgetting their tremendous losses and suffering as they adapt to new forms of political subjectivity that emphasize values such as self-reliance, individualism, and entrepreneurialism.[74] Ethnic studies scholar Yến Lê Espiritu has called for recognizing refugees as historical agents who "possess and enact their own politics as they emerge out of the ruins of war and its aftermath."[75] Vietnamese in America cannot pretend that their liberation came without a heavy price, which has produced a distinctive style of "refugee nationalism," evident, for example, in municipal and state legislation that recognizes the Freedom and Heritage Flag.[76] *Pure Land in the Making* describes how Buddhism is a form of politics through which refugees and immigrants have remade themselves in the aftermath of war.

PURE LAND IN THE MAKING

Since the late 1980s, Vietnamese refugees and immigrants have consecrated ordinary places—vacant lots, fishing camps, suburban homes, and even mobile homes—into sites for practicing Buddhism. While the spread of temples across the Gulf South appears to be a flowering of Buddhism in the region, Buddhists themselves tell a different story, one that attributes the proliferation of temples to conflicts over spiritual and institutional authority. These investments—people's expenditures of money, time, and labor as well as their aspirations of the future—should be situated within the larger regional story. Reforms of immigration policies during the Cold War dismantled the exclusion acts that had disenfranchised Asian Americans; however, postwar liberalism has not dismantled race, because it is, in fact, constitutive of liberal democracy and American nationhood.[77] Asian Americans, first excluded by immigration policies, then elevated as the "good immigrants," and later designated as a "model minority," are defined by racial difference, which left in place "a normative majority (white) population."[78] Vietnamese perform their identities as good citizens, emphasizing their adherence to anticommunism, but less visible are the ways in which they also mark their specific histories of inclusion and exclusion. Buddhist temples, in this regard, can be considered "racial safety zones," where whiteness is a marginal, not dominant, practice.[79]

Buddhism is part of public culture in the United States, but the politics of its representation have reinforced rather than dismantled histories of racial subjugation. The monastic sangha, central to Buddhism in Asia, is said to have given way to investing spiritual authority in lay followers. This process is embodied by the Oriental Monk, a solitary male who stands outside institutional lineages and delivers Asian spiritualities to Cold War US audiences.[80] But this figure obscures the importance of monk-lay exchange relations in the cultivation of merit, a key concept underpinning the sangha as a collective body and as an ideal that is difficult to achieve. Vietnamese monks and lay followers reckon with these relations as well, as they draw on competing agendas and aspirations to navigate the challenges of creating and maintaining Buddhism along the Gulf Coast.

Since the 1970s, religion has become linked to new forms of governance and political recognition. Minority or immigrant religions serve as public strategies through which immigrants and domestic minorities negotiate their place in the United States. But there are limits, which sociologist Sharmila Rudrappa calls the "trick of multiculturalism," that both obscure and entrench whiteness as a racial category that organizes US social life.[81] Thus to speak of Vietnamese Buddhism in terms of race is not to emphasize features of practitioners writ on the body; nor is it to locate the meanings of Buddhism in the homeland. It is instead to draw attention to how the history of Asians in the United States has been shaped by exclusion acts, internment, and war and materialized through people's commitments to inscribe their collective presence on the cultural landscape. Vietnamese Buddhist temples have become increasingly prominent structures in the landscape of this region. Constructing these worship halls, however, elicits controversy among Buddhist practitioners, especially over the boundaries between the social and the sacred. Is the purpose of a worship hall for prayer or display? Is the Pure Land a sanctuary from the demands of society or a threshold of existence? Large-scale construction projects amplify these questions as congregations appeal for money and support. By emphasizing not just the physical construction of the worship hall but also its social constructedness, I show how temple building entails risks for the congregation in a case study of two temples in Louisiana, each of which embarked on building a temple in order to inscribe the presence of Vietnamese on the cultural landscape.

In the ethics around death, too, monks are critical actors in addressing the traumatic past as they ritually liberate spirits trapped in the lower realms. While Buddhism is depicted by academic scholars and the mainstream media as antithetical to family and household, the multigenerational family is a key constituency for many Vietnamese Buddhists. The emphasis on the family is particularly fraught over the question of the spiritual and ritual purity of women, evident in two conflicting maternal images—the bodhisattva Quán Thế Âm as the embodiment of compassion and the accursed mother in the legend of Mulian, which is ritually enacted during Vu Lan, a Buddhist observance during the seventh lunar month. Maternal imagery also indexes the equally complex relationship many Vietnamese Buddhists have with the homeland. There is also an ethical imperative to commemorate the sacrifices of those who lost their lives, which we see in the ways people have ritualized the aftermath of war through these practices of remembrance and liberation. Ultimately, these rituals are about cultivating the self through the ethics of compassion and the aspiration to liberate all sentient beings, a practice called "repentance" (sám hối). Through bowing, practitioners reflect on their thoughts, speech, and action, thus complicating liberal notions of freedom by emphasizing bodily discipline as the source of liberation.[82]

By creating collective spaces of worship, Vietnamese Buddhists engage in political as well as ethical activities as they stake their moral claims of belonging—a Pure Land in the making—with varying degrees of success. What is instead coming into view is how the social landscape of the United States is itself changing through the spiritual negotiations of Vietnamese American Buddhists. But is this story just a first-generation story? Buddhism is regenerating in ways that defy the Asian immigration narrative and its emphasis on the fading away of traditions and values. Throughout its transmission to East Asia, Buddhism's cosmologies and supernatural figures were molded to acclimate to other philosophies such as Confucianism and Daoism. How Buddhism is transforming in its passage to the United States is still unfolding. But we can no longer see the story as primarily about the agency of US-born practitioners to the exclusion of Asian Americans and the aftermath of war. It is also a story of refugees, immigrants, and migrants and their US-born descendants. *Pure Land in the Making* tells part of that story.

CHAPTER ONE

Seeking Refuge in the Gulf South

NEW Orleans once had the greatest concentration of Vietnamese refugees, per capita, than any other city in the United States.[1] By 2010, the New Orleans metropolitan area no longer ranked among the top urban areas by Vietnamese population.[2] Hurricane Katrina in 2005 and the BP oil spill in 2010 disproportionately affected Vietnamese American households along the Gulf Coast, leading some residents and outsiders to wonder if once vibrant communities had reached an "inflection point" as younger Vietnamese Americans looked for job prospects elsewhere.[3] Why then did the metropolitan area have not just one but four Vietnamese Buddhist temples—one located in New Orleans East on the outskirts of Versailles and three on the West Bank?[4] I posed that question one evening as I sat in the living room of Mr. Trung, a Buddhist lay leader who had lived for many years in the New Orleans metropolitan area.[5] We first met during a celebration of Vu Lan in summer 2005, and I considered him a reliable guide to the city. During our conversation nearly ten years later, I noted how the number of temples in the New Orleans area must signal growing interest in Buddhism among Vietnamese in the region. Mr. Trung just shook his head. "The story isn't pretty," he warned.

Mr. Trung recounted a history of fissions and splits that led to the founding of multiple Buddhist temples in the metropolitan area.[6] The first temple was established on the west bank of the Mississippi, known also as the West Bank, in the 1980s. In the late 1990s, a disagreement among members led to a split, and a group of lay Buddhists founded a second temple, this one on the easternmost edge of the city. They recruited a Vietnamese monk from Houston, but within a year or so, a dispute arose between the monk and the board of directors, and the monk left to establish a third temple in 2003, quite close to the first temple. Later a resident monk from the third temple founded a fourth temple on the western edge of the metropolitan area. Across the Gulf South, I heard similar tales—tales of moral impropriety, struggles over financial control, disputes over elections for the board of directors, and, eventually, a group who departed to establish a new temple.[7] On occasion, the disputes took dramatic turns as monks and lay Buddhists sparred over naming rights and possession of the temple funds. Several of these disputes even ended up in court. What first appeared to me as a flowering of Vietnamese Buddhism instead was rooted in muddy struggles for control, autonomy, and visibility.

The lotus, whose petals open untouched by the mud in which it is rooted, is a popular metaphor for Asian communities in North America. But this image is also pernicious. With its emphasis on purity, the lotus may contribute to the trope of Asians in the Americas as foreigners within, no matter how many generations ago their family arrived, what their citizenship status is, or how much they identify with mainstream American culture. For Buddhists, in contrast, the emphasis on the lotus is as a symbol not of purity but of awakening. Just as the roots of the lotus are nourished by mud, awakening is inseparable from suffering, or human existence. The saying "No mud, no lotus" recognizes that awakening begins with the acknowledgment of suffering, the first of the Four Noble Truths. From this acknowledgment stems the other truths: suffering arises from our desires, we can cease our suffering, and there is a path toward enlightenment, or the Eightfold Path. The Four Noble Truths, which have suffering at their root, are the first fold of that path.[8]

The lotus is useful as a metaphor to explain the spread of Buddhist temples along the Gulf Coast because it is a rhizome. Unlike a tree, its roots grounded in place, a rhizome sends shoots from nodes that run laterally, not upward. Consequently, the rhizome defies efforts to locate a single point of origin; instead, it is a decentered and decentering organism whose connections can be made to any point.[9] Moreover, in the Gulf South, the lotus is used by Indigenous communities as a practical resource for its roots and seeds. When we see the lotus not as an exotic but a domestic plant, we may understand the spread of Buddhism across the Gulf Coast is a regional story involving the resettlement of refugees, the silencing of the histories of racial minorities, and the changing mandates of citizenship that have elevated market values over other forms of collective life. The historical and social conditions of the Gulf Coast, stretching back at least to the nineteenth century, form the mud in which the dynamics of citizenship were forged not only along a Black-white binary but also by the exclusion of the Asian migrant. As racial differences are more prominent in the United States than religious ones, the story of Vietnamese resettlement has focused on the racial designation and national origins of refugees. In the region of the Gulf Coast, by contrast, while this story has emphasized the role of Catholic faith among many Vietnamese refugees and migrants, it has neglected other orientations less resonant with the region, including Buddhism.[10] By recentering the story on Vietnamese Buddhist organizations and practitioners, we see how they are also part of the region, whether by compensating for the failures of the state, especially in light of large-scale disasters such as Hurricane Katrina in 2005 and the BP oil spill in 2010, or by expressing national ideals around freedom and anticommunism.

That evening, Mr. Trung reflected on how Vietnamese migrants arrived with the idea that in the Gulf South they would find the Pure Land, a celestial realm blessed with riches and where no one suffers. He pointed out that they did not realize that suffering takes on different forms and added, "We do not know if the Pure Land exists, which is why we need to practice." Practicing, as the following chapters show, is never complete and, in addition to liturgy or formal worship services, involves adjacent activities that are inescapably social, intractably embodied, and irrepressibly material—a Pure Land in the making.

THE GULF SOUTH AND THE LIMITS OF CREOLIZATION

The Gulf South as a cultural region resists integration into a coherent national framework.[11] Its major port cities—New Orleans, Biloxi, and Mobile—were zones of contact long before the region was brought into the Anglo-American sphere of influence. Even the influence of the Catholic Church reflects the lingering influence of Spanish and French rule, while the slow economic growth speaks to the dominance of plantation power. This historical backdrop, far from repudiated, is celebrated as endowing the region with an ethos of creativity and experimentation—creolization. Yet creolization is grounded in specific historical processes in the New World, including dispossession of Indigenous populations, the enslavement of Africans, and reliance on plantation economies. The term *creole* first denoted children of Old World settlers who were born and raised in the New World. Initially, the word implied the taint of corruption by a new environment, but it later became associated with processes of cultural creation and elaboration, heralded as erasing "old localizing strategies" of a bounded community and giving way to emergent forms of expression.[12] Among those peoples who arrived under conditions of dispossession— enslaved Africans, French-speaking Acadians, and Southeast Asian refugees—creolization may be better understood as a mode of culture building, of "using the materials in their hearts, heads and hands—as well as those materials they found lying around them," for "they were no longer going anywhere—they had, as it were, arrived."[13] Today residents on the coast still exhibit resilience, using material in their "hearts, heads and hands," in the face of increasing vulnerability, whether from extractive industries—tourism, oil, and gas—or from climate change.

The Gulf South can be defined as the area south of Interstate 10, a highway linking coastal communities, small fishing towns, and midrange metropolitan areas, but its designation as a discrete region is often invoked to distance it from the US South and its troubling history of plantation economies and racial segregation.[14] Louisiana, Mississippi, and Alabama were all part of Dixie, the nickname given to those states that seceded from the Union to form the Confederacy, and whose symbols are still visible in public places today. Even the construction of I-10 in the 1960s, the material boundary of the Gulf South, contributed to intensifying racial segregation in New Orleans. With the newly built highway, white residents evacuated the urban core for neighboring parishes, emptying the apartment complexes in New Orleans East where Vietnamese refugees would be resettled in 1975.

While the region has a long history of drawing people from elsewhere, the Gulf South is readily linked to the Caribbean and Atlantic worlds. Less visible are those connections to the transpacific, the vast networks of peoples, cultures, capital, and ideas moving between "America" and "Asia."[15] Migrants from Asia, however invisible, have been instrumental figures in debates over citizenship and remaking the region's cultural landscape. The crewmen of the Spanish empire and galleon trade were Filipinos, or "Manilamen," who occasionally jumped ship in Mexico and made their way to Louisiana, settling in the bayous, where they etched their livelihoods by drying shrimp on platforms under the sun and constructing houses built on stilts.[16] After the Civil War, sugar and cotton planters sent recruiters to Cuba to hire Chinese laborers, nearly all men, who arrived as a form of "contract slavery" to work in the sugar plantations either replacing or alongside enslaved Africans.[17] By 1887, more than sixteen hundred Chinese from California were recruited to work in lower Louisiana on plantations and railroads alongside newly emancipated African Americans.[18] By 1880, New Orleans was home to the largest "Chinatown" in the lower South. Journalists praised these residents for having "converted to the true faith of Christianity" and for paying tribute to ancestors in a manner that resembled Catholic holidays such as All Saints' Day.[19] While Chinese migrants were never as numerous on the Gulf Coast as on the West Coast, they were deemed even less worthy than free men of color by white lawmakers and Black intellectuals.[20] On the national front, these debates fueled demands for legislation to stem the number of migrants from China. In 1882, Congress passed the Chinese Exclusion Act, which banned migrants from owning land or marrying white Americans, a history that exposes how the simple dichotomy of US citizen and Asian migrant is insufficient to understand the debates around citizenship. In fact, the Chinese laborer was part of a broader politics of differently racialized groups "forced to negotiate their exclusion in relation to others."[21] Through the exclusion of Chinese laborers from citizenship, lawmakers and intellectuals produced Black domestic subjectivity. These debates would later erupt over the resettlement of Southeast Asian refugees.

In the early twentieth century, Jim Crow laws in the US South sanctioned racial segregation, a governing strategy intended to restrict Black economic, social, and political mobility. Where along this color line did Chinese and other Asians in the Gulf South belong? By the mid-twentieth century, Chinese and Japanese Americans, once seen as unassimilable, were elevated as "honorary whites."[22] The appearance of the elevation in status of Chinese in the US South may be better understood as a resolution to "racial interstitiality" in which Chinese were expected to uphold the Black-white color line in both directions, a process of "white identification and black disavowal."[23] Not limited to the US South, this model was a deeply embedded structural order of "racial triangulation," in which Asians and Blacks are alternately valorized or ostracized depending on historical contexts that shift over time.[24] By the 1960s, Chinese Americans and Japanese Americans were designated "good immigrants" and later "model minorities," exemplary free-market subjects who realized their moral worthiness and civic duty through the sanctity of economic action, family, and faith. While US policy makers heralded global integration and cultural pluralism, these strategies were ultimately designed to contain communism and quell domestic racial conflicts.[25] In the civil rights movement, Black claims for racial equality were met by white policy makers who invoked national ideals of unity and highlighted the inclusion of Asians as evidence of racial integration.

By the 1970s, the demography of the US South was changing: a region that once had the lowest number of foreign-born residents now attracted migrants from around the world.[26] Global manufacturing and new circuits of capital fueled economic growth, but these gains did not extend to the Gulf South. The old port cities of New Orleans, Biloxi, and Mobile instead occupied "the poorest stretch of major coastline in the country and represent[ed] a uniquely peripheral area within an otherwise booming New South."[27] The impoverishment of the region was attributed not to creolization but to its opposite, "plantation power," the two-century evolution of race-based practices that still govern the region's economy.[28] It was along this coastline where Southeast Asian refugees would make their homes.

This long history exposes the limits of creolization in the Gulf South. What emerges instead is the constitutive history of race as a category through which claims of belonging are contested and asserted. In this milieu, mud nourishes the conditions in which Vietnamese and other Southeast Asian migrants use "the materials in their hearts, heads and hands" to convert "mere space [into] an intensely human place."[29] In so doing, they have connected the peripheral coastline of the Gulf Coast to the transpacific while also exposing how the figure of the Southeast Asian refugee in the late twentieth century, like the figure of the Chinese migrant a hundred years earlier, has been critical to discourses of citizenship.

A NEW LAND

In spring 1975, as a victory by communist forces in Vietnam appeared inevitable, US government officials prepared for a possible evacuation of Americans and South Vietnamese. In April, Secretary of State Henry A. Kissinger estimated that as many as seventy thousand refugees would require assistance: "We consider we have a moral obligation to tens of thousands of people who worked with us."[30] By May 1, the mass exodus of evacuees was already estimated to be fifty thousand, which included US citizens and relatives of Vietnamese who had previously immigrated to the country and a second category of "high risk" people including former or present employees of the US government, US firm employees, journalists, and their parents, children, and spouses.[31] In New Orleans, the head of the US Immigration and Naturalization Service dismissed reports that three thousand refugees would arrive, insisting instead that the number would be in the hundreds, mainly relatives of those Vietnamese students already in New Orleans.[32] Lieutenant Governor James E. Fitzmorris likewise brushed aside concerns over the projected number of five hundred refugees to be resettled in Louisiana and Mississippi: "I don't think that number will affect our life or form of living to any great extent. The number is insignificant. We have to show compassion."[33] By the end of 1975, the US government resettled 130,000 Vietnamese and Cambodian men, women, and children, nearly twice the number estimated initially.

Discourses of refugee resettlement quickly shifted from a moral obligation to assist allies of the United States to a moral imperative based in Christian charity. The first coordinator for the Archdiocese of New Orleans Resettlement Bureau, who fled Cuba as a young child, framed her work in terms of anticommunism and Christian duty: "They were fleeing communism and coming to a land of opportunity: opportunity does exist for people who want to work for it." She then added, "You can't let God down."[34] In late May 1975, the Clergy Council of the Archdiocese of New Orleans pledged its support for the resettlement of Vietnamese refugees: "America is historically a nation which has provided sanctuary to those fleeing persecution and other hardships in their homelands."[35] Likewise, the archbishop of New Orleans, Philip M. Hannan, reminded congregants of their moral obligations as Christians: "[Vietnamese refugees] are dependent upon the charity of the Christian community for the basic necessities of life until such time as they are employed and can become self-supporting citizens."[36] That Christian duty and anticommunism went hand in hand is not surprising, but those rationales distanced most Americans from the plight of Vietnamese fleeing a country devastated by US military power. When the archbishop of New Orleans, along with Father Michael Haddad, director of Associated Catholic Charities (ACC) of New Orleans, visited refugees at Fort Chaffee, Arkansas, several hundred people housed at the camp staged a demonstration outside the US Catholic Conference building, demanding that they be resettled together so they could work as shrimpers, as they had done in Vietnam. Haddad acted as an intermediary between a Vietnamese priest, Tran Van Khoat, who represented the protesters, and Dave Lewis, director of the US Catholic Conference. While Lewis expressed skepticism, Haddad told Khoat the matter was under consideration.[37] By the end of 1975, more than a thousand people had resettled in the New Orleans area, and the following year, two thousand Vietnamese moved to the vicinity, transforming metropolitan New Orleans into a hub for Vietnamese resettlement and a spiritual center for Vietnamese Catholics.[38]

Discourses of Christian charity distanced Americans from culpability in instigating the war in Vietnam that produced the exodus of thousands of refugees. They also silenced refugees themselves. Once they left camps like Fort Chaffee, Vietnamese and Cambodians would continue to depend on the generosity of sponsors, neighbors, employers, and schoolteachers, leaving little room to criticize US militarism and racism.[39] Yet refugees still expressed conflicting views about their "new life," as federal agencies called the process of resettlement.[40] In July 1975, a rumor circulated among refugees at Eglin Air Force Base, in Florida, that a group of refugees sponsored by the ACC of New Orleans were said to have encountered protests by Black residents in New Orleans and sent back to Fort Indiantown Gap, Pennsylvania.[41] The camp newsletter reprinted a letter by Brother Martin Phuoc (Phạm Ngọc Phước), a former resident at the base, who assured his compatriots that all seventy-five families resettled by the ACC were doing well. While their houses were "a little far from the city," they were comfortable and their Black neighbors drove them to market and church. The letter concluded, "It is a settlement center, not a temporary camp. If some people fear discrimination from blacks, it does not exist here," assuaging people's concerns over the racial antagonism they would face in US society through the idiom of Christian charity. What reception, though, awaited those refugees who were not Christian?

Ultimately, thousands of Vietnamese refugees did resettle in New Orleans, a history that is noteworthy for several reasons. Specifically, the ACC of New Orleans rejected federal policies that recommended refugees be resettled across the United States to facilitate their assimilation into US society. Instead, the ACC selected four main resettlement areas: Versailles in eastern New Orleans, Woodlawn apartments in Algiers, the Kingston subdivision in Marrero, and Bridge City. Moreover, refugees themselves were not immobile. By 1976, many left their initial place of resettlement to live closer to family, seek out a more familiar climate, or search for employment opportunities. By 1978, an estimated seven thousand to ten thousand Vietnamese resettled in the New Orleans area, which on a per capita basis was the largest settlement of Vietnamese in the nation.[42] A supervisor at Immigration and Naturalization admitted, "They keep coming. Actually, nobody keeps tabs on these people. All we have is a rough idea."[43] Reverend Haddad, of the ACC, added that his organization tried to dissuade people from coming: "We estimate there are 7,500 Vietnamese in New Orleans. Of that number, 5,400 came here on their own. We did not bring them."[44] While the role of the Archdiocese of New Orleans may have been limited, it would still be a significant agent in defining the presence of Vietnamese refugees in the region.

New Orleans was a welcoming city, but it was also a distressed city. Unemployment rates were higher than the national average and even higher for Black adults. More than ten thousand people were on a waiting list for public housing. Black leaders in New Orleans raised concerns that the ACC directed scarce economic resources toward Vietnamese refugees rather than Black residents, but the leaders insisted that the problem was one not of racial antagonisms but of jobs and housing, a point made by Carl Galmon of the A. Philip Randolph Institute: "It is not a black against Vietnamese thing. To say that is an insult. What we are saying is Catholic

Charities should relocate Vietnamese some place where the unemployment rate is lower."[45] Across the United States, Black leaders saw the gains made during the civil rights movements in the 1950s and 1960s being eroded. Other activists drew on the region's plantation economy as a metaphor for how new arrivals contributed to the deferral of Black ambitions:

> Every time you look around, somebody is coming here and being put ahead of the blacks who were born here. We were treated as property from the beginning, never as human beings. Now we are being told to step back and make room for the Vietnamese, just as we were told to step back and make room for the Cubans and everybody else the whites wanted to put ahead of us.[46]

While leaders of the ACC acknowledged the legacy of racial segregation, they insisted the refugees themselves should not be the target of discrimination: "The decision to admit more refugees is one that will affect only the poor in this country, and it won't affect the rich or the middle class. I know that's a problem, but the problem was here long before the Vietnamese came."[47] Ultimately, the ACC voiced opposition to Galmon's nomination to the welfare board for his public criticism of the resettlement program: "His public statements, [we] believe, convey his feelings that the needs of one racial group should have priority over the needs of other racial groups. Such a position is certainly not in keeping with the teachings of the Church, nor in keeping with the ideals upon which this nation was founded."[48] What were the ideals on which this nation was founded? The statement denies the long history of racial segregation in the Gulf South, overlooking the centuries-long enslavement of Black Americans and the more recent era of Jim Crow laws as well as the nearly sixty years of exclusion acts that barred Asians from becoming citizens and culminated in the internment of Japanese Buddhist priests in Camp Livingston in northern Louisiana.

Black organizations ultimately recommended that the ACC suspend its resettlement program. In a report by the Urban League of Greater New Orleans, "Indochina Refugee Issue: Urban League Position Paper," leaders expressed worries that Black Americans were denied the rights and resources of US citizenship and laid blame on the ACC for attracting more refugees and creating ethnic enclaves. Ultimately, the report emphasized a shared dispossession among Blacks and Vietnamese newcomers. Clarence Barney, then executive director of the New Orleans Urban League, noted the commonalities between the Black community and the refugees: "The plight of the Vietnamese refugees, though derived from different circumstances, is like the black struggle, complicated by similar backgrounds of relocation and suffering."[49] For Vietnamese community leaders, what was at stake was their recognition as good citizens, as Vu Huu Chuong, vice-chairman of the New Orleans Area Vietnamese Committee, emphasized: "We hope that the leaders in the black and in the white communities will try to understand the Vietnamese, and try to explain to us clearly what the laws and the customs [are] so that we can make good citizens."[50] In Mississippi, Vietnamese residents were less conciliatory, as one fisherman expressed: "All our lives we have been at war, have known nothing but war. First it was in Vietnam. Now it is here in America—a war for our people to be accepted."[51] The archdiocese, however, saw a more powerful mandate—the performance of Christian charity and compassion toward those seeking refuge.

Where the Urban League's report did find support was among the white political leadership of Plaquemines Parish, located downstream from New Orleans. White residents saw Vietnamese as competitors who broke longstanding practices to increase their catches. Tensions flared on fishing docks when Vietnamese-owned boats were denied docking privileges, their boats were burned, and even their catches were rejected by local shrimp and seafood buyers. In Empire, Louisiana, where the Mississippi River spills into the Gulf, signs read: "No Vietnamese Wanted."[52] What was at stake was not just the assistance given to refugees but the increasing difficulties everyone faced making a living. As one fisherman said, "We got a hard enough time makin' ends meet as it is."[53] Some Vietnamese fishermen even received death threats, although no one knew whether the letters came from disgruntled landlords or Vietnamese communists who wanted to instigate unrest.[54] Eventually, the local leadership evicted all but four Vietnamese-owned boats from the parish.

Refugee resettlement in the 1970s occurred at a moment in which the contours of citizenship were changing.[55] During the Cold War, the US Congress passed landmark legislation around civil rights legislation and immigration reform. By the mid-1970s, the social mandates of the Cold War waned. The United States had been defeated in Vietnam, and US economic power appeared in decline. Popular support for refugees decreased with the emergence of a new mandate in which individuals were called to demonstrate their worth through their economic contributions.[56] Refugees were called upon to become "self-sufficient," framing belonging in terms of liberal values of individuality but masking the complicity of the state in perpetuating a system of racial hierarchy that shaped both the reception of Vietnamese refugees and the terms in which they could make themselves into worthy citizens.

As Fort Chaffee wound down its operations to house refugees in December 1975, more than a thousand Catholic refugees gathered in honor of a symbol of religious freedom, a statue of the Madonna and Child that had been smuggled out of Vietnam. The statue was destined for New Orleans, home then to the largest concentration of Vietnamese Catholics in the United States.[57] Today it is housed in Mary Queen of Vietnam Church and frequently loaned to other Vietnamese Catholic churches, thus endowing New Orleans as a "distinctive spiritual center among Vietnamese-American Catholics in the United States."[58]

The church is located in Village de l'Est, a subdivision in eastern New Orleans, better known as Versailles after an apartment complex where refugees were initially resettled. By the 1980s, its grocery stores, cafés, jewelers, and Vietnamese language services served as a beacon for Vietnamese migrants who lived as far away as Alabama, but its cohesion is attributed to the common geographic origins and faith of many of its residents.[59] Many of the families who resettled in the neighborhood had lived in northern Vietnam until 1954, when they moved south to escape religious persecution under the communist regime. These families fled a second time to escape the communist takeover of their country in 1975.

The archdiocese was a significant agent in shaping the role of Catholicism in the lives of Vietnamese refugees, even beyond their initial resettlement. While Catholic parishes generally serve a specific area or territory, personal parishes serve Catholics of a particular language or nationality. In 1983, the archbishop approved Mary Queen of Vietnam Parish for Southeast Asian Catholics, the first personal parish for Vietnamese Catholics in the United States, thus ensuring that Catholicism would be a vital institution in Vietnamese community formation across the region.[60] Mary Queen of Vietnam Parish became a model for all other personal parishes in metropolitan New Orleans, including Our Lady of La Vang Mission and parishes on the west bank of the Mississippi River.[61]

Vietnamese community leaders emphasize that Catholics still constitute the majority of the Vietnamese population along the Gulf Coast. But even in Versailles, not all residents are Catholic. In the early 1990s, most shopkeepers were Chinese or Vietnamese Buddhists.[62] Those refugees who arrived in 1975, and those who followed, were plural in their affiliations: some Baptist, some Buddhist, and others followers of syncretic practices such as Caodaism and Hòa Hảo, two movements that emerged in southern Vietnam in the early twentieth century. Mrs. Quý, who settled in New

Orleans in the 1970s, described how spiritually empty she found the city upon her arrival. She said she missed the ways in which her faith structured the rhythms of her monthly activities: "People had the habit of eating vegetarian food on the first day of the lunar month and visiting the temple, but there wasn't anywhere for them to go. Empty." Vietnamese refugees and migrants who did not identify as Christian thus faced the problem of anchoring their collective life, "finding a space and making a place," and all the ensuing activities that dwelling involved.[63] By highlighting the role of Catholic refugees, we overlook the diverse ways in which Vietnamese refugees have inhabited the Gulf Coast.

In New Orleans, and across the Gulf South, collective life is anchored by faith-based organizations, in contrast to localities like Orange County, California, and Arlington, Virginia, where retail malls serve as important nodes of community building and formation.[64] By the late 1970s, Vietnamese Buddhists had to rely on the counsel and guidance of senior monks living elsewhere, in California, Texas, and Virginia. Thus the work of making Buddhist places fell not to the ordained clergy but to lay Buddhists themselves. In 1977, a group of twenty families established the Vietnamese Buddhist Fellowship of Louisiana in Woodlawn, on the west bank of the Mississippi River. The association invited Thích Thiên-Ân to New Orleans, the senior Vietnamese monk and Zen master who had founded the International Buddhist Meditation Center in Los Angeles seven years earlier.[65] His itinerary attested to his dual role as a scholar of Buddhism and a spiritual guide for Vietnamese refugees. First he delivered a lecture, in English, titled "Buddhist Meditation in Our Daily Lives" at the First Unitarian Church, and then he met with Vietnamese residents to provide advice on setting up a lay association to support their efforts to establish a temple. The group rented an apartment to serve as a home temple in a complex that initially housed Vietnamese refugees on the West Bank. Like other home temples, its exterior conformed to the aesthetics and uses of the neighborhood, while inside people gathered to carry out rituals and prayers.

In the 1980s, a Cambodian monk described Buddha as "in hiding," alluding to the dilemmas of Southeast Asian refugees who had to reconcile the demands to be good citizens with their collective family and cultural values, which had little institutional support.[66] That people established an association, however, speaks to the long-distance spiritual resources and the local administrative experience available. Monks who provided spiritual support for these associations included Thích Thiên-Ân, who taught at universities in Southern California; Thích Tịnh Từ, who had counseled refugees as a Buddhist chaplain at Fort Chaffee; and Thích Trí Hiền, who left Japan to support

Vietnamese refugees in the United States. Later the lay Buddhists invited an elderly monk, Thích Bồ Đề, to reside in the home temple and carry out rituals, lead chants, and offer blessings to members of the group. By 1983, the association numbered more than fifteen hundred, including Buddhists from other Asian countries and people who identified as Cao Đài and Hòa Hảo.[67] The association was able to purchase land on the west bank, holding dinners to raise money. A ground-breaking ceremony was reportedly attended by more than two hundred people, exemplifying the multitude of activities such as donating, planning, constructing, blessing, and chanting that are involved in transforming a space into a spiritual dwelling.[68]

The congregation relied on guidance from the Venerable Thích Trí Hiền, who served Vietnamese Buddhists throughout Louisiana, Oklahoma, and Texas. Born in northern Vietnam, he began his religious studies at the age of six and moved south when he was seventeen. He later studied in Japan, where he became the director of a Zen Buddhist center in Tokyo, before moving to Washington, DC, to serve as vice-chairman of the Buddhist Social Service Organization in 1977. He later settled in Grand Prairie, Texas, just outside the Dallas–Fort Worth area to serve the growing population of Vietnamese refugees.[69] When he proposed building a larger center, the city council initially approved the plan, but later rescinded its support in the face of protests by residents, some carrying signs with the message "Repent."[70] Neighbors complained that Buddhists would be a "nuisance" and feared they would bring a "communist-type" of government.[71]

No protests met the association's plans to build a temple in New Orleans. The lay association eventually built what would become Chùa Bồ Đề, the first temple in the metropolitan region and, to this day, one of the most prominent and well-known temples on the Gulf Coast. What delayed construction on the temple was the municipality itself, a reminder that place-making activities are not simply acts of faith alone but must also be sanctioned by numerous state and city offices. The land purchased by the association was located in Lower Coast Algiers, across a bridge that spanned the Intracoastal Waterway. A proposal to widen the off-ramp of the bridge required the design of the temple to be modified. By November 1983, the site had been cleared and graded, but the association ran out of funding by the following April, leaving the temple half completed, with work remaining on the roof and walls.[72] These problems, whether due to protesting citizens or municipal planners, highlight how these spaces of collective worship are part and parcel of the city.

Even as late as 1989, the lay association invited monks from elsewhere to conduct rites for funerals and Buddhist holidays, leaving the day-to-day activities to the board of directors and other lay Buddhists. The temple was more than a private space where people performed their faith; it was a public stage through which community leaders gained political visibility and the congregation expressed their fidelity to American values. Such performances were overlooked by the mainstream media, with one journalist depicting Buddhism as an exotic, age-old spiritual tradition maintained by refugees who "cling to their old ways."[73] Vietnamese Buddhists, in contrast, explained their participation in terms of the American values of freedom and democracy. A twenty-two-year-old man interviewed by the journalist acknowledged his gratitude for religious freedom in America and contrasted it to the communist regime in Vietnam and its restrictions on what holidays were observed. What the journalist saw as "old ways," the young Vietnamese Buddhist described as an expression of freedom. Buddhist temples were more than places to carry out traditional practices; they were the grounds upon which people made themselves into American citizens.

Mrs. Quý, who had served on the board of directors in the 1990s, described their collective efforts to me. A savvy businesswoman, she was part of the early efforts to establish a Buddhist congregation as a lay-based organization, one that was formally recognized as a "non-profit corporation" and eventually had bylaws.

> At first, we created a non-profit corporation for the temple, and each person deposited money to buy land. [We] then held fund-raising dinners and invited a lot of people, not just Buddhists, but also people who were Cao Đài and Hòa Hảo, because they didn't have a temple either.

She described the political importance of Chùa Bồ Đề as well. The temple belonged to the community, and all registered members had the right to vote. Eventually, the board of directors recruited a resident monk, who had served as chief of the finance division of the Vietnam Unified Buddhist Church before coming to the United States in 1975, where he had resided in temples in California and Texas.[74] He eventually left the congregation over disagreements with the board of directors and returned to California. I asked Mrs. Quý if he established another temple:

> He didn't start another temple. He wanted to take over Chùa Bồ Đề and make it his, but the temple was an "association," it didn't belong to an individual, but [to] the community. . . . It belonged to all of the Buddhists, to the Buddhist community. . . . The

monk was the spiritual leader. He wasn't the director, but the
religious leader. So when it came to issues of finances or power
or whatever, he didn't have any [say].

Now there are four temples [in the New Orleans area], but
Chùa Bồ Đề was the first. Whoever wants to become a Buddhist
can do so, because the bylaws today are clear. If you wish to vote
in the election, you have to be an official member of the temple.

Even today, Vietnamese Buddhists reflect on the different organizational
structures of temples, often contrasting those governed by lay associations
(*chùa hội*) with those owned and administered by monks (*chùa của thầy*).
As Mrs. Quý emphasized, Chùa Bồ Đề was built with the money and labor
of lay Buddhists, and it gave the congregation visibility in the city, thus providing a platform that was more than a space for collective worship.

Mrs. Sang, another lay Buddhist who attended the temple, described
how the conflict between the board of directors and the resident monk led
to his departure, a feature that she said characterized those temples man-
aged by lay Buddhists.

> There isn't a temple that doesn't have a monk. But many times,
> the lay association wants to do things their way, and the monk
> wants to do things his or her way, so the monk doesn't stay
> long—whoever they invite doesn't stay long.

These stories of monks who "don't stay long" are part of the rhizomatic
spread of Buddhism across the Gulf South, propelled in ways that lead to
multiplicity through horizontal, rather than vertical, connections. Spreading Buddhism across the Gulf South happens in the mud—the disagreements over institutional control and decision-making that cannot be
comprehended when Buddhism is seen only in terms of liturgical truths
and the spaces of formal worship. Even Mrs. Quý reflected on the spread of
temples in the municipal area and admitted how she now saw the multiplicity as beneficial, rather than a hindrance, to people's expressions of
faith:

> I spoke to a monk in Houston who told me not to worry—the
> more temples the better. Why is that? I asked the monk, and he
> explained that with a lot of temples, then no temple will have a
> problem. When people aren't satisfied with the monk or the
> activities, then they can go to another temple. He really opened

my eyes. There was one, Chùa Bồ Đề, and after some problems, people founded another temple, then when that monk left, he founded another temple. So what happened when people didn't like the three? They built a fourth temple. Who is going to make trouble now? Any Buddhist who wants to come to Chùa Bồ Đề is welcome. It is the root temple [chùa gốc] and would never deny any Buddhist [Phật tử] who wanted to join, and the Buddhists at the other temples are also Buddhists of Chùa Bồ Đề.

While Mrs. Quý refers to Chùa Bồ Đề as a "root temple," we can also see it as a node, sending out shoots that spread through rhizomatic structures, not via direct transmission from a patriarch.[75] The spread of these temples, and thus the dharma, was instead nourished by the mud.

Even from a distance, Chùa Bồ Đề is impressive. Its complex includes a spacious worship hall, a monastic residence, a communal kitchen and dining room, and, for activities, a covered outdoor stage that can accommodate several hundred people. Surrounding the temple are wooded grounds where a few gardeners cultivate herbs and other plants that they offer to lay Buddhists by donation. Several years ago, the congregation raised funds to install a massive statue of the bodhisattva Quán Thế Âm (figure 1.1). Why then have the complex and its gardens not attracted as much popular or scholarly attention as Mary Queen of Vietnam Church and the fabled market gardens of Versailles? Part of the explanation may lie in how the story of Vietnamese resettlement in New Orleans has largely been told as one of Vietnamese Catholics. On the one hand, this story domesticates refugees by framing their arrival within a city that is famously Catholic; on the other hand, it obscures how Southeast Asian refugees and migrants are inscribing the Gulf Coast with new spiritual meanings, including minority ones. We also lose sight of how practitioners of minority religions play a part in regional history and how they respond to the precarity of coastal livelihoods by strengthening their investments in faith-based communities.

SPIRITUAL LABOR

The problems facing cities in the Gulf South are no different from those facing other distressed cities—population loss, joblessness, poverty, an eroding tax base, and failing schools.[76] In this regard, the force of Hurricane Katrina was not just atmospheric—damage wrought by winds and sea—it also exposed the harm done by neoliberal policies and the new

1.1 Chùa Bồ Đề in New Orleans was one of the first Vietnamese temples established on the Gulf Coast. Hoisted above the roof are the Vietnamese heritage, Buddhist, and US flags. The roof features multiple tiers and flying eaves, two elements commonly associated with pagodas in East Asia. The statue of Quan Âm featured here in 2006 has since been replaced by a much larger statue of the bodhisattva. Photo by the author.

warrant of citizenship that privileged "white property over black humanity."[77] Recovery efforts exacerbated these dynamics by channeling state-based funding to for-profit companies with the rationale that the market was more efficient at delivering state-funded resources than the state itself. These market-based solutions ultimately did not succeed because of "inefficiencies of profit," their failures compensated by the efforts of faith-based organizations and nonprofits. While these organizations provided much-needed help, they also reproduced a discourse of charity and compassion reminiscent of those justifying assistance to Southeast Asian refugees in the 1970s.[78]

Residents in the Gulf Coast turned to religious organizations as agents of recovery.[79] Faith-based groups distributed meals and materials for rebuilding homes, schools, and churches. Even national-level organizations like the American Red Cross needed to work through the existing infrastructure of faith-based organizations to reach people. Vietnamese temples and churches were also part of this spiritual infrastructure of recovery and rebuilding. They served as bases for volunteers and officials with the Federal Emergency Management Agency (FEMA), using their parking lots as distribution sites and their grounds as shelter for displaced people. Chùa Bồ Đề, for example, housed sixty people in a multipurpose building that had only been opened a few weeks before the storm. Its parking lot was a site where supplies—cash, blankets, and Vietnamese food items like cooking oil and bags of rice—were distributed to residents.[80] In 2006, FEMA recognized the importance of community and faith-based organizations and allowed these groups to submit reimbursement applications for all incurred expenses. New forms of "grassroots solidarity" and political activism also gained traction with community groups like Boat People SOS, which used its network to support the thousands of families left homeless after Hurricane Katrina, and the Vietnamese American Young Leaders Association (VAYLA) of New Orleans, which organized interracial coalitions in New Orleans East.[81] Vietnamese organizations likewise responded to the BP oil spill in the Gulf in 2010, the flooding of southwestern Louisiana in 2016, and Hurricane Michael along the Florida Panhandle in 2018. Through their disaster relief efforts, these community- and faith-based organizations have developed networks to channel support to Vietnamese residents along the Gulf Coast. Yet it has been the Catholic Church in New Orleans East that has been spotlighted for its almost textbook case of recovery.

Mary Queen of Vietnam Church emerged as a major organizing force in the city's recovery, and its contributions to rebuilding in New Orleans East have been well documented.[82] Parishioners successfully challenged the initial plan presented by the Bring New Orleans Back Commission that would have turned the neighborhood into "green space" by converting areas for flood retention. The Reverend Nguyễn Thế Viện defended the right of people in New Orleans East to return and rebuild: "Before Katrina, when we said homeland, we meant Vietnam. When my people say homeland now, they mean New Orleans."[83] Church leaders worked with Black community leaders, building an interracial coalition to protest a nearby landfill used for dumping household and demolition debris from flooded structures and opening their worship space to house displaced Black congregations that lost their buildings.[84] Nevertheless, characterizing the church's success as a distinctly Vietnamese response neglects the diversity of faith-based communities in the Gulf Coast region and their differential capacities both to provide material support and to organize these places that fostered a sense of collective belonging, or the "spatial fate" of a community.[85] What comes into view reaffirms the role of faith but also reveals how these institutions are built not out of timeless cultural characteristics but through the "active and current construction of meaning and identity performed by community members," as well as through leadership and a good dose of luck.[86] By limiting the story to Vietnamese Catholics, we lose sight of the more significant role that spirituality played for all residents in the Gulf South—whether Vietnamese or not—in the face of economic policies that sanctified the market over humanity.

Near Mary Queen of Vietnam Church, the recovery of Vạn Hạnh Buddhist Center was more uneven. In December 2005, blue tarps still covered the roof, damaged by Katrina's torrential winds. A handwritten sign posted outside the gates pleaded for volunteer groups to help rebuild the temple (figure 1.2). Early in 2006, the ceiling beams remained exposed, waiting for electrical repairs. Eventually, the Catholic pastor of Mary Queen of Vietnam Church sent his parishioners to make the needed repairs. The center's resident female monk relocated to Georgia, returning only occasionally to witness important events, so the Venerable Thích Trí Hiền, who had

1.2 Vạn Hạnh Buddhist Center was significantly damaged by wind and rain during Hurricane Katrina. For many Buddhists, the storm was a powerful lesson about impermanence. The construction of a new worship hall in 2006 is visible on the right. Photo by the author.

overseen the opening of Chùa Bồ Đề, served as a spiritual guide for the congregation, counseling them on impermanence. By May 2006, the membership board showed that only a third of the names listed had contributed their annual fees; the other names were left blank, a stark reminder of those people who had not yet returned or decided to resettle elsewhere. The storm did bring a windfall of sorts. The board of directors had purchased a hefty insurance policy that included wind damage. With the payout and the volunteer labor of members, the building was repaired and a prominent worship hall built. Still, the longer and largely undocumented process of rebuilding the temple when compared to the focus on Mary Queen of Vietnam Church highlighted the spatial fates of these two institutions—both indisputably Vietnamese and yet differentially connected to New Orleans.

In terms of resilience, the coastal city of Biloxi, Mississippi, contrasted sharply with the Vietnamese neighborhood in New Orleans East. In 1975, around fifty Vietnamese families resettled on the coast, sponsored by individuals or churches, but few remained through 1976. In 1977, Catholic social services resettled more refugees, who found employment with Biloxi seafood packers that had faced chronic labor shortages. In 1989, the Vietnamese Buddhist Congregation of Mississippi purchased a two-story house with an attached garage and converted it into a temple, and, as elsewhere in the region, the association struggled to raise money, as the vast majority of Vietnamese were Catholic. In August 2005, the congregation celebrated the opening of its temple under the direction of a senior California-based abbot, Thích Đạo Quang, who sent a younger monk, one who had arrived in the United States three years earlier, to reside in the temple.[87] The temple served a few dozen people on Sundays, but hundreds would attend Buddhist celebrations, demonstrating its importance in the cultural life of Vietnamese, not all who would identify themselves as Buddhist. When Hurricane Katrina's ten-foot storm surge roared ashore, the monk huddled in the attic of the building. If the narrative of the neighborhood of Versailles has been one of resilience, the story for many people in Biloxi was survival. Even economic recovery contributed to the displacement of East Biloxi residents, as casinos were the first businesses to reopen, while the fisheries where many Vietnamese were employed remained shuttered. Within a year, the temple had been rebuilt alongside the adjacent Vietnamese Catholic Church, and the two institutions served as staging grounds for distributing resources after Katrina. By 2007, the Buddhist congregation was fiercely divided over the role of the resident monk, underscoring the difficulties in maintaining alliances forged through the rebuilding and recovery period.

Farther along the coast, in Alabama, was a small fishing community of several thousand residents. By 2000, nearly one in ten Vietnamese living along the coasts of Mississippi, Louisiana, and Alabama worked in agriculture or fishing, drawing out the bounty of the Gulf and transforming it into economic value.[88] Eventually, Southeast Asians reworked the color line of these coastal communities by reviving seafood industries. Bayou La Batre, Alabama, where a majority held political and economic power, was transformed by the presence of Laotians, Cambodians, and Vietnamese into a "multicultural" town unified by the "culture of the sea."[89] By the 1990s, nearly a third of the three thousand residents were refugees from Southeast Asia; among the Vietnamese were both Catholics, some converted by aid workers in the 1970s and others whose families had been Catholic for generations, and Buddhists.[90] Although damage from Hurricane Katrina was significant, there was little national news coverage after the storm, reinforcing the invisibility of Asian American populations in the Gulf South.[91] Chùa Chánh Giác, one of three temples in the area, was flooded, but it emerged as a focal point for rebuilding.[92] The resident monk visited Buddhist temples across the country to seek aid, drawing on the Buddhist virtue of compassion and the resonant histories of suffering shared by so many refugees who had resettled in the United States. Vietnamese American organizations donated dried noodles and sacks of rice from around the country, and local organizations such as temples and churches then distributed the supplies, highlighting the importance of these minority faith-based communities as agents of recovery in the face of the retreating presence of the municipal and federal government.

The force of Hurricane Katrina not only demolished buildings but led to the creation of new organizations, including a monastery just outside Mobile. The tale of its creation began when Thích Tịnh Từ, the Vietnamese monk who had served as the Buddhist chaplain at Fort Chaffee, responded to a telephone call from an elderly woman. A relative of the woman recalled how that phone conversation was "fate" (duyên), as the senior monk rarely answered his phone, but on that occasion he did. The monk was familiar with the story of the woman, who fled Vietnam in the late 1970s, on a journey that led her to cross a raging river, not even knowing how to swim, with only the name of Quán Thế Âm on her lips to carry her to safety on the other side. Her survival was one of the many modern miracle tales that have bolstered the image of the bodhisattva figure as particularly efficacious for many Vietnamese Buddhists. The woman invited Thích Tịnh Từ to come to Alabama to speak to a small group of people who were interested in learning more about Buddhism. During the meeting, he invoked the storm's devastation as a reminder of impermanence, a central tenet in Buddhism. His conversations inspired the woman's extended family to convert a fishing camp into a monastery to introduce Buddhist teachings to the region, their faith inscribing the landscape with new spiritual meanings. They requested that the senior monk send someone from his monastic sangha in California to reside in the monastery and eventually transferred ownership to the monastic sangha.

These tales, spun of suffering from Hurricane Katrina, are hard to compress in a story that would define a distinctly Vietnamese or even Buddhist response. What emerges are plural responses that expose contingencies in the spatial fates, even among Buddhist communities. Yet it is not only outside observers who look for commonalities in the experiences of Vietnamese in the region; community leaders are also invested in containing difference, especially against the backdrop of long-standing religious pluralism. Thus the claim of common origins, a racializing discourse that traces descent from legendary kings, engenders a sense of obligation to provide mutual aid.

COMPATRIOTS AND THE CONTAINMENT OF DIFFERENCE

On April 23, 2006, the outdoor stage of Chùa Bồ Đề on the West Bank featured an elaborate altar at which Vietnamese gathered as compatriots and expressed a sense of collective belonging that transcended geographic, national, and even religious differences. The ceremony drew on the symbolic repertoires of village festivals and the modern state of the Republic of Vietnam, invoking a prerevolutionary past that would bring together Vietnamese residents in the region, irrespective of their religious affiliation. Instead of the five-color Buddhist flag, Vietnamese traditional festival flags were strung above a large drum bearing the words "Hùng Vương" (Hùng Kings) to welcome the several hundred people who attended. Many of the men dressed in military uniforms and the women wore flowing *áo dài*, long tunics over palazzo pants widely considered the Vietnamese national dress. A few city officials were also present to witness the event and garner votes from their Vietnamese constituents. The celebration began with a military salute by graduates of the Thủ Đức Military Academy, an officer training school of the Army of the Republic of Vietnam in Saigon. A three-member color guard approached with three flags—the US flag, the flag of the Republic of Vietnam, and a Vietnamese festival flag. Unlike the Tet festival held at Mary Queen of Vietnam Church that year, the celebration did not receive any press coverage.

People had gathered to pay homage, not to Buddha but to the Hùng Kings, revered as ancestors of the Vietnamese nation. The Hùng Kings are said to have descended from the legendary union of Lạc Long Quân, a dragon king from the sea, and Âu Cơ, a mythical phoenix or fairy from the mountains, who laid a sac of eggs from which sprang a hundred children. Eventually, the two parted ways, each accompanied by fifty children and promising to provide mutual support to the other. Vietnamese describe themselves as "children of the dragon, descendants of the phoenix," or more commonly by the Vietnamese term *đồng bào*, or "from the same sac," often translated as "compatriot."

The legend is highly malleable, emphasizing how the metaphor of "sac" contains seemingly irreconcilable differences.[93] Historians of Vietnam attribute the story to the adaptation of seafaring people to a delta environment, while others consider it an origin myth of an independent state whose founders predated the first Chinese emperor.[94] For Vietnamese in the Gulf South, the legend bridges religious differences, allowing people who gather to experience a sense of collective unity in spite of diverse spiritual orientations. In the 1960s, political tensions between Buddhists and Catholics in the Republic of Vietnam ran high. Many Buddhists thought that the Catholic communities that resettled in the south in 1954 were recipients of state-sponsored programs that privileged Catholics, who accused Buddhists of being communist sympathizers. While the tensions did not entirely dissipate in the United States, these differences are muted by reference to common origins, "the children of the dragon and the grandchildren of the fairy," and the promise of mutual aid.

The emphasis on common origins is an element in these spiritual negotiations. Buddhist congregations call upon compatriot Buddhists (*đồng hương Phật tử*) when they organize festivals and other celebrations. The Vietnamese phrase invokes both the idea of *đồng bào*, or descent-based relatedness, and *quê hương* ("homeland"), or place-based origins; thus compatriotism engenders a discourse of obligation and mutual aid to solicit participation from those people who are only casually, if at all, interested in Buddhism. Invitations and full-colored posters, banners strung across temple gates, and open speeches welcome these compatriots. Since not all Vietnamese identify as Buddhists, calling upon compatriots expands the social field to include those participants who may not attend a Sunday service but still enjoy the convivial atmosphere of these occasions.

Compatriotism cannot be expressed by memory alone. People require spaces for their gatherings, where they can carry out celebrations like the one that honors the Hùng Kings. In New Orleans, a dedicated temple to the national ancestors now stands near the Vạn Hạnh Buddhist Center and is a site of the festival and of gatherings for the lunar New Year. But in the months and years after Hurricane Katrina, it was in Buddhist temples and Catholic churches that people performed mutual support that transcended otherwise irreconcilable differences in religious orientation. Traditionally celebrated on the tenth day of the third lunar month, the Hùng Kings festival often falls near April 30, which marks the fall of Saigon in 1975. Both occasions celebrate Vietnamese collective identity by honoring ancestors around an explicit display of anticommunism, a loosely constructed platform that opposes the current Vietnamese government while celebrating American-style capitalism.[95] In doing so, these communities distinguish themselves from the Socialist Republic of Vietnam, where celebrations of the Hùng Kings' Death Anniversary have been embraced as a model of statecraft to present the Vietnamese Communist Party as "the legitimate successor to the exceptional Hùng Kings."[96]

Along the Gulf Coast, both events draw on a moral vocabulary of the Cold War, emphasizing the value of heritage and freedom. In 2003, Louisiana was the first state to recognize the flag of the Republic of Vietnam as the "Vietnamese American Freedom and Heritage Flag." The legislation forbade the flying of the flag of the Socialist Republic of Vietnam, over objections by the Vietnamese Embassy.[97] While the heritage flag is meaningful to Vietnamese Americans, its display at these events signifies how Vietnamese assert their particular form of citizenship in the United States. Celebrations of April 30, the lunar New Year, and even Buddhist festivals like the Buddha's birthday (Vesak or Phật Đản) often include special guests such as US veterans, thus underscoring how these collective spaces of worship serve as "strategic memory projects" that transcend religious difference.[98] Today religious festivals at both churches and temples observe a minute of silence to honor those who lost their lives either in fighting for the republic or by fleeing the country, binding Catholics and Buddhists through common rituals and symbols of mourning that have come to define Vietnamese subjectivity in the United States.[99]

The Hùng Kings' Death Anniversary, organized by community leaders, brings people together to demonstrate their symbolic kinship as children of the dragon and descendants of the phoenix. These ancestors are neither Catholic nor Buddhist, nor are they particularly efficacious. In other words, they have little power to answer people's prayers or offer spiritual refuge. For most Vietnamese, the Hùng Kings are models of virtue, but they cannot help people with the everyday vicissitudes of their lives, leaving residents along the Gulf Coast to express their dignity, not in terms of the market but in terms of their spirituality and faith.

◆ ◆ ◆

The story of Vietnamese refugee resettlement along the Gulf Coast has emphasized the role of Vietnamese Catholics. While this story shows the creolizing dynamics of the administrative power of the Archdiocese of New Orleans with the faith of Vietnamese practitioners, it also reinscribes the Gulf South as a Catholic landscape. How then do we make visible those refugees who are non-Christian? How do we understand their efforts to create places to dwell and sanctify their dignity? The Gulf Coast is a muddy place, yet it is the mud that nourishes new forms of collective responses, which is all the more reason to include non-Christian groups in how we understand recovery efforts in the region. Both Vietnamese churches and temples provide material infrastructure as they inscribe the landscape with new spiritual meanings. At times, however, people endeavor to dissolve faith-based differences by drawing on a collective sense of responsibility or "staying Vietnamese." The call to compatriots is a notable feature in these spiritual negotiations.

The spread of temples is indeed about the struggle of institutional control, and these sites are best understood as lateral shoots, running through the mud of the Gulf South, nourished by people's suffering. It is also within the mud that we can understand the spread of Buddhism, not because of a centralized effort to plant more temples but rather through the rhizomatic structure of diaspora. The spread of these temples has compelled Buddhist lay leaders to reflection. For Mr. Trung, the story of their spread was not pretty, but neither were the conditions that faced Vietnamese refugees and migrants. The spread of these institutions is a regional story, a response to US empire, war, and refugee resettlement, the color line, and a vulnerable coastline, buffeted not just by hurricanes but also by neoliberal policies that have long emphasized the logics of profit over human dignity. Numerous Buddhist temples now stand where there once were none, evidence of a long history of spiritual negotiations arising from other, not so pretty, stories. These places provide people a refuge in which to construct and perform their identities as Buddhist—a refuge not in age-old tradition or an abstract philosophy but one in the making.

CHAPTER TWO

Recruiting Monks

I N 2005, the members of a newly built temple in Mississippi gathered for a special celebration—the formal acceptance of the temple by its California-based abbot and the installation of its first permanent monk. Fifteen years earlier, Vietnamese Buddhists had begun gathering for services in a garage attached to a two-story house purchased by a lay association in 1989.[1] Once they paid off the mortgage, they turned to raising funds for a temple built largely by members of the congregation, which opened in 2002, a common pattern in which the first temples were established by lay Buddhists (*chùa hội*), who then recruited a monk to serve as the spiritual leader.[2] On that day, the newly installed resident monk observed that in the United States, there were more Buddhist temples than monks, a skewed ratio that raises the question of what the role of Buddhist clergy is in making the Pure Land.[3]

Buddhism in the United States is often characterized by laicization, a model in which lay practitioners, rather than ordained monks, hold administrative control. *Laicization* is an elastic term, referring to the act by which an ordained monk returns to secular life, to the leadership of lay members, and, more broadly, to those practices adopted by lay members once reserved for ordained clergy. Laicization is also heralded for exemplifying new ideals around the democratization of Buddhism, which we saw in Mrs. Quý's claim that a temple belongs not to the monk but to the community.[4] While laicization is too often attributed to a gradual process of Americanization, much like congregationalism in the Protestant tradition, empirical studies suggest the factors in laicization are more complex.[5] Laicization, for example, does not explain why monks and lay Buddhists may break away to establish a new temple, often on property purchased by the monk. Lay Buddhists refer to this model as a "monk's temple" (*chùa của thầy*), where the

2.1 A procession from the monastic residence to the worship hall. The monks wear their (darker) golden ceremonial robes and the lay Buddhists wear pale gray practice robes (*áo tràng*). Children may be included and carry fresh flowers to place on the altar. Photo by Quang Huynh.

monk is not only the spiritual leader of the temple but also its administrator. Yet the difficulty in recruiting monks remains, reflecting the challenges of creating a sangha in the Gulf South, both as an institution and as an ideal.

Historically, laymen and laywomen have been part of the sangha, particularly in Mahayana traditions of practice. Yet even within the sangha, the distinction between monks and lay Buddhists is still maintained (figure 2.1). The precepts or rules of behavior for monks number in the hundreds, while lay followers who take refuge in the Three Jewels vow to adhere to five precepts or codes for moral conduct.[6] The ideal of the sangha, however, lies not just in the vows that govern conduct, as Master Deep Awakening explained:

> We use the word *sangha*, but we add a word, *monastic* sangha. You shave your hair, you take a vow. Whether you are a novice or a senior, you are considered part of a monastic sangha. If you are lay, you say "lay sangha," but the true definition of the word *sangha* is "harmony," so the word *sangha* means "harmony." As long as you practice Buddhist teachings and you live in harmony and awareness, you consider yourself sangha, lay sangha or

monastic sangha. If I shave my hair and live a monastic life and I don't teach people, I don't share [the dharma], I don't live mindfully, I don't live in harmony, I cannot consider myself a monastic sangha, only maybe the form, but just a shell.

Master Deep Awakening pointed toward those external signs that *appear* to define a Buddhist monk—shaving one's hair, taking a vow, and living a monastic life. But these signs are only the form, "a shell," and cannot alone create sangha, or "harmony," a collective body whose meaning lies in the Sanskrit root conveying a sense of unity, without schism.[7] Sangha means to live together with the Buddha and the Dharma as a collective body, the third of the Three Jewels (or refuges) of Buddhism.

While the sangha is an indisputable focus of Buddhism, its role can be difficult to grasp for outside observers. Colonial scholars in Asia, for example, associated the sangha with the rise of modern nationalism, attributing more unity to the Tibetan and other sanghas than warranted.[8] In the United States, some practitioners de-emphasize the monastic sangha in favor of a more expansive definition based on shared Buddhist practices or devotion to a particular teacher, which resonates with laicization, or the diminished authority of the Buddhist clergy. For Vietnamese Buddhists, the role of lay associations reflects temporalities of migration. Few ordained monks fled Vietnam in 1975, but arrived later, as refugees themselves or through family reunification policies. Later, with the normalization of diplomatic relations between Vietnam and the United States in 1995, monasteries in Texas and California sponsored the visas of monks who emigrated as religious specialists. Today even small associations recruit monks ordained in Vietnam, although the politics of the diaspora still influence how people evaluate the sincerity of these monks. Thus laicization overlooks the historical conditions and sociological importance of monk-lay relations in making the Pure Land, both as a specific institution, offering a viable vocation, and as a collective body. It also misrecognizes the strategies by Vietnamese migrants to build Buddhist institutions in the Gulf Coast region, where there once were none.

Even before the arrival of Southeast Asian refugees in 1975, popular understandings of Asian spiritualities reflected new forms of Orientalism in Cold War American culture. These politics of the Cold War continue to shape how lay Buddhists evaluate the sincerity of monks, from preoccupations with material prosperity in the United States as a hindrance to Buddhist practice to anxieties over the Vietnamese state's control over spiritual life. Recruiting monks is not an easy task, for senior monks or for lay associations. Consideration of monk-lay relations within their historical, social, and even material contexts illuminates why the ideal of harmony within these spiritual communities has been so challenging to realize in the Gulf South.

THE ORIENTAL MONK

Popular depictions of Buddhism in the United States often feature a solitary monk, not a sangha. That there is no similar institution within Anglo-Protestant religious traditions may help explain this blind spot.[9] This way of seeing Asian spiritualities emerged during the Cold War. As the United States attempted to contain communism, American audiences were introduced to new ways of representing Asia.[10] It was in this context that representations of the Oriental Monk, a celibate male figure detached from the sangha as a collective body, began to circulate.[11]

When individuals enter monastic life, they are said to renounce their secular or worldly identities. In Vietnamese, the act of renunciation, *xuất gia*, can be translated as "leaving the family." In Asia, individuals do not so much renounce their family ties as enter into a new kinship structure as the sons and daughters of the Buddha. Vietnamese monastic names carry the surname Thích, the Vietnamese translation of the last name of the historical Buddha (Shakyamuni), and the names of female monastics are further marked by Nữ, or "female." Monks' dharma names (*pháp danh*) are composed of two words, the first designating their place in a lineage by identifying their affiliation to a master and the second conveying a quality of the individual. Dharma names, like given names, thus tell a story—a story of origins and affiliation, of roots and belonging. Likewise, lay Buddhists who undertake the formal ceremony of initiation as Buddhists known as taking refuge in the Three Jewels (*quy y Tam bảo*) are also given dharma names to signify their relationship to their teacher, the monk who performed the ceremony.[12] Unlike monks, they do not carry the surname Thích.

Monasticism does not exhaust the meanings of how people practice. Lay Buddhists, or householders, have long held important roles as scholars and leaders. Cultivating the virtues of compassion and wisdom that lead to liberation through practice (*tu*) is an aspiration held by monks and lay Buddhists alike. Householders engage in cultivating those virtues in a practice that takes place in the family (*tu tại gia*) rather than in the pagoda (*tu tại chùa*). The Vietnamese saying "First is practicing at home, second is practicing in the market, and third is practicing in the pagoda" (Thứ nhất là tu tại gia, thứ nhì tu chợ, thứ ba tu chùa) ranks the level of difficulty, uplifting the efforts of those who attempt to carry out their practice in the family or in business above those who are in a pagoda.[13] The saying is also invoked to show that while monks may be respected, they are not always revered. In contrast, many Americans have little exposure to monasticism or even to individual monks, and certainly not to the lampooning of monasticism so common in Asia. Consequently, monks are often regarded as embodiments of an ideal rather than as individuals with human foibles. Part of that misrecognition can be attributed as well to the popularity of the Oriental Monk.

As the United States escalated its involvement along the Pacific Rim, new figures representing the Orient began to circulate. The term *Orient* is intentional; it alludes to the colonial knowledge project in which scholars produced truth claims about their subjects in Asia to justify their dominance. American Orientalism is a homegrown variety, a project whereby American popular culture consumed representations of Asia while simultaneously rejecting Asians themselves.[14] One example was the Oriental Monk, who imparted spiritual knowledge to US audiences as a friendly and subservient icon of Buddhism and Hinduism but did not threaten the national body.[15] The Oriental Monk served as an "ideological caregiver," instructing Americans so they could "reimagine themselves as the protectors, innovators, and guardians of Asian religions and culture and wrest the authority to define these traditions from others."[16] Representations of the Oriental Monk included actual historical figures such as D. T. Suzuki, the Zen translator, and fictional characters like Kwai Chang Caine, of the action-packed television series *Kung Fu*, reminders of how these individuals did not overturn Orientalist assumptions even as they presented Buddhism's appeal as universal.[17]

If the Oriental Monk mediated new forms of US-Asian integration in popular culture, it is important as well to note that white Americans traveled to Asian countries to learn firsthand about their spiritual traditions.[18] These travelers encountered Buddhism already infused with modernist aspirations. In nineteenth-century Burma, after British colonial authorities stripped the Burmese king of his powers, monastic sanghas sought to regain institutional support from lay practitioners. By the early twentieth century, Burmese monks developed meditation as a lay practice, stressing the values of collective well-being as well as aligning Buddhism with nationalist sentiments.[19] In the 1960s and 1970s, a few Americans traveled to Burma, Thailand, and Japan and studied under monks; some even became ordained and were conferred certificates of transmission. These Americans later established meditation centers in Massachusetts and

California and adapted the teachings to make them accessible to new audiences. Through their combined efforts, these monks and their American students presented meditation as the heart of Buddhism but also as a practice easily detached from the sangha itself.[20] Even though these Americans studied under Burmese and Thai monks, the institutionalization of insight meditation reinforced a dynamic similar to American Orientalism, in which white practitioners supplanted Asian monastics. Meditation was repackaged as mindfulness and moved into secular arenas, including medicine and psychiatry, further distancing meditation from monasticism.[21] Moreover, the emergence of a unified dharma was credited to the "open, diverse society" of the West, where "isolated Asian traditions [were] meeting for the first time in centuries."[22] Thus did the Oriental Monk hand spiritual knowledge to predominantly white disciples for safeguarding, marginalizing Asian American Buddhists in the United States.

The Oriental Monk is ultimately a character made for and by US national culture, a solitary figure reinforcing liberalism, or the right of persons to be free from external constraints, and affirming an individualist model of spiritual fulfillment over the collective obligations that arise in relation to family, community, and society.[23] The Oriental Monk diverts attention away from the importance of the monastic sangha, obscuring the patronage and service to the sangha that has underwritten Buddhism as an institution for centuries. It is not just monasticism that is difficult to transmit but the spiritual value monks are said to confer or merit, "the glue that holds the community together through religious ceremonies based on the exchange between the monks and lay people."[24] Monasticism and merit are entwined, both vital to making the Pure Land.

MERIT AND SPIRITUAL ECONOMIES

The spiritual economy around merit has been invoked as a dividing line between Buddhist modernism and traditional Buddhism. For many Americans, monks are regarded as models of a renunciatory lifestyle, pursuing vocations free from materialist desires.[25] While they may be familiar with the concept of karma, they do not attach importance to merit-making activities.[26] Yet for the monastic sangha, the "invisible merit economy" is the foundation of its material support, perhaps even more important than karma in understanding what motivates people's economic action to support temples and the monastic sangha.[27] As "karmic virtue," merit is produced through moral behavior and ritual action, and it requires the monastic sangha as a "field of merit" for those behaviors and actions to be realized and multiplied.[28]

Academic scholarship on merit has focused on Theravada Buddhism in Southeast Asian countries such as Thailand, Myanmar (Burma), Cambodia, and Laos. Merit-making activities are public acts. Monks go on daily rounds, carrying their alms bowl, head down and barefoot. Lay Buddhists place food in the bowls to cultivate generosity, while monks accept those gifts to cultivate humility; these acts also produce something more, merit. In Thailand, these exchanges bind conceptions of family well-being with the monastic sangha as young men enter temples for short periods and, in a ritual process, acquire merit, which they then transfer to their parents. In medieval China, merit was central to institutionalizing Buddhism: a gift of land was the most meritorious act a lay Buddhist could make. Not only did the gift secure the economic and cultural livelihood of the sangha, but it also memorialized the reputation of the donor, whose generosity was attested to by a stele or monument.[29] Zen teachings, in contrast, are replete with stories of kings failing to make merit. The most famous rebuke is when Emperor Wu of Liang asked the Bodhidharma, the founder of Zen Buddhism in China, how much merit he had earned from sponsoring monks and building monasteries. The Bodhidharma replied, "None, as good deeds that have worldly intent may bring good karma but no merit." What then is merit, that even an emperor's worldly acts of supporting the sangha could not ensure its production?

Merit is said to be the seeds of good fortune, actions that offset negative karma and propel one out of samsara, the cycle of death and rebirth, and into the Pure Land. In the Lotus Sutra, merit describes the magnificent benefits bestowed upon those who read, recite, copy, and uphold the sutra. People engage in both spiritual and physical labor when they painstakingly copy lines from the sutra. Some have painstakingly written out the entire sutra over several years. In May 2007, I joined a group of women who wrote out lines on strips of paper and then placed the paper under statues of Amitābha Buddha and the bodhisattva Quán Thế Âm, thereby endowing their ritual action with even more power. While the men positioned the statues on the altar using forklifts, the women carried out a different but no less important activity related to constructing the new worship hall. But merit is not just an invisible substance produced by listening to dharma talks or donating food and money. These ritual activities are said to loosen the grasp of one's ego by cultivating ethical behavior such as generosity, discipline, and patience. Thus the emphasis on practice, a combination of moral effort and ritual action, binds lay Buddhists and monks in an economy that produces collective well-being, the sangha.

In societies where market values prevail, these forms of ritual action are dismissed as "baggage," remnants of cultural values and beliefs that migrants carried with them from the homeland. Such forms of action have little place in models of Buddhism that focus on the interior life of the practitioner rather than collective well-being. Consequently, merit-making activities by lay Buddhists, such as supporting temples, attending dharma talks, and reciting Buddha names, are often dismissed as devotional, that is, expressions of faith rather than productive activities. The difficulty is that merit appears to produce no material, equivalent value—just a supplement. Monks are key actors because they receive worldly gifts from lay Buddhists and convert those donations into otherworldly merit, a process that anthropologists would recognize as the return gift—the field in which the seeds of merit are planted.[30] For practitioners, the monastic sangha is the field for cultivating merit.

Merit is also said to accrue almost money-like qualities: it can be accumulated, saved, or spent, and because it is fungible, it can be transferred to others.[31] In Thailand, for example, Buddhists carry out merit transference as a "form of spirit insurance" by redirecting merit or the results of their good deeds to deceased relatives or even to all sentient beings.[32] Merit is thus a means of communicating with the spirits of deceased family members. Buddhist practitioners transfer merit to the dead, ensuring their rebirth in the Pure Land and reinforcing a conception of the social life premised on intergenerational continuity. When people make merit, they do so for themselves and also for family members at a distance, ancestral spirits, and even unborn descendants. In other words, through the moral action of making merit, people also cultivate collective well-being. When merit-making activities are dismissed as a cultural practice, or an invisible spiritual economy, we miss their import as an ethical alternative to the sovereign individual. Other explanatory models likewise reject such economistic metaphors, describing merit instead as the flame of a candle that can light another candle without diminishing its own brightness. Master Deep Awakening described her practice of accumulating merit as a means of offsetting karmic conditioning, or a form of wealth intimately connected to well-being:

> Like when you work, the more money you have in the bank when
> a crisis comes. You don't break out, you don't get stressed,
> because you have something to pay for it. But let's say you don't

save your money. Now when you work, when a crisis comes, when you are laid off work, where's the money now? So it's the same thing with a spiritual bank, the spiritual merit bank. Everything you do, from contributing your time, from donations, from taking care of other people, through your work, your actions, your good deeds, those are merit that you put into your merit bank, and when karma comes to you, when an accident happens to you, you have something to pay, so your merit makes it lighter.

In her explanation, merit differs from karma, which arises from causes and conditioning, one's habitual thoughts, feelings, and deeds. Because Buddhists like Master Deep Awakening conceptualize merit as lessening the consequences of karmic actions, they engage in the spiritual work, donating their time and money to support the sangha in order to stockpile merit. If karma is conceptualized as a form of debt (*nghiệp*) that must be repaid, then merit is sheer plentitude, a store of value to be accumulated and transferred to others. The formal worship services I attended always closed with a prayer to transfer merit to all sentient beings.

Practitioners readily invoked merit as a rationale for supporting Buddhist temples along the Gulf Coast. In 2008, the director at one temple in New Orleans arranged to host a tour of Buddhist relics, the bejeweled remains of famous Buddhist masters after their cremation. These relics were viewed not merely as historical artifacts but as spiritual objects that conferred merit, not because they themselves were magical but because of the expenditure of effort on the part of the viewer. The director of the temple asked for my assistance in advertising the event. I wrote a press release framing the tour as an opportunity for people in New Orleans to support a Buddhist temple that had recently been rebuilt after Hurricane Katrina. At the time, it did not occur to me to promote the relic tour in the idiom of merit, and likely doing so would not have appealed to New Orleanians who attended as a gesture of solidarity in the citywide effort to rebuild after the storm. On the final day of the tour, the president of the board of directors, pleased with the turnout, proclaimed that my two children would enjoy the merit from my actions. On another occasion, I was contacted by a monk in Alabama to carry a box of specially embroidered gray robes back with me from Vietnam to the United States. I agreed, more out of obligation than in the spirit of moral effort. At the airport, I reluctantly paid the surcharge to transport the tightly sealed box. When I delivered the box to the temple, the monk asked how much I was owed, and as my irritation had subsided, I brushed aside the cost. The monk nodded approvingly, noting that the act would bring me merit. These actions do not have to be meritorious; they could be simple acts of pitching in or even gestures of solidarity. However, by framing these exchanges through their supplement, merit, practitioners engage in labor that is also spiritual insofar as it underwrites the institutionalization of Buddhism. But even among Buddhists, these ideals of generosity are hard to maintain.[33]

Gift economies are said to mask economistic calculations that underlie exchange relations.[34] Because monks depend on lay Buddhists to support their vocation, they must cultivate strong relations with lay practitioners, whom they are expected to guide and on whose good favor they depend. One male lay practitioner referred to these exchanges as "customer service," observing that monks needed to make people happy if they wanted them to "open their wallets." Such comments underscore, then, the difficult position of the monastic sangha in an "elaborate relation of gift-acceptance from the [laity]," especially as the laity now judges the sangha by the sincerity or purity by which its members adhere to monastic discipline and monastic vows.[35]

Even the discourse of merit does not extinguish conflicts arising in how money flows through Buddhist temples. Mrs. Quý, a lay Buddhist, expressed the difficulties in managing donations. While at her temple the monk in residence collected donations, the board members were responsible for paying the expenses:

> Salaries, contributions, donations, and because there was only
> one temple, the monk became very wealthy. But people had to
> run their businesses, go to work—they couldn't be there to
> supervise [him]. The temple had to mail invitations for all the
> members each time there was a ceremony, so people would
> know. The temple had to pay for the plane tickets. It was really a
> lot of money, but the monk wanted to protect himself, so he
> didn't want another monk to reside in the temple.

Mrs. Quý saw the donations as money because the board was responsible for paying the expenses associated with maintaining the temple. Lay Buddhists and the resident monk, in contrast, regarded those donations as gifts or modes of payment for the monk's blessings. No wonder the ideal of the sangha as a harmonious community is so difficult to realize.

Monks see their role as creating the conditions for Buddhists in the United States to practice ethics such as generosity. Brother Pure Diamond entered monastic life at the age of eleven and completed his training at a Buddhist university in Vietnam before immigrating to the United States. As we talked, he brushed aside my questions about the differences in monastic life in the Gulf South by referencing the importance of moral action:

> In general, Buddhism is the same anywhere. The main point is to provide people with the opportunity to practice. Temples are a spiritual house [một nhà tâm linh], so people have a life that is light and free [nhẹ nhẹ và thong thả]. That's the way it is everywhere. We also transmit the teachings, so people know how to practice what is right every day.

Yet even spiritual houses, that is to say, temples, require ongoing financial support. Transmitting the teachings is not easily separated from the day-to-day household expenses, whether paying the mortgage or the utilities. Merit sustains these institutions but also threatens to expose how they organize these exchanges in ways that bind monks and lay Buddhists. What both lay Buddhists and monks see as a threat to the sangha is material plentitude. Brother Pure Diamond, for example, noted that few young Buddhists entered into monastic life, because it was challenging for those raised with so many material comforts.

> In the United States, children don't enter monastic life, because there is enough. The material conditions are enough, children have enough things, so entering a temple [in the United States] isn't like in Vietnam. In Vietnam, people who enter monastic life learn [that way of life] from a young age.

Given these challenges, monastic sanghas confront a threat not only to their patronage but also to their reproduction in the United States.

WHO WANTS TO BE A MONK?

The Buddhist monastery in Alabama overlooked a small lake surrounded by tall pines and sturdy oaks. Just before daybreak in September, an elderly monk walked through the hall, ringing a handbell to awaken the lay Buddhists still asleep in a shared sleeping room. She continued out the front door and down a dirt road that led to the Buddha Hall, a worship hall used for formal ceremonies. She opened the glass doors and took a seat next to the Great Bell (Chuông Đại Hồng), usually rung in the mornings and the evenings. There she sounded the bell, its deep reverberations carrying across the lake, awakening all sentient beings, seen and unseen. Back in the monastic residence, a young monk entered the smaller meditation hall usually reserved for the monastic sangha. She placed a steaming cup of tea on a napkin in front of each seat cushion. One by one, the dozen or so lay Buddhists entered the room, each wearing a gray robe. They faced the statue of Bodhidharma and then sat down on one of the cushions as far as possible from the altar and the gold cushion reserved for the senior monk, who had arrived from California. The resident monks, all women, entered the room and took their seats closer to the altar. Everyone sat quietly, their hands resting gently in their laps, their eyes gazing at a spot just in front of them. Only after the senior monk entered the room and rang the Blessing Bell (Chuông Gia Trì) three times did they pick up their cup in both hands, allowing the warmth to stave off the morning chill, and sip their tea. At that moment, people experienced not just their physical bodies but the collective body of the sangha. The warmth of the tea, the vibrations that penetrated the body each time the master struck the bell, the chanted prayers to transmit merit in four directions, and even the master's reminder to breathe in and breathe out produced the sense of being part of a harmonious community.

The senior monk looked around at the attendees and asked jovially, "Who wants to become a monk?" A woman in her thirties, her hair pulled back tightly in a ponytail, raised her hand. He looked at her in surprise and then asked how old her children were. "Five and nine," she responded. She had left her two children in the care of her husband's parents to attend the three-day retreat by herself. For the moment, she was free from her social obligations as a mother and wife. The master smiled and then gently reminded her that she had not yet "repaid her karmic debt" (*chưa trả nghiệp*) as a mother to two sons. He then turned to three unmarried women, all in their twenties, and asked which of them wished to become a monk.

Scriptural accounts describe how the sangha was initially limited to male followers of the historical Buddha, but his aunt requested that she and her companions join the sangha. In deference to his aunt, the Buddha established a female monastic order, *bhiksuni*, but required the women to adhere to eight additional rules, placing them under the protection of male monks.[36] Sometime between the eleventh and twelfth centuries, the Buddhist order of nuns disappeared, marginalized because of beliefs that the more virtuous the recipient, the more merit a donation would accrue.[37] During this period, the participation of lay Buddhists was likewise restricted, transforming the sangha into a mostly male, monastic order. In Thailand, where Theravada Buddhism is practiced, women have struggled to reestablish the order. Female renunciants are instead called "nuns," or *mae chee*; while they renounce secular life and signal their vows by wearing white robes and shaving their heads, they cannot take full ordination as men do.[38] Despite this lesser position, their liminal status of *mae chee*—neither lay Buddhists nor fully ordained monks—enhances their educational and professional roles as meditation teachers and practitioners.[39]

Mahayana Buddhism, in contrast, has long emphasized the sangha as inclusive of laypeople and ordained male and female monks. Mahayana teachings explicitly challenge the assertion that women's abilities to attain enlightenment are less than men's, as made evident in the figure of the bodhisattva Quán Thế Âm, who is said to assume the form of a female goddess and a male householder.[40] Yet there were limitations even though male and female monastics "lived the same lifestyle, did the same practices, and even looked alike, both having shaved heads and identical robes."[41] Sexual difference was still seen as grounds for elaborating distinctions between male and female monastics. In China, Taiwan, and Vietnam, women are ordained as monks, but for ritual purposes they are subordinate to male monks. Even though a female monk may have taken her vows years earlier than a male monk, she is expected to follow male monks in formal processions. During services, male monks hold the microphone, their voices carrying over the public address system. In Vietnam, Buddhist monasteries are predominantly segregated by sex, a practice difficult to maintain in diaspora, where male and female monks may reside in the same temple. Along the Gulf Coast, some practitioners viewed having both female and male monks as an accommodation, but others saw it as potentially breaking the precepts or vows that govern their daily life.[42]

The claim that male and female monastics "look alike" dismisses how differences shielded by monastic robes are materialized and embodied in other ways. Even everyday activities where monks stand and sit made visible the reckoning of these gendered hierarchies. Lay Buddhists expected female monks to be hardworking and diligent. They judged them by their willingness to care for the temple, especially in relation to meal preparations. Male monks, in contrast, were praised for the richness of their voices and their jovial demeanors, drawing people around them with their lighthearted, joking manner. Some female monastics resisted hierarchical arrangements. When I referred to female monks as "nuns," Master Deep Awakening corrected me by pointing out that she dedicated herself as fully to her vows as any male monastic. She introduced herself to English speakers as *master*, using a title in which gendered distinctions are not marked. Other female monks, however, used the term *sister*, maintaining horizontal relations with lay practitioners.

Monks evaluated themselves against different ideals in relation to physical rather than spiritual labor. One monk saw his role as using "his mind as an instrument, not his body" (*dụng tâm đừng dụng thân*). In contrast, a senior monk who had overseen the construction of several monasteries emphasized that only those monks willing to work "with their arms and legs" (*bằng tay, bằng chân*) would succeed in planting dharma seeds along the Gulf Coast, attesting to the physical work building temples entailed. These models of labor are not singular but suggest how monks hold varied aspirations for realizing the vows of their vocation.

These differences remind us that acts of renunciation are spurred by individual desire. Indeed, when both male and female monks discussed their decision to renounce their secular lives, they often referred to an ideal embodied by the equanimous demeanor of a senior monk. Surprisingly, they also described having to conceal their aspirations from their family, a contrast to popular explanations that position the decision to enter monastic life in terms of merit and family status. Even in those societies where Buddhism is the majority religion, people's attitudes toward the ordination of children are decidedly ambivalent.[43] Likewise, monks come to the United States for many reasons. While most are college-educated, as a degree in Buddhism is often required before one can immigrate to the United States as a religious worker, some harbor ambitions of fame.

Other models of renunciation exist as well. In Vietnam, men and women may renounce their secular life not in their youth but later in life, often in their fifties or sixties. On the Gulf Coast, this dynamic is also evident. Sister Deep Justice, a woman in her sixties, described becoming a monk as a lifelong wish, even when she was a young girl in Vietnam. She eventually married, which she described as her fate (*duyên nợ*), and had two sons before she immigrated to the United States in 1996. After her sons were grown and married, she took her monastic vows, framing her decision as having repaid her "debt" (*nghiệp*) accumulated during "this lifetime and that lifetime" (*kiếp trước, kiếp khác*). She noted that, as a woman, her debt was "heavy" (*nghiệp nặng*) because, unlike men, she had been entrusted with the care of others and had little time to perfect herself, thereby offsetting her karmic debt. In Vietnam, female lay Buddhists expressed a similar view; however, they explained their actions in terms of continuing in their roles as caregivers once their children had grown.[44]

Even unmarried women framed their decision to take monastic vows within the idiom of fulfilling obligations to their parents. Master Deep Awakening attributed her decision to become a monk to a vivid memory from when she was just four years old and still in Vietnam. Her parents brought her to a monastery, where over twenty female monks resided, and when the abbot came out to greet the family, she recalled, she asked if she could stay, but her mother just laughed.

> But that was the moment when I saw this monk, the head monk, and I just said, "This is what I want to be. I want to be just like her." And so I told [my] mom, "I want to stay here today. I want to stay here forever." My mom and dad just smiled and said, "No, you have to come home." They picked me up [to bring] me home. I was crying and trying to reach out to the monk: "Pull me back, please. Don't let my parents take me away from this place." They all tried to calm me down by saying, "You will come back." And I said, "When?" I asked my dad, "When?"
>
> "When you grow up, when you are in college, you finish college, that's when you come back."
>
> I said, "How far from here to there?"

A year later, her family left for the United States. She recalled how in California, people knocked on the door of their house and invited the children to go to church. Buses picked up people in the neighborhood, and one of her siblings eventually joined a Sunday school. Worried they might convert to Christianity, her father sent his children to study in a Buddhist temple in Stockton, California, each summer. When she and her brother expressed their wish to become monks, her father insisted they complete their university education. After she received her bachelor's degree, Master Deep Awakening turned down medical school to enter monastic life close to her family. As she recounted her personal history to me, she paused to reflect how her father did not want her to become a monk even though he ensured that she was trained in multiple traditions of Buddhism. "It's strange," she said, "he didn't want me to become a monk, but he gave me all the access." Yet she acquiesced to one request by her parents.

> The strange thing is, when I was young, I wanted to go back to Vietnam and find a teacher there, somewhere in the mountains. . . . It had to be in Vietnam, in the mountains,

somewhere in a remote area. But I was told by my parents that if I wanted to become a monk, I had to stay in the United States, where they could take care of me. One of the dharma teachers told them, "She can't study in Vietnam, she was raised here, so it just makes more sense that she practices here in the United States." So my dad said, "If you want to become a monk, then go to [the] monastery about fifty minutes from [our] house."

While Master Deep Awakening did not use the phrase "repaying karmic debt" (trả nghiệp), she did frame her biography in terms of meeting the expectations of her parents, both by finishing her university education and by not acting on her desire to find a master in Vietnam.

The stories of Master Deep Awakening and Sister Deep Justice underscore how the Vietnamese expression for renunciation, "leaving the family," fails to capture the dynamics of people's biographies and their lived experiences as monks. Both women described their wish to become monks as something they desired early in life, but their obligations to their families—as daughters, wives, and mothers—shaped their decision. Moreover, having renounced secular life as an act of leaving the family did not mean that monks no longer cared for their parents. Quite the contrary. Some monks would return to Vietnam to care for their elderly parents or dharma teachers, underscoring how their lives as renunciants are still structured around obligations and caring for family members. Other monks relied on their extended families for supporting their vocation. Thus popular conceptions of monasticism, much like merit, obscure the centrality of monk-lay relations in maintaining the sangha, and by extension Buddhism, especially on the Gulf Coast.

In both of their accounts, Sister Deep Justice and Master Deep Awakening described the role of nearby Buddhist temples, an indication of the spatial politics of Buddhism on the West Coast in contrast to the Gulf Coast. For monks ordained in California, the Gulf Coast was a new area, an "outpost," insofar as there were few temples and Vietnamese Buddhists, exposing them to vicissitudes of support by lay Buddhists.[45] With a smaller population of Buddhists, the values, opportunities, and even ideals of the sangha have little reinforcement on the Gulf Coast, as Master Deep Awakening described:

At that time, I didn't want to go to [the Gulf Coast], I wanted to stay in [California] and practice more, because I knew it was a lot of responsibility. I have to be able to teach lay friends, to organize whatever needs to be done and coordinate a monastery [that way]. I was not ready, and I didn't want to go, but because I was put in the position that I must do it, I had no choice.

When I asked if she felt that she could not refuse, she replied,

I could not refuse, I couldn't voice myself then, because they made the point that I can speak Vietnamese, I can speak English, and I am ready to do administration work, I have both cultures in me, and [the Gulf South] is a very new area. But I know other people are not taking responsibility, because there aren't a lot of Vietnamese in the area or a lot of activities. Others had the ability, but they didn't want to.

The question "Who wants to be a monk?" is not just an invitation. In English, it can be inverted, exposing the irony, which is what happened during that same retreat at the monastery in Alabama, revealing tensions in the reproduction of the monastic sangha. While washing dishes after lunch, the three young women who earlier had been asked that question joked among themselves. "Who *wants* to become a monk?" one said with a shrug. Once they put away the dishes, the three women pulled out their cell phones to exchange profiles on social media. Their casual dismissal at the suggestion was not an expression of disdain for Buddhism, but it did expose the tensions in reproducing the monastic sangha in the Gulf South. By turning around the question, they revealed the shifting contours of the monastic sangha in making Buddhism.

RECONFIGURING THE SANGHA

Mahayana and Theravada resolve the role of lay Buddhists in the sangha in different ways. Theravada Buddhism is often described as preserving the monastic precepts as handed down by the Buddha, whereas Mahayana Buddhism emphasizes the bodhisattva path as a spiritual paradigm available to everyone. How then do monks embody and perform their authority in ways that mark them as different from lay Buddhists? The differences cannot lie only in external signs, as Master Deep Awakening noted in her definition of sangha, for such signs are only forms.

Monks signal their identity by shaving their heads and wearing robes, acts that are "technologies of the self," insofar as they transform identity and conduct as a means of controlling desire.[46] The historical Buddha marked his transition from householder to ascetic by cutting off his hair, which is today ritualized by initiates in their transition to monastic life.[47] During the ordination of a young man in Louisiana, the presiding monk turned to the lay Buddhists gathered to witness the ceremony and noted, "Shaving the head is easy, but shaving the heart is difficult." By comparing the head (đầu) and the heart (tâm), where wisdom is centered, the monk reminded attendees that renunciants must undergo both an internal and a social transformation. The young man first turned to his mother and father and prostrated himself once. He then bowed three times before his Buddhist teacher or master, signaling his submission to the Buddha, the Dharma, and the Sangha. Dressed in new robes and having just had three tufts of hair clipped from his head, the young man entered into a transpacific lineage that stretched from Louisiana across the Pacific to Asia. The members of the temple had gathered to witness the young man's ritual transformation as a novice but also to console his parents, who were losing their son, at least symbolically.

Wearing robes, like shaving one's head, is a sign of a monastic identity. Cloth has long been attributed as a mark of a person's interior state. In Asia and Africa, for example, colonial officials turned the body's surface into a "central terrain on which battles for the salvation of souls and the fashioning of persons were waged," through their insistence that clothing converted colonial subjects into Christians.[48] Monastic robes likewise fashioned new forms of discipline and ritualized bodies, part of the "habitus," or "way of being or acting synonymous with virtue."[49] In the early twentieth century, monks educated in Bangkok returned to Cambodia with new ways of wearing and even folding their robes, signaling the circulation of new Buddhist identities.[50] In Vietnam today, this process of fashioning of Buddhist identities continues. In southern Vietnam, robes worn by lay Buddhists indicate not only regional but also doctrinal differences. Gray robes worn by lay Buddhists (áo tràng Phật tử) are associated with Zen and the fashioning of a modern Buddhist identity in Vietnam. These robes mark a form of devotion and piety separate from other domains of spiritual life where ritual specialists also wear brown robes. Robes thus signal membership within the collective body of the sangha and an interior state of devotion.[51] During ceremonies, monks sometimes request that participants wearing gray robes sit closer to the altar, emphasizing their proximity to Amitābha and the Pure Land. If robes are the material for fashioning identity as a monastic or a lay Buddhist, they expose the problem of how and when monks are perceived as embodying spiritual authority.

Unlike lay Buddhists, monks wear robes at all times. Vietnamese monks own three sets, each a different color—gray, brown, or gold—signaling the spatial distance from the worship hall. Whenever monks leave the grounds of the temple, they wear brown robes, and when they attend to daily activities on the grounds of the monastery, they wear gray robes. However, when they enter the worship hall to conduct a formal ceremony, they wear golden or saffron robes.[52] The ceremonial robes of monks are not interchangeable, as they have stitched folds, each one marking a year since the monk renounced secular life; thus the gold robe designates the monk as a field of merit, a disposition that must also be ritually produced by the proper setting. Because the colors of the robes signify the social field in which monks circulate, as monks move outside in society their spiritual authority diminishes as well. On one occasion, a male monk invited several people to a popular café in New Orleans. His purpose was to request help in advertising a meditation class to lay Buddhists. One of the women teased him that she was not afraid to turn down his request while he wore his brown robes, but she would never dare refuse his request when he was wearing his gold robes. When monks wear their gold robes, they are models of Buddhahood, elevated above the laity. Just as microphones amplify the voices of monks during the service, the gold robes also signal closer proximity to the Buddha. However, as the woman made clear, the monk's status did not extend to the New Orleans café; instead, his status required the power of ritualization in the proper setting of the worship hall.

In the Mahayana tradition, monks participate in secular life as a condition of their bodhisattva vows. They attend English classes at local community colleges, purchase building materials at home-improvement stores, attend hearings to secure building permits, and even visit the boardwalks of coastal communities. Florida's Gulf Coast, renowned for its white beaches and warm waters, was an attraction for monks as well. On retreats, monks and lay Buddhists visited cafés, went on afternoon picnics, and even ate at pizzerias on crowded boardwalks in the evening. On such occasions, people passing by did not give a second look. The first time I went swimming with a group of monks, I wondered what protocol to follow. The female monks wore their brown robes into the water, while the senior male monk wore a yellow swim shirt and yellow swimming pants, emphasizing his status even in the warm Gulf waters. At first, I did not think much of the female monks wearing their robes into the water. In Vietnam, it was common for people to wade into the ocean while dressed in their street clothes. Later, however, I attended a one-day retreat with a group of twenty monks who were on their way home from a weeklong trip to the Florida coast, and I was reminded that the solution for bathing was not so obvious. As we sat in a circle and took turns asking questions, one man asked what may have been on everyone's mind. What he wanted to know was whether the monks had worn swimming suits. Everyone laughed at the question, for its impertinence but also its intrigue. A monk in her mid-twenties, who had arrived from Vietnam less than a year before, replied that she was embarrassed to look at her "brothers" and wore sunglasses so they could not see her eyes. She then pointed out that while a male monk had worn just long shorts into the water, she and the other female monastics had worn their short brown tops and pants, which quickly became waterlogged, making it difficult to swim. The senior male monk leading the discussion teased her, "Sister, you are giving away our secrets!" He may have sidestepped the practical question, but he reminded everyone in the room that the brown robes were tangible reminders of his ordination vows.

As with robes, terms of address and naming practices also serve as reminders of the status and role of persons. In Vietnamese, lay Buddhists refer to themselves as "child" and the monks as "teacher" (*thầy* for men and *cô* for women). Even the word *teacher* may not express differences in rank and training. Master Deep Awakening, for example, requested that lay Buddhists address her not just as *cô*, or "teacher," but as *sư cô* to acknowledge her vocation as a dharma or spiritual teacher (*sư*) and to distinguish her status in relation to the other female monks. How Vietnamese monks address lay Buddhists is not so straightforward, revealing ambiguity in the relative status of monks vis-à-vis lay Buddhists.

In Vietnamese, terms of address denote the speaker's relationship to the addressee. While speakers choose from among a number of strategies, including a proper name or a common noun, in general, kin terms are preferred irrespective of whether the speaker and addressee are actually revealed, a preference that indicates "a pervasive orientation to and awareness of social hierarchy, rooted in a model of the extended, multigenerational family but mapped onto the social world as a whole."[53] Terms of address are paired (e.g., mother-child), but they are not reciprocal. Whereas in English, speakers refer to themselves as "I" and the addressee as "you," in Vietnamese, the terms of address encode an ideal social model. A mother, for example, may refer to herself as "mother," or *mẹ*, and address her child as "child," or *con*, and the child, in turn, calls himself *con* and addresses his mother as *mẹ*. Monks address lay Buddhists by their dharma name or their first name or a term appropriate for their relative age and gender, revealing the asymmetries in constructing monk-lay relations. Lay Buddhists use self-referential terms to show deference to monks who stand as their spiritual guides, while monks construct that relationship on different, sometimes more egalitarian but also deferential, terms.

The asymmetries of status in the ritual setting of the worship hall and those activities that take place in the temple complex are especially evident in relation to communal cooking and eating. If meals are occasions for expressing both solidarity and rank, they are also occasions that expose the difficulty in maintaining those hierarchical arrangements. After Sunday services, the members of the kitchen committee prepare a vegetarian meal, an occasion to produce the collective body of the sangha but also to regulate the boundaries between the monastic and lay communities. At some temples, monks retreated to their residence. In other temples, the lay Buddhists ate with the monks and practiced a meditative activity of eating in silence. At still other temples, lunches were boisterous occasions in which people conversed loudly with friends. On one occasion at Hồng Ân Monastery in southwestern Louisiana, the formal service took place under the hot August sun. Beneath a covered pavilion, one of the few shaded spots, members of the temple laid out food for the vegetarian lunch that would follow the ceremony. Yet during the ceremony, visitors gathered alongside the long tables laden with platters of fried noodles and rice to serve themselves. Several members urged them to wait until the monks were served first before filling their own plates. But the visitors gestured to the children as if to explain why they were bypassing that protocol.

The model of the multigenerational, extended family further confounds the relationships of monks and lay associations. When the board members of a temple recruit a monk, they are said to be taking a "daughter-in-law" (con dâu). Vietnamese family structures tend to be hierarchical and male-oriented. Women in their role as daughter-in-law are expected to serve their husband's family. Monks, as "daughters-in-law to a hundred families" (dâu trăm họ), are expected to serve the association, which, in turn, is the rightful owner of the house or the temple. While a woman gains status by giving birth to sons, thereby ensuring the continuity of the patriline, that strategy is hardly available to monastics.

In likening the role of a monk to that of a daughter-in-law, people acknowledge the limited role played by monks in resolving disputes over administrative control. In December 2007, the local newspaper reported that the police had been called after a fight broke out at a temple in Biloxi.[54] The dispute was between different factions over whether to retain the head monk, who was up for reelection that month. Some members accused the monk of financial improprieties, while other members accused former leaders of wanting to retain control. While the monk remained in residence after the election, he eventually left Biloxi and moved farther away, to where he had better relations with lay Buddhists. Today he maintains distance and caution in his relations with lay leaders so that he may remain unhindered in his activities, exposing how difficult it is to sustain the ideal of the sangha, harmony. The incident was not isolated but reflected the structural difficulties in reconciling the moral community of the sangha, in which the monk was the recognized spiritual guide and day-to-day manager of the temple, funded by the donations of lay Buddhists.

The asymmetries in monk-lay relations is momentarily resolved during the formal services. Both monks and lay Buddhists turn toward the image of Amitābha Buddha to express their intent to seek refuge in the Three Jewels by bowing three times. Monks wear gold robes, and their voices are amplified by a microphone, guiding lay Buddhists as they recite Buddha names and chant mantras to the steady beat of a drum and broadcasting prayers to those unseen beings who reside outside the temple walls, emphasizing the collective power of the sangha. In such moments, harmony is produced through these technologies of the body and sound—hands held in prayer, bodies prostrated at the sound of the small bell, voices carried beyond the worship hall. The ceremony closes with the dedication of merit, not to one's relatives but to the world, thus enacting the ethics of Mahayana Buddhism premised on collective well-being. How, though, people evaluate sincerity, among both monks and lay Buddhists, alerts us to how the sangha is being made and remade in the Gulf Coast region.

THE POLITICS OF SINCERITY

The identity of Buddhist monks is conveyed by external signs—wearing robes and shaving their heads. These signs alone cannot guarantee the "authenticity" of monks. US newspapers have reported on the problem of "fake monks" in New York City.[55] In these stories, monks approach people for donations to an unnamed temple, often in exchange for an amulet or small charm, but when asked to name their temple or Buddhist sect, the monks communicate that they do not understand English and then disappear. While begging is associated with the cultivation of generosity, the tactics employed by these men were described as "strong-arming" and "shaking down" tourists. The monks are "fake" because their interest is revealed to be only about money.

Similar anxiety over fake monks has accompanied the revitalization of religion in Vietnam. When I lived in southern Vietnam (2000–2002), people advised me to watch whether a monk's gaze was on his alms bowl or the street, as if the gaze itself held a clue about the monk's interest. Yet the distinction between men in robes and monks was also blurred. In the late 1990s in southern Vietnam, for example, people would joke that Buddhist monks were often the first to enjoy material goods, such as mobile phones and motorbikes, by turning the word for Thích (a homonym in Vietnamese for "like") into a pun, *thích tất cả*, or "likes everything," exposing how some monks were seen as violating their vows of poverty.[56] Fake monks have been reported as well in Singapore, but their presence is linked more to the anxieties of residents in the city-state over border crossing and the spiritual marketplace than to whether the monks are actually fraudulent.[57]

In contrast, Vietnamese monks who carry out their practice in non-Buddhist countries risk being seen as insincere as they negotiate how the contingencies of everyday life conflict with the ideals they are supposed to embody.[58] Such concerns are rooted in the lingering effects of the Cold War that have shaped Vietnamese subjectivity, and Buddhists, especially monks, are vulnerable to such accusations.[59] People draw on conflicting models— some more political than doctrinal—when assessing the sincerity of monks, which in turn introduces schisms into the sanghas and jeopardizes support for temples in the Gulf South.

The problem of sincerity arises from the politicization of religious institutions in postwar Vietnam. In 1976, Buddhist leaders endorsed the revolutionary regime, stating that communism did not threaten Buddhism and that Buddhists would have a role to play in building a new society. Even as late as 2015, Vietnamese in the United States still questioned the sincerity of monks trained in Vietnam, perceiving them to be "contaminated" by the socialist state. Lay Buddhists relied on senior monks, some who had fled as refugees themselves, to vet younger monks. The fact that these senior monks escaped from Vietnam after 1975 served as a sign of their fidelity to anticommunism, a value held by many first-generation Vietnamese in the Gulf South. Some monks perform fidelity to these ideals by displaying the Vietnamese Freedom and Heritage Flag, which once flew over the Republic of Vietnam, or by attending ceremonies that mark April 30 to mourn the defeat of the republic and express their allegiance to the diaspora. One monk who did not display the flag brushed aside my question with the simple reply, "It's complicated." Yet the flag also serves as an object lesson for reflecting on how dualistic thinking—who won and who lost the war, for example—contributes to people's suffering, as Brother Bright Awakening explained:

> [Displaying the flag] is a sign of respect for the past of the Vietnamese people, because any war involves bloodshed and loss of life. The wounds of war are the same everywhere. We can't distinguish the Republican from the Communist because the Republican is the Communist, they are both just people, differing only in their ideology.

Yet it is not just the renunciation of communism that matters; material comforts that define American life are seen as threats to the sincerity of one's practice as well. A lay Buddhist was adamant in her evaluation of monks: "If you are a person who worships Buddha, you shouldn't own anything." She pointed out that monks in Vietnam were often self-sufficient and did not expect to "be taken care of" (nuôi, a term used for rearing children or raising animals). She explained that the board of directors must decide if and how to compensate monks for their work and whether the temple should provide items indispensable to life in the United States, such as cars. Some monks have stipends for spending, but she believed that monks should live by donations. She pointed out that the expenses for maintaining temples were not incidental. Temples provide airfare for visiting monks, along with a gift (cúng dường) of several hundred dollars, lodging, and meals. In closing, she stated that a sincere monk would turn down the envelope of cash: "To be a monk, you have to give up material wealth," but then added that no monk ever did.

While the popular Oriental Monk is reduced to external signs—"his calm demeanor, his Asian face, his manner of dress"—these are not the signs that Vietnamese lay Buddhists read.[60] They are looking for something both more and less: a resonant voice to lead the congregation while chanting, a willingness to perform physical labor, a sense of respect for the financial sacrifices made by lay Buddhists to support the temple, and a joyful demeanor. One woman described the arrival of a new resident monk: "He set aside his ego to live with us, always smiling and laughing, he's never angry [and he never] reprimands us when we have made a mistake, [but] he gently scolds us." Here we see lay Buddhists who want a monk to "set aside his ego," a quality expressed both in the monk's comportment in the worship hall and in his interactions with the lay Buddhists. While setting aside his or her ego seems to be precisely what one would expect from a monk, the lay Buddhist's observation underscores how relations between monks and lay Buddhists are "delicate" (té nhị), especially as monks must cultivate good relationships with a wide swath of people who bring diverse expectations, engage in different spiritual orientations, and make various demands. Not all lay Buddhists seek out monks who impart theological insight. And most reject supporting monks who wish to be served. They look instead for spiritual guides worthy of their financial sacrifices and who make them laugh and work on behalf of the congregation. This critique exposes how the institutional power of Buddhism depends not just on the moral worthiness of the resident monk but also on supporters' evaluation of the monk's sincerity.

Vietnamese monks must contend with yet another problem, the sheer breadth of the spiritual marketplace, even in the Gulf South. Vietnamese Buddhists encounter other models of what it means to be Buddhist and practice Buddhism. Some people now see Pure Land as "traditional," steeped in superstitions and thus not as authentic as Tibetan Buddhism, Zen, or Theravada, a perspective reinforced in the United States as well as in Vietnam and China. Some people seek what they regard to be more authentic and thus more powerful versions of Buddhism than the ones they associate with Vietnamese temples. In urban Vietnam, some Buddhists seek out Theravada Buddhist monks, who are seen as doctrinally pure because they have eliminated the "magical and animist practices" associated with Mahayana Buddhism. Some Khmer monks now direct their teachings toward the Vietnamese rather than their Khmer compatriots, whom they deride as "just lighting incense and praying for their fortune and ancestors," which is itself a paradox, insofar as Khmer monks profit from the perception by middle-class Vietnamese that the monks' practices are more authentic.[61] Some Vietnamese also see Tibetan Buddhists as more authentic, redirecting their financial support to these monks, some of whom visit Vietnamese temples for donations or to sell various items.

Finally, it is the monks' aspirations that lead them outside the gates of the temple as they, too, turn from serving Vietnamese Buddhists to pursuing education or establishing parallel congregations, a practice that has been widely effective for many Thai Theravada congregations.[62] Monks recruited from Vietnam expressed their desire to learn English so that they could adapt to life in the United States and also impart Buddhist teachings to a younger generation of Vietnamese Buddhists. But pursuing education takes monks outside the temple or monastery, leaving the sangha behind and exposing them to critiques by those lay Buddhists who support their vocation.

Recruiting monks exposes a predicament for reproducing Buddhism in the region, especially when temples outnumber monks and Vietnamese

Catholics still outnumber Buddhists. In the Gulf South, the population of Vietnamese Buddhists is far smaller than in California, Texas, or even Georgia. That monks are watched and evaluated by lay Buddhists leads to their vulnerability when they are deemed no longer worthy of support. Likewise, contention over what it means to be a monk or to be a layperson has been renegotiated, compounded by anxieties over the recruitment of monks primarily, although not exclusively, from Vietnam, raising questions about their allegiance to the Socialist Republic of Vietnam. The question then of "who wants to be a monk" reveals the competing ideals facing the reproduction of Buddhist orders in the Gulf South. Monks are obliged to interact with laypeople, who provide the requisites necessary for the sangha to survive. Part of making Buddhism in the region lies in how lay practitioners and monks must continually negotiate the expectations and requirements they have of one another. These negotiations can falter when monks are perceived not to adhere to the values of frugality, still valued by many Vietnamese who struggled when they first arrived in the United States. As lay Buddhists impose restrictions on the use of air-conditioning and the purchase of a new set of plates and glassware, they define the expectations and requirements of monks. Monks fall short of the ideal they are supposed to embody when they come too close to living like laypeople, thus confusing the categories of monastic and layperson that organize and sustain Buddhist monasteries.[63] In the end, when lay Buddhists withhold their time, labor, and money, monks seek refuge in another sangha.

◆　◆　◆

In 2015, as the activities wound down after the celebration of Buddha's birthday at a monastery in Alabama, the tensions between the lay Buddhists and the monastic sangha reappeared. A woman described her regret that her children no longer visited the temple. She recalled how they once camped under the moonlight and would stand silent as deer approached them. But as relations between the lay Buddhists and the resident monks became strained, the children stopped attending. Later that day, one of the elderly female monks described the physical toll of her daily routine. In the morning and evening, she chanted; in the afternoon, she offered rice porridge at a small shrine; in the evening, she recited the Great Bell Sutra, and then she fell asleep. She confided her wish to live in a nursing home where all she needed to do was push a button and someone would meet her needs.

Indeed, the monastery seemed to weigh heavily on all participants, resident monks and lay Buddhists alike.

As I listened to these recountings of troubles, the serenity of the monastery suddenly seemed more foreboding. Even the physical structure of the buildings showed strain. The wooden porch was beginning to crack, and the floor of the worship hall was weakened by water damage. Several bathroom stalls bore handwritten Out of Order signs. In 2015, the statue of Quán Thế Âm lay on its side, covered with a blue tarp to protect against the rain and wind, its installation deferred for lack of funds. The erosion of the built structures of the temple complex signaled that not only had financial support waned but so had the support of lay Buddhists to ensure maintenance of the monastery.

Vietnamese Buddhist complexes are not hermitages where monks retreat to perfect their practice. They house diasporic communities that depend crucially on the financial support and physical labor of lay Buddhists. Monks and lay Buddhists alike see tending to these temples—cutting grass, maintaining buildings, advertising events, collecting donations, and preparing meals—as dharma work that expresses one's ethical subjectivity. Yet this common vision does not banish the tensions. Difficulties arise in part because of the new configurations of the sangha, in which lay Buddhists are expected to support the temple and the vocation of monks, who in turn must fulfill the expectations of lay Buddhists. This model of the sangha is far more complicated than that portrayed by the Oriental Monk. Monks must navigate their status even as the sangha is reconstituted under conditions in which lay Buddhists exercise democratic rights and exert financial control. It is no wonder that monks only risk investing their energies in building a worship hall once they have control over the property itself.

CHAPTER THREE

Building a Hall for Buddha

I N the 1980s, Buddhists in the Gulf South gathered in tucked-away places—rented apartments, converted garages, and vacant offices that functioned as collective spaces of worship. These spaces still vary in type and size, from repurposed mobile homes to large complexes situated on spacious tracts of land, but newly built worship halls now showcase the presence of Buddhists along commercial corridors and suburban streets in the port cities of the coast. If Southeast Asian refugees initially found little support for their notions of personhood and collective life in different domains of American life, today Buddha is no longer "in hiding."[1] Repurposed and renovated within existing built structures, these buildings now provide a cohesive public identity recognizable by features such as Buddhist flags and outdoor statues of the bodhisattva Quán Thế Âm.[2] More than spaces for formal services, these worship halls are promoted by monks and lay Buddhists as key structures for preserving a distinctive ethos or way of life, a claim made popular by the poem "Remembering the Pagoda" (Nhớ chùa).

The poem was composed by the late Venerable Thích Mãn Giác (1929–2006) under the pen name Huyền Không in 1949. Today it serves as an anthem for congregations raising funds to build worship halls.[3] Singers and speakers invoke the final lines of the poem:

> Mái chùa che chở hồn dân tộc   Its roof protects the national soul,
> Nếp sống muôn đời của tổ tông   An eternal way of life.

The Venerable Thích Mãn Giác fled Vietnam as a refugee himself and resettled in Los Angeles, where he promoted Buddhism in the United States in his roles as abbot of the Vietnamese Buddhist Temple in Los

Angeles and president of the Vietnamese United Buddhist Churches of America. Upon his death, his followers recalled how he had wanted Buddhism to adopt American ideals of "equality, freedom, and nondiscrimination."[4] These ideals are not inconsistent with those held by Vietnamese Buddhists who also fled as refugees. As the poem "Remembering the Pagoda" makes clear, Buddhism conveys a distinctive ethos (*nếp sống*) closely bound to ancestral culture that is under threat:

Chuông vẳng nơi nao nhớ lạ lùng	Distant bells anywhere stir strange memories.
Ra đi ai chẳng nhớ chùa chung	When leaving, who does not remember the common pagoda?
Mái chùa che chở hồn dân tộc	Its roof protects the national soul,
Nếp sống muôn đời của tổ tông	An eternal way of life.

Composed during a time when Vietnam was plunged into war with its former colonizer, France, the poem is marked by a sense of longing.[5] It opens with a scene from the Vietnamese countryside—the meandering path, a bamboo hedge, and a temple bathed in sunlight.[6] The sound of the pagoda bell and the sweet scent of burning incense draw villagers near. This scene arises not before the narrator but from his memory, and the tone abruptly shifts. The picturesque countryside and the pagoda are threatened by the ravages of war:

Biết đến bao giờ trở lại quê	Who knows when I will return to the countryside?
Phân vân lòng gởi nhớ nhung về	My troubled heart longs to return.
Tang thương dù có bao nhiêu nữa	Whatever vicissitudes may come,
Cũng nguyện cho chùa khỏi tái tê	I pray for the temple to escape pain.

Building a worship hall is thus a project understood not in the temporality of modernity, linear and progressive, but in ancestral time, in which past, present, and future are melded. Today the poem, set to music by Võ Tá Hân, inspires people to donate money to support the construction projects of temple complexes. Calls to lay Buddhists to fund these projects as a means of "protect[ing] the national soul" (*che chở hồn dân tộc*) appear resonant with how these institutions are conventionally classified as ethnic or heritage Buddhism. However, those designations overlook how people draw on their spirituality to repair "experiences of dislocation [and] generational fractures," both in Vietnam and in America.[7]

A stand-alone worship hall is one of the most ambitious and expensive construction projects undertaken by a congregation. These projects require actors from outside the congregation—construction crews, engineers, and government officials—whose participation carries risks. They may defile the site, reject permits, and enforce municipal guidelines, waylaying completion. The act of building worship halls carries other risks as well. Fundraising for these projects often takes years, drawing upon financial support from lay Buddhists beyond the core group of members. Two congregations in Louisiana each embarked on building a chapel or worship hall, the heart or "central chamber" (chánh điện) of a temple complex, during the period I carried out this study (2013–17) and provide examples for this chapter. Each had been founded several years earlier by a monk who had first resided in a temple run by lay Buddhists (chùa hội). In both cases, the monk and his supporters left to establish another temple nearby, a pattern that has contributed to spreading Buddhism across the Gulf South. The first temple, which I call Hồng Ân Monastery, occupied a house in a semirural area in southwestern Louisiana, and the second is Vạn Minh Pagoda, a former storefront along a commercial corridor in metropolitan New Orleans. If the "pagoda roof protects the national soul," it is not because of the built structure alone but because of how people embody that space, creating a social field recognizably Vietnamese *and* Buddhist. As we will see, this field is neither straightforward nor without controversy but instead elicits multiple and even conflicting ideas about the Pure Land, especially whose labor is acknowledged and how. The focus here is not on the physical construction of the worship hall—the architectural designs, the permits and inspections, or even the actual construction work. Rather, it is on how participants voiced conflicting visions of whose labor transforms the Gulf South into the Pure Land.

PARALLEL PRACTICES

The idea of other-power is fundamental to Pure Land. It refers to the contributions of buddhas and bodhisattvas, in contrast to self-power, which denotes those of the practitioner. By reciting the name of Amitābha Buddha—silently or aloud, in groups or alone, with or without accompanying musical instruments—practitioners express their intention to be reborn in the Pure Land, where they will be able to perfect themselves without attachments or suffering and eventually attain enlightenment. Some people play endless loops of recordings of monks reciting the names of buddhas and bodhisattvas, a tactic derided by others as "easy practice." Yet practices that are seen as relying on other-power are also understood to exhibit "right effort," a step along the Eightfold Path, a principal teaching in Buddhism.[8] Invoking the names of Amitābha Buddha and Quán Thế Âm for protection is a means by which practitioners prevent unwholesome states of mind from arising, as an American man explained to me. He recalled walking across a field in Alabama with a Vietnamese friend, when they came upon a copperhead, a common but poisonous snake. His friend urged him not to kill the snake but instead to recite "A Di Đà Phật" several times. As he did, the snake slithered away. Later, while walking with his grandson, the man saw another snake and told his grandson to do the same, and, again, the snake disappeared. Through these small miracle tales, the other-power attributed to buddhas and bodhisattvas is manifested in the world, but practitioners also conceptualize their practice in terms of effort or self-power. Thus self-power and other-power are better understood not as oppositional but as complementary, "a cooperative venture in which the devotee and the Buddha contribute to the process of achieving rebirth."[9] In Vietnamese, this cooperative venture is summed up by the phrase "Zen and Pure Land are parallel practices."

Despite the emphasis on their union, these practices exhibit long-standing tensions and debates that play out in how people ascribe value to different activities and forms of spiritual labor. These tensions not only arise in diaspora but have long shaped representations of Pure Land, from a celestial realm of Amitābha Buddha of the Western Paradise to the human realm achieved here and now, not after death.[10] As early as the tenth century, the Zen master Vĩnh Minh Diên (904–975) emphasized the importance of Buddhist practices that had broad appeal:

> Zen without Pure Land, then ten people meditate, but nine lose their way. . . . Zen with Pure Land, ten thousand people meditate, and ten thousand are reborn. See Amitābha Buddha, there is no need to worry! With Zen and Pure Land, it is as if the tiger also has horns.[11]

The Pure Land tradition of practice in China and Vietnam thus makes space for lay Buddhists. During formal services, for example, in unison, monks and lay Buddhists chant sutras and recite Buddha names (tụng kinh niệm Phật) to the steady beat of a wooden drum. While these practices are associated with other-power, that is, relying on the vows of these celestial beings, Buddhist monks themselves describe chanting and name-recitation as a form of concentration. Some lay practitioners readily admit that they do not understand the meaning of this sutra or that mantra, but the words are not where they attribute power. Instead, the value is in the effort of reciting Buddha names or chanting, an explanation that resonates with anthropologists' reassessments of the role of prayer as an embodied practice that fortifies an individual's belief.[12] People chant mantras not for their meaning but to achieve a state of consciousness that is compassionate, concentrated, and calming, suggesting that the line between lay and monastic practices may be more a matter of "intensity, expectations, and access."[13] Even non-Vietnamese speakers explained to me that listening to the collective chanting calmed their mind, allowing them to sit in repose, which they were unable to do when sitting in silence. While they did not understand the chanted words, they followed along as the drum beat steadily, like a metronome, the experience of praying not in the words themselves but in the collective soundscape of drumming and voices.

Just as chanting has elicited diverse views, so has the act of silent meditation. As I sat in the living room of Mrs. Sang, a woman in her late sixties, I asked about the role of silent meditation in these temples. She made it clear that the temple was no place for "just sitting around" (*ngồi không*) and meditating.

> [Lay Buddhists] have work to do in the temple; no one just sits around and just meditates. People are busy with work, with business, so when they are free, they go to the temple. But they don't do the daily work of the temple. They don't do the work of reciting sutras a few times every day. That's the work of the monk, who must also tend the grounds and take care of the pagoda.

Mrs. Sang drew a sharp distinction between what she saw as the "work" of lay Buddhists and monks and the "sitting around" that meditation entailed. Lay Buddhists set aside their responsibilities in business to spend their free time at the temple. Monks likewise recited sutras not once but several times a day in addition to maintaining the pagoda. She emphasized the physical and spiritual labor that is materialized in these spaces. While these activities may be understood to generate merit, that merit is a return on their expenditure of effort. In contrast, she dismissed silent meditation as involving no visible or material effort, just "sitting around."

Mrs. Sang and her family were steadfast patrons at Buddhist temples, and I often met her or her adult daughter at fund-raisers and Sunday services. During our conversation, she showed me a photograph of her mother, who had renounced secular life in her fifties in Vietnam. Before I left her house, she took me to a room where she had an altar and a CD player. In this space, she listened to dharma talks by renowned monks and chanted sutras, engaging in forms of spiritual labor that would generate merit. When she had time to attend formal services, she exerted effort, a point that is often dismissed when those activities are described as "devotional." Mrs. Sang as well as other women I interviewed made clear that they were working—whether cooking in the kitchen, tending the temple grounds, or chanting in the worship hall.

In contrast to Mrs. Sang's emphasis on the labor entailed by these temples, the Pure Land is often described by the soteriological goals of practitioners as a celestial realm of rebirth. For some, the Pure Land is a "reward" land and for others, a "transformation" land, where they may perfect their practice before attaining enlightenment. Master Deep Awakening drew on the idea of the Pure Land as a celestial realm on earth when she described the monastery in Northern California where she was ordained:

> [The monastery] is up in the mountains, so when you [are
> there], you feel like you are in the Pure Land—there is energy
> around, you feel very strong and very clear, and very powerful.
> Even now, when I talk about it, I feel goosebumps, an experience
> I have had ever since I was a child. It's more than two thousand
> feet in elevation, so you feel like you walk on clouds, because
> there's fog, even in the summer. And you have a view—there's
> [the] bay, you can look over [the city], you can see the whole
> view. So for me, [the monastery] is like the Pure Land.

The monastery, located high in the Santa Cruz Mountains, was the Pure Land by its very elevation and its magnificent features—a view of the bay, the towering redwoods, and fresh air. Her description invokes the idea of the Pure Land as beyond the human realm, where one, no longer burdened by suffering, could instead focus on one's practice and "feel very strong and very clear, and very powerful." The Pure Land, as a world apart from samara, or the realm of suffering, however, is difficult to sustain alongside the Mahayana emphasis on nonduality, in which nothing exists external to the mind.[14] A few moments later, Master Deep Awakening returned to how the Pure Land is attainable in our everyday lives, likening her work in administering and managing monasteries to a form of spiritual work.

I don't have to reach Pure Land when I die, I want to make the Pure Land right here, right now. So there's peace in every step, and if I don't apply [that idea], I think I will be stressed . . . just thinking of the mortgage, thinking of teaching my students, thinking of coordinating on the ground and running back and forth between two monasteries. If anything happens [at the other monastery], I have to take responsibility, too. If something breaks, I have to make a phone call—who can fix it? So I'm dealing with a lot of expectations, from the residents [monks] to the outside [visitors] to the grounds to running the monastery, from the administration work to construction work and building work. You can see, if I don't build my own Pure Land, through my work, how would I be able to breathe?

Master Deep Awakening describes the Pure Land not as lying beyond human comprehension but as attainable in the present moment, through practices of mindfulness. She drew on mantras such as "peace in every step," which is associated with the practice of the Venerable Thích Nhất Hạnh, whom she considered one of her dharma teachers. Through the conflicting views of Mrs. Sang and Master Deep Awakening, we see how people value their spiritual and physical labor.

These views inform people's evaluation of the aesthetics and design of worship halls. In these spaces, the main altar usually features a prominent statue of Amitābha Buddha flanked by two bodhisattvas (bồ tát), supernatural beings who deferred enlightenment to ensure all sentient beings would be released from their suffering. On one side is Quán Thế Âm, who perceives sounds and responds to the suffering of others, and on the other side is Địa Tạng, who tends to those souls not yet released to the Pure Land. In other meditation halls, especially those used by monastics, there may be a single statue of the scowling, bearded Bodhidharma, said to have transmitted Zen (Chinese: Chan) to China in the fifth or sixth century. Some monasteries have two different spaces, a small meditation hall used primarily by the monastic sangha and a larger Buddha Hall, open to all, for formal services and ceremonies.

Because Pure Land is imagined as a celestial realm, the main altar uses decorations to convey its marvelous features. Blinking colored lights strung around the back of the altar and large, ornate vases filled with artificial flowers are forms of "bling" that some practitioners find distracting.[15] A monk who proposed offering classes in Zen meditation found that the adornments in the worship hall distracted from the core teachings around emptiness he wished to impart. On one occasion, I walked with him through the worship hall of a temple run by a lay association. He confided that he had asked the board of directors to remove the towering vases, the colored lights, and even the red apples and water bottles stacked on the altar, but they denied his request. They did, however, allow him to use a back room for Zen meditation classes. The room had not been in use for months, perhaps years, and was filled with cobwebs and dust. Within a month or so, with the help of volunteers, the walls were freshly painted, and bamboo curtains were hung so that people could practice a Japanese version of meditation, in which they faced the wall rather than each other or the altar. On Sundays, the monk performed formal services in the Pure Land tradition, and during the week, he offered meditation classes. Thus Zen and Pure Land were unified in the same temple complex, but each was practiced in a different location with different aesthetics and with a different audience.

The worship hall as a built structure is empty until practitioners constitute themselves as a sangha, or harmonious community, when they gather to pray, chant sutras, and listen to dharma talks. Participants remove their shoes and cover their street clothes with gray robes, marking the worship hall as separate from ordinary activities. They show their intention to take refuge in the Buddha, the Dharma, and the Sangha by bowing three times before the altar. During the service, a monk or lay Buddhist maintains a steady rhythm on a wooden drum (*cái mõ*), each beat marking a syllable, and the chime of a bell signals to participants when they have recited the name of a buddha or bodhisattva or chanted the Great Compassion Mantra (Chú Đại Bi) the requisite number of times, creating a distinctive soundscape. By removing their shoes, covering their street clothes, and blending their voices with the drumbeat and bell chime, participants make the social body of the sangha.

The sounds of the wooden drum and the chimes are not those that called the villagers in the poem "Remembering the Pagoda." What drew them was the sound of the bronze Great Bell (Chuông Đại Hồng). For older Vietnamese, the deep tones of this bell are familiar and comforting, reminding them of their childhood. Inside the worship hall stands a set of instruments, the Great Bell and the Drum Tower, both impressive in their size and sound (figures 3.1 and 3.2). This set is called the Bell Drum of Wisdom (Chuông Trống Bát Nhã).[16] The instruments are not heard during ordinary services but are used for ceremonies to announce the procession of monks and for repentance (*sám hối*) services. During these processions, the beats become faster and louder, stirring people's memories of festivals

3.1

This bell is rung in the mornings and evenings and on ceremonial occasions to announce the procession of monks into the worship hall. Together with the drum pictured below, the set is called Chuông Trống Bát Nhã, and their sound is considered a dharma teaching to awaken all sentient beings. *Bát nhã* is a Vietnamese transliteration of the Sanskrit word *prajna*, meaning "wisdom." Photo by the author.

3.2

The Drum Tower (Trống Bát Nhã) stands on the other side of the Great Bell. Photo by Quang Huynh.

in Vietnam and evoking "ancestral time," when Buddhist pagodas were part of daily life. In Vietnam, only monks are allowed to touch these instruments. In the Gulf South, it is lay Buddhists who invite the instruments' sound, further blurring the distinction between monastics and lay practitioners. With the sound of the bells, the beat of the drums, and the collective voice of practitioners, sometimes accelerating to an electric buzz, it is not just the roof of the pagoda that protects the national soul, but the sangha as well.

Most of the time, these worship halls stand empty. Unlike Christian chapels, with their rows of pews, the worship hall has no fixed seating, a symbol of emptiness. But *empty* also refers to the common practice of keeping the gates to the temple locked, a precaution against the theft of cash from donation boxes or even statues. Locking the temple gates also keeps out laypeople and casual visitors, in contrast to the openness of pagodas in Vietnam, where people stop by to light incense and say prayers, especially on days close to the full moon and the new moon. And despite the spaciousness of the worship hall, it is not used for meetings or discussions. Instead, people gather in the dining room to discuss fund-raising or administrative issues, with the exception of elections for board members.

Separating spiritual and secular matters is not always easy. At one service, I was surprised at the turnout, but it soon became clear why so many people had attended. A respected community leader stood up to address the congregation following the service. He reminded participants that he had called all the members the week before to request that they vote on the board of directors. The election had already generated discussion among members. One woman who had previously served on the board confided that she wanted lay leaders to take turns on the board, although she insisted that she did not want "contested elections." Another woman, who attended a different temple, called it a "family-run business," one "owned" by an extended family. On that evening, however, the community leader presented the slate and asked for the support of the people present. No one dissented, and the board was unanimously approved. The election of the board was sanctioned not just by the members' vote but also by the setting, the worship hall. At other times, the worship hall offered a different kind of refuge, especially during celebrations of Buddha's birthday or Vu Lan. Its enclosed space provided air-conditioned relief from the summer heat or festival crowds. Children entertained themselves while the adults ate lunch or watched cultural performances outdoors. Sometimes even adults would retreat into the hall to take afternoon naps, rolling up the square cushions as makeshift pillows.

If we look closely, however, the Buddha Hall serves as an important setting to sanction the requests that monks make of lay practitioners to donate their time and money to support the institution. In front of the altar are wooden boxes labeled "support the temple" (*úng hộ chùa*) or "contributions" (*công đức*), reminders that both the vocation of monks and the maintenance of the temple depend on the ongoing support of lay practitioners. The topography of donations is complex, and so it is no wonder that disagreements ensue over the flow of money in these temples. In answer to my question, "Where does one donate money?," a lay leader summed up the various ways someone could support the temple. If the donor wants a receipt, he explained, he or she should write a check to the temple, and the funds would pay for utilities and upkeep; otherwise, the donor could offer cash directly to the monk leading the service. He then pointed to a glass-doored refrigerator stocked with Vietnamese specialties and standing near a counter, where he would sit, waiting for people to pay their dues or make a donation. The resident female monk had prepared foods such as vegetarian sticky rice cakes wrapped in banana leaves to sell as a fund-raiser to support an orphanage in southern Vietnam. Finally, he pointed to a glass counter where there were prayer beads and books, all offered by donations. Through these various ways of channeling money, the temple solicited support from visitors and lay Buddhists. But other, more spectacular forms of raising money involved showcasing ritual objects, whether relics from the remains of respected Buddhist masters or a magnificent statue that toured the world.

HOSTING THE JADE BUDDHA

The most ambitious project that a congregation can undertake is building a stand-alone worship hall. Shorter projects might include constructing dormitories for retreatants or even restroom facilities, which may be completed in several months. Practitioners can readily transform the garages and living rooms of suburban houses into collective spaces of worship, and even a backyard gazebo or sitting room can be converted into an altar. But building a worship hall may take years, which was the case for the two congregations I describe. The head monk may travel to Vietnam to purchase statues and roof tiles or oversee the smelting and blessing of the Great Bell. Congregations also invite monks from distant temples to witness land-blessing and ground-breaking ceremonies. They also open their gates to festivalgoers, construction crews, and city inspectors. Call it goodwill, blessings, or destiny, but building a worship hall requires more than just money. For Buddhists, this something more is a store of accumulated merit (*phước báo*).

The two communities in Louisiana did not embark on building a stand-alone worship hall until they had each hosted the Jade Buddha of Universal Peace. These temples were just two stops in the Jade Buddha's nine-year tour to 125 cities throughout the United States, Canada, Australia, and Vietnam before reaching its final home at the Great Stupa of Universal Compassion near Bendigo, northwest of Melbourne.[17] Despite its lengthy tour around the world, the jade statue was largely ignored by Buddhist media outlets, pointing to the difficulty in reconciling Western Buddhism's emphasis on detachment with the amount of time, effort, and money necessary for these congregations to construct and display the statue.[18] The Jade Buddha is eight feet tall and was created from a massive boulder unearthed in Yukon, Canada, in 2000. Thai and Australian artisans spent five years carving the huge piece of jade, their labor funded by the sale of smaller Buddhas made from fragments of the stone, and upon its completion, monks blessed the statue in Sydney, Australia. People who visited or hosted the statue received blessings or merit, not just because of their proximity to the Jade Buddha but through the intentional act of seeing the image, an expenditure of effort that generates a return, merit. In the two cases I describe, the congregations understood hosting the Jade Buddha as a blessing that would sanction their efforts to build a stand-alone worship hall.[19] For visiting monks, however, the Jade Buddha signaled a dilemma—how to convert people's interest in seeing the Jade Buddha into support for the ongoing work of the monastic sangha in making Buddhism in the Gulf South.

During the event's opening ceremony at Hồng Ân Monastery, a senior monk from California stood onstage. He reminded the audience of their own power, not just because they stood next to the image but because they could express their own Buddhahood in their smiles and through their donations to the Buddha Hall. He urged the audience to support the monastic sangha, especially the young monks who had left their homeland to plant the seeds of the dharma in the United States.

> You see the Buddha statue, it is very beautiful, especially if you
> look at the hands, the skillful hands. Pay attention to your hands.
> Your hands look like Buddha's hands because you do many
> different things, every moment, every day. So the Buddha stays
> there for you to look at, and you look at yourself. You see, you are
> the Buddha. I hope everyone opens their mind and shares a little,
> donates to us, and later you will come to see the Buddha Hall and
> the living Buddha inside.

By drawing attention to the concept of skillfulness, the senior monk voiced a critique that trailed in the wake of the Jade Buddha—the misrecognition of spiritual power. The monk would later describe the statue as nothing more than a massive rock transported around the world, mobilized by the strength of people's beliefs. That afternoon, however, only a few listened to his speech. The majority lined up to take photographs in front of the statue or purchase souvenirs, replicas, or postcards of the Jade Buddha.

As I later learned from members of each temple, the money raised from the tour hardly covered the outlay of expenses in hosting the event. The congregations sponsored monks to give talks and singers to perform, and members prepared food to sell to attendees. Much of the money, however, flowed back to the organizers of the tour, who were raising funds for their own Buddha Hall in far-off Australia. Nevertheless, the benefits of hosting the event could not be reduced to monetary profits. By hosting the display, the congregations contributed to disseminating the teachings of Buddhism, thereby acquiring a vast store of merit. Over the next three days, once the crowds had dispersed, dozens of monks from around the United States who had gathered to witness the event then carried out an elaborate ritual to liberate the souls of the grievous dead. Thus, hosting the Jade Buddha and raising awareness of its benefits blessed each congregation's own ambitious project, the construction of a stand-alone worship hall.

BLESSING THE CONSTRUCTION SITE

Hồng Ân Monastery was not the first Buddhist temple in southwestern Louisiana. In 1986, Laotian refugees built a temple to support a cluster of households.[20] It was also not the first temple founded by Vietnamese Buddhists. A group of lay Buddhists formed an association and, over the years, invited several monks to reside in their temple to serve as spiritual guides. One of those resident monks petitioned to leave and then solicited financial support from Buddhists in the area, including his own relatives. He eventually purchased a ranch-style family home on four acres of land. Thus Hồng Ân Monastery was the third Buddhist temple in the heart of Cajun country.

The monastery was located on a county road where neighboring houses on large tracts of land advertised businesses such as income-tax preparation and tailoring. Initially, few changes were made to the exterior of the property, a tactic of home temples to blend into their surroundings. Only later did the congregations present a more public face of Buddhism by erecting a large wooden gate and installing two stone lion statues at the entrance. The first modification to the property, however, was not visible from the road at all.

A long, paved driveway led from the street to the back of the house, where French doors opened to a splendidly renovated worship hall. Next to the doors, the Great Bell hung from an ornately carved wooden frame on one side and the Drum Tower stood on the other side. The altar featured the trinity of statues, Amitābha Buddha in the middle, flanked by two bodhisattvas. On the wall hung charts of the expenses associated with specific projects, such as paving the driveway. Members of the congregation paid monthly dues to maintain the monastery, and they also signed their names to a pledge to cover the cost of these projects. These charts were not permanent fixtures of the worship hall—indeed, they changed depending on whatever project was underway—but their prominence in the worship hall attested to the importance of maintaining accountability to the monastery's benefactors.

The worship hall also proclaimed its node in a transpacific network. On the left-hand side of the hall was a small table with an incense holder surrounded by vases of arranged flowers, candles, and plates of fruit, together with photographs of deceased family members, some who had resettled in the United States and some who had died in Vietnam. But it was not just in serving these spirits that the transpacific was materialized. All along the walls of the worship hall ran three shelves that displayed golden statues of the historical Shakyamuni Buddha (Thích Ca Mâu Ni Phật), each featuring the engraved name of its donor, from the United States or as far away as Australia. These statues proclaimed more than the reputation of the donor; as a collection, they signaled the sheer scope of support required to transform Cajun country into the Pure Land.

When I first visited the monastery in 2013, I saw the temple complex as a finished project. For the abbot and members of the congregation, the layout was inauspicious. Where the public face of the temple complex, the Buddha Hall, should have been was the monastic residence: the front door opened to the living quarters, the intimate space where the monks cooked, ate, and watched television. A small hallway led past the bedrooms to a side door that opened to the worship hall. It would take several years and fundraising projects, including hosting the Jade Buddha, before the congregation embarked on a multiyear construction project to build a stand-alone worship hall that would present a public face of Buddhism.

In the meantime, the members continued to make improvements to the monastic complex. Especially welcome was the new communal kitchen that replaced the small area where women jostled over several gas burners as they prepared the vegetarian lunch on Sundays and meals for upwards of one hundred people for festivals. The new kitchen was outfitted with two restaurant-size refrigerators and long counters to accommodate the dozen or so women who would gather to cook and converse. Standing at the counters, the women peeled squash and potatoes, stripped stems from leafy greens, and chopped tomatoes, work that, while so vital to the collective life of the monastery, was not always harmonious. Tensions sometimes simmered because of the demands made by a visiting monk or the hasty arrangements to ensure enough rice noodles would be delivered to meet the larger than usual crowds. The covered patio next to the kitchen served as a buffer where people gathered to purchase snacks or enjoy a steaming bowl of soup, transforming the work of the kitchen crew into merit.

That the kitchen would be one of the first projects attests to the importance of food in gathering a sangha. Even the grassy area behind the temple complex demonstrated the importance of cultivating food. There several members planted fruit trees, built a chicken coop, and even tended a small garden with a muddy area for "water spinach" (*rau muống*), a leafy green not widely available in US grocery stores. By 2015, with the grassy field behind the buildings used for parking when hundreds of people would gather for cultural celebrations and Buddhist holidays, the complex had no more room for expansion. The remaining improvement, the construction of a worship hall, was both the most expensive and the most ambitious.

Building a Buddhist worship hall requires a financial commitment on a scale that necessitates raising money, not over months, but often years. Large-scale construction projects require hiring architects, obtaining the proper permits from city officials, and employing a construction crew. Many also rely on the labor of their members. The abbot estimated that the cost of building the worship hall, including materials, permits, and labor, would be almost eight hundred thousand dollars. In the face of so much money, the unseen world loomed large. This invisible presence was not just wayward local spirits but also rumors and dashed expectations among supporters of the project. Not only would breaking the ground displace spirits in the vicinity, but supporters could also turn their back on the project. About the time the congregation initiated construction, stories circulated that the first Vietnamese temple had faltered over concerns about its board of directors. The rumors came to a head just six months later when local newspapers reported that the presiding monk of the nearby temple stood accused of gambling thousands of dollars at a nearby casino.[21]

The head monk invited a dozen or so monks to witness two different ceremonies—setting the cornerstone (*lễ cúng đặt đá*) in 2014 and breaking the ground (*lễ động thổ*) in 2015. The collective body of monks acknowledges the accumulated history of a particular place by calling upon the invisible presence of spirits who linger in the area. These ceremonies also serve to stitch together the different Buddhist organizations around the United States, especially in the Gulf South, into a social body of Vietnamese Buddhism. These monks witness the ceremonies and pray for their success, and they may even bring donations raised from their congregations.

These ceremonies are common among Buddhist congregations. Anthropologist Jiemin Bao describes how a delegation of more than 150 Thai monks witnessed a similar ceremony at a temple in Silicon Valley, California, their presence not only a ritual of purification—their accumulated merit cleansing the site of "bad spirits"—but a regulatory means by which Thai monastic authorities acknowledge the legitimacy of the chapel. Such sanctioning is not just in adhering to the requisite local building codes and standards but also in the acceptance of the new chapel by the official sangha in Thailand.[22] Vietnamese Buddhist communities in the Gulf South, however, are not subject to the stringent Thai monastic code, nor do they enjoy the substantial financial support that flows from the Thai monarchy as the guardian of the dharma. Still, these ceremonies serve to sanction the construction project through the participation of Buddhist monks drawn from across the region, converting the accumulated capital of resettled Vietnamese refugees and immigrants in the Gulf South into the Pure Land.

In 2015, Hồng Ân Monastery sponsored one such ceremony to mark the actual ground-breaking ceremony. More than twelve monks, both male and female, had been invited from as far away as Oklahoma and California to witness the event. On the night I arrived, laywomen and laymen and more than a dozen male and female monks filled the worship hall. Master Pure Word, a senior monk from California, settled down on a cushion to give a dharma talk (*pháp thoại*). Rather than praise Buddhist teachings, he used simple and direct words to convey his vision for the monastery. He counseled the laity not to build a Buddha Hall but to purchase more land. With that land, they could provide a path for walking and thereby create conditions for people to experience the Pure Land, not beyond the threshold of human existence but in the present moment. Like the Venerable Thích Nhất Hạnh, whose most influential teachings emphasize that the Pure Land is realized in the present moment, Master Pure Word urged the congregation to consider the grounds of the monastery as more than just a place to park their cars. He spoke approvingly of a monastery in Florida, whose signature feature was a mile-long walking path that traced the perimeter of the temple grounds. Investing in land, he advised, would be not only for the present generation of Buddhists but for future generations as well, by ensuring the monastery remained a refuge from the demands of

3.3 Walking meditation is considered to be a mindfulness practice. Practitioners may take a step after each full breath or breathe in with one step and exhale on the next step. Monasteries with spacious grounds have walking paths. At temples in urban settings, this walking practice, if it occurs at all, takes place inside the worship hall or around the parking lot. Photo by Quang Huynh.

everyday life (figure 3.3). Pressing his point, he joked that this monastery was the only one he regularly visited where he feared for his safety on his morning walks, which took him down the nearby county road. The narrow route was flanked not by sidewalks but by ditches, common features for draining water but hazardous for pedestrians in a rural landscape that privileged driving over walking.[23]

The monk's advice was timely, as both adjacent tracts of land were up for sale, but they were not cheap.[24] By building a worship hall now, he warned, the community would foreclose the opportunity to create a refuge from the demands of modern life. Finally, he reminded the congregation of the distinction between pagodas and monasteries. While in this book, I collapse pagodas and monasteries into a single category, "temple," the distinction is still instructive for understanding how people ascribe different meanings to Buddhist centers. Pagodas in Vietnam are places people visit to make offerings in the hope that such actions will accrue merit and to gather in celebration of Buddhist holidays such as the first day of the lunar New Year. Monasteries, in contrast, are located on remote but spacious grounds and provide a sanctuary from the demands of everyday life. While both the pagoda and the monastery offer refuge, monasteries are where individuals gather to perfect the skills of wisdom and pagodas are centers where people come together to celebrate. Hồng Ân Monastery had elements of both—an active laity that provided substantial financial and social support and an abbot whose own training and aspirations were expressed in his naming the institution a monastery. Master Pure Word gently reminded everyone in attendance that they were in a monastery, not a pagoda. At that moment, a young woman called out, "Teacher, tomorrow we'll buy [the land]" (Thầy, mai mua cho). The attendees laughed, dispelling the tension in the hall. The young woman drew attention to the donations of those in the room—people who worked as fisherfolk, welders, manicurists, restaurant owners, and hourly employees. It was their work and donations that would raise the worship hall in the fields of Cajun country, not just the spiritual labor of ordained monks. The monastery depended on the financial contributions of migrants like herself, and so it needed to meet her needs as well.

The next morning, fog shrouded the ranch-style house, its gable roof visible like a mountaintop. Master Pure Word's speech did not stop the congregation from proceeding with the construction work as planned. The project manager, a Vietnamese American man, arrived with a burly white man and a large front loader to level the ground. Members busily set up an altar—men carried out rolled-up carpets and women laid out plates of freshly stir-fried water spinach, mangoes, fried spring rolls, and bitter melon stuffed with tofu, as well as bottles of water and bowls of uncooked rice. When the ceremony began, the lay members stood facing the monks, who prayed for the success of the project and blessed the land where the worship hall would stand (figure 3.4). Master Pure Word addressed the two men in charge of the construction project as they both stood respectfully with their heads bowed. He paused to ask the name of the man who would be grading the land. With a broad gesture of welcome, he emphasized that many agents were needed to build the worship hall and that, in turn, the worship hall was for all beings:

> We hope the new Buddha Hall will be built as soon as possible by
> you and our Vietnamese brothers and sisters, who are not only
> praying but building it with our skillful hands. It is difficult for
> Vietnamese refugees in the area, but, step-by-step, soon we will
> have a Buddha Hall not only for Vietnamese but for all our

3.4   Monks bowing down at a ceremony to bless the land. To the right are
members of the temple, and to the left are the men overseeing the construction
project. Photo by Quang Huynh.

> friends who want to learn the teachings and cultivate loving-
> kindness, compassion, and to share with all sentient beings.

Master Pure Word addressed the construction worker much as he would
those spirits, both seen and unseen, on whose support the success of the
project depended.[25] In so doing, he also invoked the arrival of Vietnamese
as refugees who had met with difficulties but through their expenditure of
effort would build a Buddha Hall to be dedicated to "all our friends," to
spread the ethics of loving-kindness and compassion to all sentient beings.
Through the built structure of the worship hall, not only would Vietnamese
Buddhists in the region make the teachings of Buddha available for all, but
they would also inscribe their presence onto the cultural landscape.

After the ceremony, the lay Buddhists cleared away the altar, and the
construction worker climbed into his front loader to level the ground. The

concrete foundation would be poured later that afternoon, so there was no time to consider Master Pure Word's advice to postpone building a Buddha Hall and instead purchase the adjacent land. I then joined the women and men who sat at the long tables to eat steaming bowls of spicy rice porridge for breakfast. The fruit and cooked dishes that had adorned the altar were now in the kitchen and quickly divided up by those in attendance, as they now signified Buddha's blessings, or *lộc*. People would later bring the fruit home, channeling those blessings back to their family and friends. Here the labor of the lay Buddhists in the kitchen stood in sharp contrast with the spiritual practice of mindfulness. When sitting in silence or walking slowly down a path, the connections to the realm of spirits and the family are less obvious, so people do not recognize these activities as spiritual labor. For monks such as Master Pure Word, emptiness is precisely the point, but for practitioners, such emptiness does not acknowledge their expenditure of effort, a key ethical disposition. I do not mean to suggest that the monks and the temple-goers did not find value in the teachings of monks like Thích Nhất Hạnh. Quite the opposite. On the wall of the living room in the monastic quarters hung a photograph of the abbot and several lay members who had visited Magnolia Grove in Mississippi, a monastery affiliated with the legendary Zen master. As we sat in the kitchen, the women joked with each other about the senior monk's advice that they purchase more land, both rejecting the monk's vision for the temple and replacing it with their own. For these people gathered in the kitchen, the monastery served a role in reconstituting and repairing their own lives by providing a roof to shelter their ancestors and compatriots alike. Unswayed by the senior monk's advice, the small gathering in the kitchen recognized how their work was as important as that of the invited monks who carried out the ritual ceremony of blessing the construction site.[26]

CELEBRATING BUDDHA, CELEBRATING THE DIASPORA

Vạn Minh Pagoda sat in a commercial corridor on the west bank of the Mississippi River, in metropolitan New Orleans, a location visible to a steady stream of cars that passed by daily. After having hosted the Jade Buddha, the congregation initiated an even more ambitious project, constructing the largest Buddhist temple between Houston and the Florida Panhandle, a landmark to the presence of Vietnamese along the Gulf Coast. The worship hall would be fifty-four feet tall and measure seventy-two hundred square feet. Its sheer size was not its only distinguishing feature. The hall would also showcase artisanal pieces handcrafted in Vietnam.

The abbot proudly showed me the ornately carved wooden doors, the statues of Amitābha Buddha and bodhisattvas, and the altar, created from a thousand-year-old tree, all products made in the homeland, transported across the Pacific, and displayed on the Gulf Coast. The hall did more than materialize the homeland: over the several-year construction period, the project served as a stage for showcasing the presence of Vietnamese Americans along the Gulf Coast.

Like Hồng Ân Monastery, Vạn Minh Pagoda initially repurposed an existing structure, a street-front building, into a worship hall. Separate monastic quarters were in a back building. Within a few years, the congregation erected an activity hall, a large barn-like structure that housed the communal kitchen, an open area for dining, and an upper-floor space used by a small group of convert Buddhists who met once a week to meditate and discuss Buddhist teachings. While a new Buddha Hall was not needed to resolve the spatial dilemma, as we saw with Hồng Ân Monastery, it was intended to resolve another concern. The repurposed building, with its low-pitched ceiling, did not summon the grandeur associated with urban Buddhist temples.

Before construction began, the congregation moved the altar to a temporary space in the multipurpose building so the existing worship hall could be razed. For the next four years, the front area of the temple complex was a construction site, with steel beams stacked in piles and a bright yellow front loader parked in the yard. Eventually, the frame of the hall was erected, its steel beams stretching four stories into the air and towering over the adjacent buildings. Even the outdoor statue of the bodhisattva Quán Thế Âm was dwarfed by the worship hall in the making.

The size of Buddhist temples elicits commentary, whether in Vietnam or along the US Gulf Coast. Some people admire the sheer size of temples for their social power. At a retreat attended by both Vietnamese and non-Vietnamese participants, one of the monks showed a video of Dhammakāya Temple in Thailand, which has animated the long-standing tension between wealth and authentic Buddhist piety and practice. Scholars and practitioners, shocked by such overt displays of prosperity, lament how its immense size has diverted resources away from other Buddhist temples.[27] The monk who screened the video, however, was clearly impressed by its size and the number of retreatants. Yet Vietnamese lay Buddhists sometimes measure the spiritual worth of a temple inversely to its size. The saying "Small temple, big Buddha, big temple, small Buddha" (Chùa nhỏ, Phật lớn, chùa lớn, Phật nhỏ) emphasizes how piety cannot be expressed in the idiom of global capitalism, where moral worth and relative size are thought to be mutually reinforcing qualities. Some lay Buddhists also comment that monks who build elaborate temples are "chasing after form" (*chạy theo hình thức*), underscoring the difficulty inherent in such projects. Consequently, donations for these projects can sometimes run dry. Quyền, a woman in her late forties who occasionally attended the temple, described the efforts of the congregation in terms of "fate" (*duyên*):

> Everything is up to fate. Even families are that way. The [monk] sees people have a lot of money. But one has to do these projects a little at a time. If you don't have the money, you have to wait to build. Sometimes you wait your whole life. It's difficult. Just waiting for money.

In contrast, Mrs. Thu was more adamant in explaining why she no longer supported the building efforts of the temple: "A temple should not have any fun or outside people. It's a place of worship, like a church." She was not alone in her views; the size of the proposed building led other people to question why such a large Buddhist worship hall was needed in the region. During one celebration, only a handful of people attended, and the scene of row upon row of empty folding chairs served as a visual reminder of the difficulty of maintaining support during these large-scale and long-term projects.

Urban temples are subject not only to the scrutiny and gossip of lay Buddhists but to the oversight of local government authorities as well. The buildings must conform to municipal codes in ways that temples in rural areas do not. In metropolitan New Orleans, one of the most strictly enforced regulations concerns the number of designated parking spots. While Hồng Ân Monastery used the grassy area behind the temple complex for parking overflow during festivals, Vạn Minh Pagoda had no such solution. During the week and even for Sunday services, the need for parking was limited; however, whenever festivals and other celebrations were held, parking was scarce. Buddhist complexes are blessed with "flexible topographies."[28] When the project manager filed for permits to build a multipurpose building, he categorized the structure as a library rather than a place of worship, a designation that required fewer parking spaces. By designating the temple as a library, he cleverly framed the construction project within the widespread perception among Americans that Buddhism is a philosophy, not a religion.

Even flexible topographies have limits. When the main altar no longer had a designated space marked off from the secular rhythms of the kitchen and dining room, the limits became obvious. That monks and lay

Buddhists remove their shoes and wear special robes marks the space of the worship hall off from ordinary activities. This distinction was harder to maintain once the main altar was moved to the ground floor of the activity hall. The large room was divided in two, with one area for storing the carved wooden doors from Vietnam and the other used as a flexible zone, providing a worship area for Sunday services and for family members to offer prayers to their deceased relatives. After the services, people would set up folding tables for the communal Sunday lunch, as they had done before construction began, but most of the time people just ate at the long tables in the kitchen. While the arrangement appeared to work, the flexible topography also created confusion. People kept their shoes on when they walked through the large room; thus symbolic boundaries, once held apart by separate physical spaces, collapsed. On one hot afternoon in August 2015, as I sat inside to escape the heat, a woman entered the dining room that temporarily housed the altar and looked around with some confusion. She asked a group of men sitting at a table if she should remove her shoes, glancing toward the seat cushions and small prayer books. One of the lay members shrugged and replied, "Mệt rồi" (Tired), conveying a sense of the labor required to maintain the distinction between the sacred and the profane amid so much construction.

The Vietnamese presence in the city was showcased not only by the anticipated size of the temple. One of the fund-raising strategies of the community was to sponsor performances of well-known and up-and-coming singers. The events followed Buddhist celebrations—special days honoring the bodhisattva Quán Thế Âm, the Buddha's birthday, or the Vu Lan festival. In contrast to temples where the cultural programs followed the Buddhist service, at Vạn Minh Pagoda they were held at night, transforming a religious ceremony into a cultural event to appeal to a broader audience than would otherwise attend the service.

On one occasion honoring Quán Thế Âm, the formal Buddhist service took place on a Saturday night. The temple was strangely quiet when I arrived; only four or five cars were in the parking lot. Twelve or so women were in attendance, setting up cushions and lighting incense in front of the memorial board (*khung thờ hương linh*), where photos of deceased family members were displayed. The visiting monk began his dharma talk with little fanfare as a few more people filed in, discreetly bowing in front of the altar and then quietly taking their place on a cushion. When the monk finished, he slipped out of the room and moments later reentered with the presiding monk in a formal procession. After the ceremony, the monks and lay Buddhists filed out of the building and crossed behind the construction site, muddied after a hard afternoon rain. Pieces of plywood were laid down, and the procession walked over to the statue of Quán Thế Âm and circled the small area three times. Women jostled to find a dry spot and then knelt and touched their heads to the ground. After the prayers, people placed their candles around the base of the statue and walked silently back to the activity hall before leaving in their cars.

The following night, a much larger crowd sat on white folding chairs set up in neat rows on the concrete foundation of the worship hall. Members of the temple sold various Vietnamese specialties from wooden stalls, erected almost overnight (figure 3.5). While the previous evening featured the slow procession of monks and lay Buddhists around the statue of Quán Thế Âm, the activities this night focused on earthly pleasures—food and song. People crowded around the row of stalls to buy vegetarian versions of well-known Vietnamese foods such as steaming bowls of the spicy noodle soup *bún bò Huế* and a turmeric-infused noodle dish known as *mỳ quảng*, as well as standard festival fare like snow cones and popcorn. The atmosphere was

3.5 Vegetarian to-go dishes are a popular draw at festivals. Featured here, at a different temple, are steamed rice cakes wrapped in banana leaves, steamed dumplings, and bags of fried sesame balls. Behind the tables are stacks of sugarcane to be pressed into juice. Photo by the author.

rowdy and loud as people sat at long tables and children gleefully sprayed each other with Silly String.

On that evening, several singers were slated to appear, including Đan Nguyên, a popular young male singer featured on Trung Tâm Asia's syndicated music series. His role that evening was to entertain the crowd and solicit contributions by approaching members of the audience with a donation box. After he performed two songs, he asked what else the audience wanted to hear. People responded enthusiastically, calling out "Where Is My Vietnam?" (Việt Nam tôi đâu?) and "Who Are You?" (Anh là ai?), two songs written by composer Việt Khang, a Vietnamese national arrested in 2012 in southern Vietnam.[29] As Đan Nguyên belted out the first song, he wound his way through the rows of chairs and people eagerly reached out to put cash in the box he held. His second and final encore, "Who Are You?," elicited even more applause and cash. His voice carried through the night air, and as he sang out the plaintive lyrics in Vietnamese, a two-story-tall digitized image of Quán Thế Âm hovered over him:

> Who are you to arrest me,
> What have I done wrong,
> Who are you to beat me without mercy,
> Who are you to keep me from proclaiming my love for this land?

In Vietnam, the lyrics were understood as a rebuke to the Communist Party for not defending its territorial rights in the South China Sea. For many Vietnamese in America, the lyrics also addressed Vietnam's continued repression of dissident opinion, and so that year the song was regularly performed on occasions including the lunar New Year and April 30, which marks the fall of Saigon. Đan Nguyên and other singers mobilized Vietnamese in the region to contribute money toward building a worship hall, thereby aligning the construction project not just with Buddhism but with the politics of Vietnamese Americans. The popularity of singers like Đan Nguyên speaks to the widespread culture of Vietnamese video music, a "highly mobile technology" that allows Vietnamese Americans to envision and articulate post-refugee identities.[30] In this case, Đan Nguyên's performance invoked the suffering of people who had been displaced and subsequently fashioned a sense of community through expressions of anticommunism.

A Vietnamese American community leader once estimated that fundraising events in the New Orleans area easily net as much as fifty thousand dollars in a single evening. However, raising money by selling vegetarian food and nonalcoholic drinks is not as lucrative. Over the next two years, monks and lay members regularly sponsored cultural performances at Vạn Minh Pagoda to raise funds for the construction. These performances became as much a ritual as formal services. Large crowds gathered, and cars lined up along the road and filled the neighboring parking lots. The head monk would step onstage to welcome guests and humbly request that people "once or twice" give money to complete the construction project, intended for the entire Vietnamese community in Louisiana. He encouraged the people in the audience, "Buddhists and compatriots" (*các Phật tử, quý đồng hương*), to support the efforts of the congregation. The master of ceremonies, a jovial man who was Catholic, called on people to contribute and "build a worship hall that will be really grand" (*chánh điện thật to lớn*), inadvertently reminding many in the audience of the moral dilemma presented by the size of the hall. The singers cheerfully asked the audience to contribute as they dutifully wove their way through the rows of chairs to solicit donations. People waved them down to drop in a five-, ten-, or twenty-dollar bill, often asking the singer to stop so they could take a quick selfie as a souvenir. The singers called on people to give "a lot or a little" and reminded them that the temple was not only for Buddhists by pointing out that the master of ceremonies was Catholic. Sometimes the singers teased the audience about pulling out their cash by asking if they were out of "big bills" and complimenting the men about how handsome they were. One singer called out that the temple had already spent $267,000 but still needed $700,000 because the fees were so high. She asked the people in the audience to call their friends so the temple would receive their support, while another singer walked through the audience like a hostess, inquiring if they were enjoying the space and whether they had enough to eat and drink, pausing now and then to thank people for their contributions.

On one occasion, the monk addressed the question that had been on people's minds and tongues—why was the proposed worship hall so large? It spoke to people's anxieties around financial accountability but also the difficulties many people faced as they struggled to earn a livelihood in the Gulf South. The monk was joined onstage by a community leader, who also served as project manager for the construction. The man took the microphone and held up a golden statue of the young Buddha to address the scale of the worship hall. He proclaimed that ten thousand Buddha statues would line the walls of the hall, each in its own shadow box with the name of the donor inscribed on a plaque beneath the statue. The master of ceremonies later appealed to attendees to donate money for the roof tiles, to be imported from Vietnam at considerable expense, more than $150 per square meter. Toward the end of the evening, one of the female singers announced how many of the $200 statues had been purchased. They were at sixty-two, a long way from the goal of ten thousand Buddhas.

Fund-raising, far from being peripheral to liturgical truths, is integral to making Buddhism in the Gulf South. The construction site itself stood as a visible symbol that confirmed both the money raised was being used and why more funds were still needed to complete the project. The progress was incremental, and each step was another occasion to ask for more money. For one event, the earth had been graded; for another event, the concrete foundation had been poured; for yet another event, the steel beams to support the walls had been erected. While such gestures acknowledged people's skepticism, we can see how Buddhist monks must assuage not only local spirits but lay Buddhists as well.

· ◆ ·

Building a worship hall exposes the politics of Pure Land in the making. The two settings of the temples profiled here—one in a semirural neighborhood on several acres of land and the other in an urban commercial area hemmed in by other businesses and parking lots—reflect different tensions over whose labor transforms the Gulf Coast into the Pure Land. The scale of these construction projects required solicitation of support not just from members but from compatriots in the vicinity and even around the world. Is the power of a worship hall in its size and ability to draw people from across the region? Or is a monastery a meditative place where people can escape the demands of daily life? Such debates are also contentious in Vietnam and elsewhere in Asia, underscoring how the meanings of these structures are neither stable nor coherent.

Buddhism in the making is an ongoing, dynamic process in which people inscribe the postsuburban commercial corridors of the West Bank and the semirural fields of southwestern Louisiana with new spiritual meanings that are both undeniably Buddhist and inescapably Vietnamese. This transmission happens not only in the worship hall but in kitchens and large cultural events. While people distinguish between "pagodas" and "monasteries," the former referring to a space that draws crowds attracted by music and food and the latter designating an area of refuge, in practice these sites need to fulfill both roles. The young woman who interrupted the dharma talk of a senior male monk by calling out, "Teacher, tomorrow we'll buy [the land]," reminded everyone in attendance that it was with the donations of hardworking lay Buddhists that the worship hall was built.

If building a Buddha Hall takes years, so does the work of raising funds. Buddhist communities hold dinners at banquet halls, inviting well-known singers to perform. These fund-raising events also risk turning away lay Buddhists, who see such activities as violating the vows of monks, much as when temples are rumored to sell beer or allow gambling during the New Year to attract more people. Several women mentioned to me that they no longer attended services to avoid the constant appeals for money. One woman who had supported Buddhist temples in New Orleans since the 1970s expressed her disappointment: "I believe in Buddha, I believe in Buddhism, but I do not want to follow an individual monk."

These large-scale construction projects carry risks. The biggest threat may be not a wayward monk who absconds with temple funds to play the slot machines at a nearby casino, but rather the loss of support from lay Buddhists. People who once enthusiastically attended temples sometimes retreat to their own homes or sponsor a monk to establish yet another temple or monastery. In my interviews, some people stressed how they retreated to practice inside their own homes. One woman showed me her bedroom, where she had displayed an image of Buddha and three framed pictures of the bodhisattva Quan Âm. Another woman had arranged a small sitting room just off her front entryway, where she could chant sutras and recite the names of buddhas and bodhisattvas. A man who had long attended one temple confided that, while he meditated at home, he still attended the temple to enjoy lunch with his friends. In different ways, each of these practitioners had found a way to address their spiritual needs beyond the space of the formal worship hall.

How then do temples pull Vietnamese Buddhists back? One strategy is by cultivating a sense of filial obligation through invoking the sentimental figure of the mother and, by extension, the homeland.

CHAPTER FOUR

Honoring Mothers

THE setting sun cast a warm glow over Hồng Ân Monastery in southwestern Louisiana as people made final preparations for Vu Lan, one of the most solemn ceremonies of the Buddhist ritual calendar. The presiding monk called upon everyone wearing gray robes to gather in the worship hall. On that August evening in 2015, even the few children present wore the loose robes, perhaps more in deference to their parents than as a self-conscious declaration of their identity as Buddhist. Moments later, a dozen monks walked slowly down the center aisle toward the main altar. Their voices carried through the night air as they called upon the spirits of the dead to be released from hell and reborn in the Pure Land. When the service ended thirty or so minutes later, both monks and lay Buddhists filed out of the worship hall. As we left the hall, a monk handed each of us a candle and a sheet printed with Chinese characters, on which we were to write the name of a deceased relative. Then, one by one, people made their way to the outdoor pavilion, where a temporary altar had been created. After another round of prayers, people placed their candle and sheet on the altar. As soon as the ceremony ended, the head monk jovially invited the lay members to spend the night in the monastery. "Is one night too much to ask," he called out in Vietnamese, "for your parents, who sacrificed so much for you? Spend the night with the spirits who have gathered here to be pardoned!" Through the night, the candles burned, tendrils of smoke carrying the prayers of the living across the porous membrane that separated them from the afterworld, as distinctions between the living and the dead, the worldly and unworldly, momentarily fell away.

By the next morning, the candles were burned down to small stubs. Members of the temple turned their attention from pardoning the dead to welcoming visitors from as far away as Mississippi and Alabama. Women no longer wore the loose-fitting gray robes but had put on colorful *áo dài*s, long, figure-hugging tunics worn over palazzo pants, and pageant-inspired sashes printed with "Vu Lan" in italicized script to identify them as hostesses. Under the covered pavilion, where the night before we had gathered to chant sutras, two women collected donations for the monastery and sold souvenirs—calendars, prayer beads, and bouquets of flowers. Later that afternoon, visitors would enjoy performances by a well-known Vietnamese American singer from Houston and bid on Vietnamese proverbs rendered in calligraphic script to raise funds for the monastery. The first stop for many visitors was the open-air statue of the bodhisattva Quán Thế Âm, who is revered as a gentle mother (*mẹ hiền*). Some people bowed; others posed for photos. Almost everyone then walked over to the patio, where they could purchase specialties such as freshly squeezed sugarcane juice and steamed dumplings wrapped in banana leaves. The solemnity of the previous evening had yielded to a celebration of motherhood and homeland.

In the United States, Vu Lan is popularly known as Vietnamese Mother's Day, a label that transforms the Buddhist observance into a holiday comfortably familiar to other Americans. Mother's Day originated in Philadelphia as a day to celebrate Christian mothers. Not until 1914 was it commemorated as a national holiday to sustain the morale of soldiers deployed overseas, thereby fulfilling a social function "beyond the purely personal mother-child relationship it ostensibly honored."[1] Vu Lan likewise fulfills a social function, one that has provided a compelling narrative told and retold over the salvation of "impure and sinful women, in particular, mothers."[2]

In Asia, Vu Lan is also known as *Ullambana*, a Pali term meaning "to release (those souls tormented in hell)."[3] Classic sources associate the legend of Mulian (Master Mục Kiền Liên in Vietnamese) with the Yulan Bowl Festival, in which people give bowls of food to monastic sanghas on the fifteenth day or full moon of the seventh lunar month. Unlike many sutras, the legend of Mulian does not have any counterpart in South Asian sources.[4] Mulian, a disciple of Shakyamuni Buddha, is said to have descended into the lower realms of hell to liberate his own mother. When he failed to do so, Buddha counseled him that only when the entire sangha carried out rites would his mother be released from her torment. For many Buddhists, the legend offers an exemplary tale of filial piety—even an exalted monk who had renounced his family could not forget his debt to his mother. Vu Lan thus goes hand in hand with the celebration of filial piety, a moral value that obligates the child to respect and care for the parent, even after death.

While the festival celebrates filial piety, it also reveals an ambivalence toward maternal imagery that is not unique to East Asia. Maternal imagery in South Asian Buddhism also oscillates between two models, universal love and particular love.[5] On the one hand, the image of the mother is the very model for monks wishing to cultivate loving-kindness and compassion, a boundless love emblematic of buddhas and bodhisattvas. On the other hand, mothers are seen as deeply attached to their own children, which inhibits women's possibility of liberation. Their karmic debt weighs more heavily because of their social roles as daughters, wives, and mothers. Yet paradoxes abound: while mothers expose the limits of universal love, monks as sons and daughters still owe their mothers a debt of gratitude. Mother-love is thus a "double-edged symbol," one that succeeds because of its intensity but simultaneously fails because of its particularity.[6] The mother figure presented in the Vu Lan legend mediates this tension by being caught in the realm of samara or desire, the very opposite of the Buddhist ideal of emptiness and liberation.

If maternal imagery links the sangha to the family, then maternal imagery also links the sangha to the ancestral homeland. Two maternal figures are of interest here: the bodhisattva Quán Thế Âm, affectionately known as the gentle mother, and the accursed mother depicted in the legend of Vu Lan. These mother figures mediate two different forms of love, the universal and the particular, the tension between which is instructive for understanding how Vietnamese Buddhists position themselves in relation to the ancestral homeland. People's love for family and nation are core elements in making Buddhism in the Gulf South, and it is love in its particularity that some monks recognize as not yet universal, in which the labels "here" and "there" fall away.

AN ACCURSED MOTHER

At first glance, a Buddhist celebration of filial piety is puzzling. Buddhism is depicted in academic scholarship as concerned more with death than with the welfare of families. Monks, for example, rarely sanction births or marriages, as other religious specialists do.[7] Moreover, renunciation as a ritual process is predicated on leaving the family of origin and constructing an alternate identity.[8] What does Vu Lan reveal about how Buddhists navigate family obligations through the very institution premised on renouncing those obligations?

For societies influenced by Confucianism, filial piety (hiếu) is regarded as the basis of a broader economy of sentiment that children must be taught early on. Filiality inaugurates the moral debt that structures the parent-child relationship, what some scholars claim is "the core of Vietnamese culture, dominating everything else" but others cautiously describe as "partially of Western manufacture and mold."[9] Moreover, expressions of filial piety vary widely, both in contemporary East and Southeast Asia and among transnational migrant families.[10] Among Chinese students in the United States, for example, the sanctity of parent-child relations is the basis of "filial nationalism," in which the object of loyalty is the nation, likened to a long-suffering parent, flawed to be sure but still deserving of their devotion.[11]

How Buddhism accommodated its teachings in those societies where Confucian values like filial piety prevailed has long been of interest to scholars.[12] By the sixth century, Buddhist monks aligned the sangha with popular religious practices like the Ghost Festival, centrally concerned with ancestor worship and even animal sacrifice. Monks, once renouncers of the family, were positioned as crucial actors within the "circle of reciprocity between descendants and ancestors."[13] More significantly, the legend of Mulian shifted the locus of obligation from father and son to that of mother and son: Mulian's mother, cast into hell, was liberated through the collective efforts of the sangha, effectively "co-opt[ing] the basic Confucian value of filial piety to Buddhist projects."[14] The enduring popularity of the legend reinforced depictions of female impurity by showing women as more prone to desire and thus "in greater need of salvation from the torments of hell."[15] For these reasons, the Buddhist version of the Ghost Festival in East China may be considered one of the "world's great religious inventions and rivals the Passion of Christ in all but one way: no one in the West cares about it."[16] If no one in the West cares, it may be because the legend invokes a cosmology premised not just on filial children but also on ghosts.

Across China and Vietnam, Vu Lan is celebrated on the full moon of the seventh lunar month, a time when the boundary between the world of the living and the dead is said to be especially permeable and the spiritual powers of the monastic sangha are at their peak.[17] The Ghost Festival, known as Rằm Tháng Bảy in Vietnam, is a public spectacle as households make offerings to "hungry ghosts," those wandering spirits who are not celebrated within the family; nameless and placeless, they remain caught, unable to be released into the cycle of rebirth. During the seventh lunar month, people mark these ghosts as external to the household and ancestors, whose altars are inside the house. Instead, people set up small tables on sidewalks with bowls of rice, salt, and water, as well as sugary treats, trivial amounts of money, and votive or paper offerings of money and clothing of a lesser quality than what one presented to ancestral spirits. The spectacle of people tossing out offerings to the streets as young children grasp for the candy, fruit, and cash materializes the invisible presence of ghosts in the avenues and alleyways of Vietnam.[18]

In the Gulf South, these ghosts have all but retreated from public life. People still make offerings at Buddhist temples, those spaces culturally encoded and legally sanctioned as private, and they are carried out throughout the year. What is significant is how Vu Lan differs from these streetside rituals—it is not a nameless ghost whom Mulian endeavors to save but his own mother. What he learns from Buddha is that neither his accumulated merit nor his filial piety is sufficient to do so. Only with the power of the entire sangha will his mother be released from the lower realms of hell.

If filial piety as a moral virtue influences the self-fashioning of transnational subjects, how then has it shaped Vietnamese Buddhist practices in the Gulf South? One answer lies in how Buddhists express their devotion toward the ancestral homeland even as they also remain antagonistic toward the Communist Party still in power. Vietnam is conceptualized not as the motherland but as an ancestral land, *tổ quốc*, and the temple serves as a guardian or protector of ancestral time, a way of life that flattens the distinctions between the past, present, and future. Ancestry may be formally traced through the father or patrilineal relations, but kinship structures are premised on both solidarity and hierarchy, a dichotomy between inside and outside relations. This dichotomy is expressed explicitly in language—the father's side is "inside" (*bên nội*) and the mother's side is "outside" (*bên ngoại*).[19] While the structural emphasis appears to privilege the inside or patrilineal descent, a dynamic in which a daughter's loyalty is said to be transferred from her parents to her husband's family, those models are never complete or totalizing.[20] Most people engage in a far more flexible bilateral model, in which the "outside" responds to the exegencies of everyday life. Consequently, it is the mother who is associated with sentimentality and the home, rather than the father, who is associated with duty. During the American War in Vietnam, wartime songs invoked kin-based or geographical nostalgia by appealing to maternal imagery. The song "Mother of the Native Place" (Bà mẹ quê), widely performed during the conflict, depicts a woman waiting for her children to return from the front, opening with a famous proverb of maternal love: "Mother's feelings are as expansive as the Pacific Ocean."[21] Maternal love is intense and compassionate, much like the love that bodhisattvas are said to possess. The Vu Lan festival can be said to capitalize on the tremendous debt binding people to their mothers, and by extension to the homeland. But in doing so, the festival and legend also stage the ambivalence that is at the heart of Buddhism as a diasporic religion—is being both Buddhist and Vietnamese an expression of heritage? If so, is liberation from this debt relation possible?

In the US Gulf South, people's devotion to the homeland extends not to the actual nation-state of the Socialist Republic of Vietnam but to "ancestral time," conjured by images of a maternal figure.[22] At Hồng Ân Monastery in southwestern Louisiana, a large banner with a huge photo of an elderly Vietnamese woman in a conical hat and the checkered scarf of the Mekong Delta draped around her neck hung behind the altar set up in the outdoor pavilion. The image was not of anyone's mother in particular but was a stock photo that staged ancestral time. Not everyone's mother is elderly or even resides in the Vietnamese countryside, but this image stood in for heritage and the homeland, allowing the temple as an institution to claim the "sacralizing power of ancestral authenticity."[23]

Buddhist institutions mediate between ancestral time and aspirational values for the futurity, between the homeland and the land of resettlement. People gather as compatriots to perform their piety, both to their mothers and to the ancestral homeland, with a glass of sweetened sugarcane and the strains of familiar songs in Vietnamese. In turn, temples solicit these compatriots as possible donors, drawing on their sense of duty and obligation to support the sangha as keeper of ancestral time, realizing the late Venerable Thích Mãn Giác's vision of the temple as protecting "the national soul." Vietnamese practitioners—monks, lay Buddhists, and compatriots—bridge the distance between the Gulf South and the homeland through maternal imagery, transforming the temple into a crucial infrastructure for remembering the homeland. And it is on these occasions that the temple community presents its vision of futurity by calling on compatriots to fund capital projects as a way of expressing gratitude toward their own mothers, thereby ensuring that the spiritual meanings—of longing and loss, duty and love—will be inscribed on the Gulf South.

A GENTLE MOTHER

One does not have to look far to find an image of a boundless, compassionate love on the grounds of Vietnamese temples—the outdoor statue of the bodhisattva Quán Thế Âm. Extolled as a "gentle mother," the figure of the bodhisattva gazes toward the street, a gentle smile on her lips as she hears the cries of people's suffering. Statues of the bodhisattva are also installed on the main altar inside the worship hall, signaling the bodhisattva's place as an attendant to Amitābha Buddha. But outside, Quán Thế Âm stands alone, an image familiar and approachable. For many Vietnamese Buddhists, the most popular and beloved bodhisattva is Quán Thế Âm, and her statue is a defining feature of temples along the Gulf Coast (figure 4.1).

In Mahayana Buddhism, bodhisattvas are supernatural beings who participate fully in this world, having deferred their own enlightenment so they may relieve the suffering of others. Also known by the Sanskrit name Avalokiteśvara, the bodhisattva was initially an attendant to Amitābha Buddha, one who guided souls to the Western Paradise. In the sixth century, the figure accrued new meanings as traders and scholars carried religious texts and images of the bodhisattva along the Silk Road.[24] The most significant transformation was the conversion of the male Avalokiteśvara into the female Kuan-Yin, the Goddess of Mercy, or Quan Âm, as the figure is known in Vietnam. In the broader process of domesticating Buddhism in East Asia, Kuan-Yin stood outside the official cosmology of the triad—Heaven, Earth, and the Emperor as the Son of Heaven—and therefore was not subject to hierarchies of class, gender, or even moral worthiness.[25] Still, the bodhisattva did not destabilize gendered relations so

4.1

On the grounds of a temple, a statue of the bodhisattva Quán Thế Âm holds a vessel symbolizing boundless compassion. Visitors leave lit sticks of incense in the urn in front of the statue. The newly constructed frame of the worship hall is visible in the background. Photo by the author.

much as reinforce patrilineal ties—one of the most sought-after powers attributed to the figure was sending sons to people who called her name.

For many Vietnamese Buddhists, Quán Thế Âm invokes the transpacific as a powerful symbol of how people experienced crossing from Vietnam to the United States.[26] One of the many variations of the bodhisattva is Quan Âm Nam Hải, or Quan Am of the South China Sea, a feminine figure dressed in flowing robes, holding a vase or a willow branch, and hovering over water.[27] In China, the figure is associated with a major pilgrimage site on Mount Putuo, an island located near a major trading hub in the East China Sea, ensuring that representations of the bodhisattva's powers—miracle tales, inscriptions, images, and travelogues—spread throughout the wider region.[28] Some Vietnamese in the United States attribute their rescue as they fled Vietnam to the bodhisattva, revivifying earlier miracle tales through their modern-day stories of refugees adrift at sea. Like seafaring people of centuries ago, Vietnamese refugees circulated the name of Quan Âm through these retellings.

During one ceremony at a temple I attended in Mississippi, an elderly monk quietly yet forcefully reminded the laity in attendance of the bodhisattva's power. The ceremony was held at sundown. Colorful lanterns swayed in the night breeze as people sat on reed mats in front of the outdoor statue of Quán Thế Âm. In a barely audible voice, the monk addressed the fifty or so people gathered that evening. Some in attendance had made harrowing journeys from Vietnam; others were born in the United States; still others had only recently immigrated to the United States. Everyone, though, listened intently as he recounted his own story. After 1975, he fled Vietnam in a small boat with thirty other monks. A tempest left the boat adrift for days. Nearby, on a US naval ship, a junior officer awoke to the sensation of someone tapping his shoulder and asking him to save a group of people lost at sea. The officer informed his commanding officer, who went on deck, spotted the tiny boat, and eventually rescued the refugees. In this tale, the US naval ship was an instrument but not an agent of rescue. The monk's story attributed the rescue to Quán Thế Âm, reinforcing the other-power, or faith in the power of the bodhisattva's vow to relieve the suffering of all sentient beings. He also overturned the prevailing narrative that credits the United States with having rescued refugees and instead endowed the bodhisattva with that power, raising the question of who then deserves the gratitude of refugees.

The monk's story and others like it reinforce the powers ascribed to Quán Thế Âm, or the "Perceiver of Sounds" in the Lotus Sutra, in chapter 25, which details the bodhisattva's supernatural powers to rescue those who call her name:

If you are cast adrift on the vast ocean,
menaced by dragons, fish, and various demons,
think on the power of that Perceiver of Sounds
and the billows and waves cannot drown you![29]

The Lotus Sutra is not just a sacred scripture chanted as an act of devotion but an affirmation of the vivid stories of people who survived their transpacific crossings and are now bound by a Vietnamese Buddhist diaspora. Refugees who crossed the Pacific with Quán Thế Âm ascribe their new land in a Buddhist vernacular of suffering and compassion, invoking her image, both nowhere in particular and everywhere, filling the immense gulf between the "here" of the Gulf South and the "there" of Vietnam. These stories affirm the vows of the bodhisattva to relieve people's suffering and remind sons and daughters of the debt they owe to their own mothers.

Quán Thế Âm is not only a significant figure of crossing for many Vietnamese Buddhists but also a key element in dwelling, or processes of home-making that "orient individuals and groups in time and space, transform the natural environment, and allow devotees to inhabit the worlds they construct."[30] One of the most significant donations people make is to a statue of the bodhisattva to be installed on the grounds of a temple. A monk in Louisiana recounted the story of a husband and wife, he a fisherman and she a manicurist, who visited the monk's temple and asked him what he needed. The monk was surprised, as the couple had only visited the temple once or twice before, so he suggested that the temple needed a garden where they could install a large statue of the bodhisattva. The couple agreed and presented him with a check for fifty thousand dollars. Today the statue is installed in a pavilion with landscaping and welcomes people who gather to express their gratitude toward the "gentle mother," Quán Thế Âm. This story is instructive because it highlights the role of monks in guiding practitioners to see the bodhisattva as worthy of their investment, just as evangelicals work to experience God talking to them.[31] In other words, such devotional activities must be cultivated, and thus are not nearly as straightforward as we may think.

In the figure of the bodhisattva, we can see how self-power and other-power complement each other by invoking Quán Thế Âm through the power of prayer. It is not that people simply invoke the name of the bodhisattva; it is how they express effort in doing so. Master Deep Awakening recounted how she had prayed for someone to donate a statue of Quan Âm to the monastery in Florida, where there were few Buddhists. She relied on financial support from her own family and friends, who lived elsewhere, but she felt strongly that the statue had to come from someone in the community.

> I prayed to Quán Thế Âm to bring someone who lived in the area to come here and donate the statue. About two weeks [later], a lady who came, . . . she wanted to become my Buddhist lay student. She said she was fond of me and felt a connection to me. I shared some of the Buddhist teachings and then conducted the taking refuge ceremony. After that, she came and wrote me a check to contribute to the statue. So you see, the statue is a miracle. I made a vow that it had to be someone here who donated the statue; it could not be someone where there was no connection to the people here, to the monastery here. I still think of it as a miracle, a mixture of miracles and blessing and spiritual potential, those three words together.

The statue affirmed the power of Quán Thế Âm to respond to people's requests, her presence in the Gulf South thus inscribing the landscape with meanings especially resonant for many Vietnamese American Buddhists.

Lay Buddhists make a place for the bodhisattva beyond the gates of the temple as well. People place statues of the bodhisattva on their altars at home. They tuck laminated cards of the bodhisattva in the glove compartments of their cars and wear pendants of the bodhisattva around their necks to enjoy her protections. Grocery stores and restaurants offer cards with her image and sheets printed with the Great Compassion Mantra, an eighty-four-line mantra that many people have learned by heart. Through these acts—some highly visible, others more mundane—Buddhists domesticate the supernaturalism they attribute to the figure lovingly called the "gentle mother."

Yet Quán Thế Âm as a model of compassion is also "free and detached from living beings through the wisdom of emptiness."[32] She is the mother of all because she is the mother of none. Some scholars suggest that the maternal imagery detracts from the polymorphic nature of the bodhisattva—even the transformation from the male figure of Avalokiteśvara into the female figure Quán Thế Âm reinforces rather than dismantles the dualistic thinking of gender. Instead, the manifestation of Avalokiteśvara in the form of a woman is an example of the skillful means of the bodhisattva, not an essential quality.[33]

However, the supernatural potency attributed to Quán Thế Âm resonates with other female figures in Vietnam, including Liễu Hạnh, associated with the Mother Goddess religion, whose name spread via the mobility of female merchants and entertainers in the sixteenth and seventeenth centuries.[34] In southern Vietnam, Bà Chúa Xứ, or "Lady of the Realm," offers a modality of power that is open to multiple ethnic influences but whose power emanates from the geographical frontier of the modern Vietnamese state. Likewise, the maritime goddess, Mazu, forges links across diasporic Chinese populations in Southeast Asia, challenging the sanctity of state-based identities and engendering a distinctive coastal realm of the South China Sea, or Nanyang.[35] While monks may draw a line separating Buddhism and the religion of spirits (đạo thần), for many people, these goddesses are an incarnation of the bodhisattva, thus incorporating other deities into Buddhist cosmology.[36] These feminine figures, like Quán Thế Âm, embody a source of power unbound by hierarchical orderings of the household or the nation-state or derived from the margins of these collective formations and therefore signify a more inclusive vision of belonging. Yet discourses of femininity are conflicting, both in Vietnam and in its diasporas. While women are valorized as defenders of national tradition and the bearers of culture, they are also vilified for succumbing to the temptations of the market and pursuing their desires, a trait exhibited by the figure of Mulian's mother.[37]

VU LAN, VIETNAMESE MOTHER'S DAY

Quán Thế Âm is not the only maternal figure. The universal love represented by the bodhisattva is coupled with the figure of particular love, the mother of Mulian, who stands for the mother-child relationship. In contrast to the miracle tales of Quán Thế Âm, who responds to the cries of all sentient beings, the legend of Mulian highlights people's attachment to their own mothers, inscribing a very different model of liberation. Mulian's mother is a "hungry ghost," accursed by her desires. Ultimately, her liberation comes not through the spiritual powers or meritorious acts of her son but from the collective offerings of the entire sangha, which alone has enough merit to liberate the aggrieved mother from the underworld.

More is at work in Vu Lan than staging the rescue of Mulian's mother. After all, the legend has mingled with the Hungry Ghost Festival since the medieval period.[38] Much as scholars in medieval China argued for adapting Buddhist teachings to their audiences, monks today see festivals such as Vu Lan as "bringing practice into life" (đem đạo vào đời) or widening the audience for Buddhist teachings. In the Gulf South, these teachings involve not just the ritual labor of liberating deceased relatives but also the bridging of distance between the Gulf Coast and the ancestral homeland, Vietnam.

Congregations promote festivals like Vu Lan widely, sometimes at considerable expense. Invitations are printed on cardstock with images of a mother cradling an infant or an elderly woman in the warm embrace of a young girl, underscoring the festival's emphasis as less the liberation of tortured souls than the celebration of a reverant form of filial devotion (*báo hiếu*). Acts of devotion include prayers for the living and the dead. Along with the invitations are forms for prayers of peace for the living (*cầu an*) and remembrance for the deceased (*cầu siêu*) and a return envelope. Lay Buddhists bring the filled-in form and envelope with cash to the service or simply mail them back to the temple. The payments are donations to the monks, who recite the names of those individuals to be prayed for during the ceremony.[39]

During the late summer of 2013, I attended four consecutive Vu Lan ceremonies across the Gulf South, one on each subsequent weekend. Because of their importance in supporting the monastic sangha, these festivals are staggered to ensure that monks can travel from one temple to the next to witness the ceremony, and the celebrations attract sizable crowds. All four ceremonies were held outdoors to accommodate the larger-than-usual gatherings. The formal service included chanting excerpts from the Vu Lan and Filial Piety Sutras and a short dharma talk, in which a guest monk explained the legend and cajoled people into showing respect for their parents. Through the collective act of chanting the sutras, monks and lay Buddhists alike recalled the boundless sacrifices of mothers—the pain of pregnancy, the burden of giving birth, the lack of sleep, the worry over providing food and clothes. Fathers are described in this teaching, too, but Vu Lan holds a special place for the mother, just as the legend itself emphasizes the particular love of the mother-child bond. The sacrifices of the mother were described in surprisingly vivid terms, as the excerpt below shows:

Nhớ nghĩa thân sanh	Remember the one who gave birth
Con đến trưởng thành	After you (the child) have grown up.
Mẹ dày gian khổ	Mother suffered hardships,
Ba năm nhũ bộ	Three years of suckling and spoon-feeding,
Chín tháng cưu mang	Nine months of pregnancy,
Không ngớt lo toan	Endlessly worrying,
Quên ăn bỏ ngủ	Forgetting to eat and sleep,
Ấm no đầy đủ	[So you would be] comfortable and content.[40]

The work of these festivals happened not only during the formal service but alongside and at the edges as well, emphasizing how people fashion themselves as Buddhist not just in the formal service or through the recitations of Buddhist liturgies but also through donating money, dressing in *áo dàis*, and even taking photographs in front of the outdoor statue of Quán Thế Âm.

As the sangha expressed its collective power to release ancestral spirits, the temple members presented their vision of the future. During these festivals (*đại lễ*), the members displayed to the people in attendance the temple's expansion plans, or their "horizon of expectation" that would propel these projects into the future, thus providing a sense of "solidarity, purpose, identity, and futurity."[41] In 2013, the architectural blueprints for the worship hall at Hồng Ân Monastery were available for people to view. In Florida, another monastery presented plans for building huts to accommodate participants on retreats, while in Alabama, a lay member directed people's attention to a poster depicting an ambitious project to install a statue of Quán Thế Âm in the middle of a lake. Visiting monks also recruited participants to fund their projects. At one festival, monks asked attendees to purchase raffle tickets for an upcoming fund-raiser at a banquet hall in a major metropolitan area a six-hour drive away. Such solicitations underscored how temples appealed to their compatriots as potential funders for the expansion of Buddhism itself. Requests for donations were not only cast in the idiom of merit; monks and lay Buddhists also emphasized the role of these temples as guardians of Vietnamese heritage and purveyors of future prosperity. Some monks even sold lottery tickets promising prizes of a bar of gold, a smartphone, or even a new car. In so doing, the sangha—both lay Buddhists and monks—presents itself as having the power not only to save Mulian's mother but also to serve as guardians of ancestral time and fulfill people's aspirations for material blessings.

While the four celebrations of Vu Lan exhibited similarities, it was their differences that exposed the plurality and plasticity of Vietnamese Buddhism along the Gulf Coast. In Mississippi, the lay Buddhists were eager to introduce their temple to other Vietnamese residents in the area. I attended a meeting that took place about a month before the celebration, where members rather than the monk took the lead in organizing the festival, discussing what songs they would perform and what they should wear. On the day of the festival, most of the female members wore *áo dàis*, their outfits signifying their fidelity to remaining Vietnamese. While Buddhist lay robes are uniformly gray and loose fitting and sometimes used communally, *áo dài*s are awash in striking colors and bold patterns and are custom-tailored. The appeal of the *áo dài* exemplifies how Vietnamese in the United States have reconstructed the pageantry of the homeland they lost, now displayed during Vu Lan through celebrating both motherhood and the homeland.[42] But it also underscores how women shoulder the responsibility of representing the nation.

On the day of the festival, a banner welcoming "compatriot Buddhists" was strung across an outdoor tent. Like the *áo dài*, the epithet "compatriot Buddhists" underscores how participants are bound together by a geographically distant homeland and common descent but also by their political subjectivity as Vietnamese Americans, symbolized by the display of three different flags—the five-color flag of Buddhism, the yellow-and-red striped Vietnamese Freedom and Heritage Flag, and the US flag. The phrase "compatriot Buddhists" acknowledges that festivals such as Vu Lan appeal to those people who do not regularly attend services or consider themselves members of that particular temple. But festivals are also an opportunity for members to visit different temples, sometimes accompanying a monk invited to witness the ceremony, and other times with friends as a leisure activity. I quickly realized that I was not the only person who had attended more than one Vu Lan festival that year as I greeted people I knew who had traveled from other temples in neighboring states. That these festivals draw people from other temples is part of the political work of gathering dispersed peoples into a Vietnamese sangha in diaspora.

How can we see fund-raising activities as also part of the ritual labor of liberation? In the Vu Lan Sutra, it is the assembled monks who have the power to liberate Mulian's mother. Buddha counseled Mulian that his mother would only be liberated by offerings made by the sangha, a lesson that can be extended to the collective activities of preparing and purchasing food. At the temple in Mississippi, people quickly filled up the rows of folding chairs set up under a large tent. Alongside the service, lay members sold a steady stream of cups filled to the brim with sweetened porridge (*chè*) and plates of vegetarian spring rolls and fried sesame balls with a sweet mung bean filling (*bánh cam*), as people piled the food in small boxes to take to their cars. Most of these snack items were prepared to go, tightly wrapped in cellophane and sold in plastic cups and disposable containers. The buying and selling hardly paused during the formal ceremony, as monks solemnly led the congregation in chanting the Vu Lan Sutra to the steady beat of the wooden drum. By supporting the temple, people bring home the very material artifacts that create and maintain diasporic identifications—the sweetness of the porridge, the crunchiness of the sesame balls, the spiciness of the peanut dipping sauce. By channeling the merit produced by the sangha back to their own families, they fulfill the "circle of reciprocity" that binds these temples to the larger Vietnamese diaspora.

Such diasporic identifications are not inevitable. In Florida, in a popular tourist area on the Gulf Coast, the draw of Buddhism was much weaker than in Mississippi. The monastery was just as new as the one in Mississippi, but it was affiliated with a wealthier monastery in Northern California. Several weeks before the Vu Lan festival was organized, I attended a regular Sunday service in Florida, where Master Deep Awakening instructed the laity about the celebration's importance in sustaining monastic life. She asked for volunteers to provide food and drink to be sold on behalf of the temple during the festival. The twenty or so attendees hesitatingly raised their hands. One woman offered to bring soft drinks, another suggested paper plates. No one offered to make anything that resembled a traditional Vietnamese dish. The monk did not insist that temple members bring something; she did, though, gently remind those in attendance that Vu Lan was traditionally the time when the laity presented monastics with gifts.

Like the other festivals I attended, the one in Florida was held outdoors. On this occasion, there was no banner welcoming compatriot Buddhists, only a string of Buddhist flags. One woman had driven two hours to set up a small stand to sell sandwiches (*bánh mì*), iced coffee with sweetened condensed milk, potato chips, and candy bars. Only a handful of attendees wore gray robes. People celebrated their lack of discipline with good humor. After a group of girls performed a fan dance as part of the after-lunch cultural program, a man called out plaintively, "Can we go home now?" Later, one of the lay Buddhists who had helped organize the festival loudly teased her friends for refusing to sing onstage, calling them out for being "hung over" from the night before.

Different still was the celebration at a monastery in Alabama, also organized by Master Deep Awakening, but whose participants had been disciplined in practices of mindfulness. No state flags were displayed, no anthems were performed, and no snacks were sold. Several young girls dressed in loose gray robes led the procession from the monastic residence to the worship hall. After the service, the lay Buddhists returned to the main building, where we lined up on the wooden deck. It was hot that August day, and the few children bounced up and down on the soles of their feet but remained silent as they waited for their turn to enter the dining hall. The food, plates of vegetarian sushi and fried noodles, had not been prepared in the kitchen, but was donated by a patron who owned a hibachi restaurant. No one said a word as we filled our trays, maintaining a practice called Noble Silence, and took a chair at the long tables. Only when the senior monk rang a bell did people raise their bowl to their head and chant three times in union "Homage to Shakyamuni Buddha" in a distinctive cadence before they lowered their bowls and ate in silence. After fifteen minutes or so, the senior monk stood up and walked around the tables, greeting people and offering them fruit and steamed dumplings from his plate. Later, he called on lay Buddhists by name to perform songs, not those replete with sentimental romance, but ones that celebrated a mother's love for her children.

Vu Lan is celebrated as well in Vietnam, but its significance is noticeably different than what I observed at these four temples. It is considered a time to reflect on one's ancestors and the teachings of Buddha. People present gifts of fruit, medicine, and other necessary items to monks. They also visit the gravesites of deceased family members. In the United States, the promotion of Vu Lan as a Vietnamese Mother's Day underscores how the Buddhist observance is being negotiated in a new setting, the Gulf Coast. While the teachings still emphasize the role of the sangha in liberating Mulian's mother from the underworld, the festival also presents the temple as a guardian of ancestral time. The meaning of Vu Lan lies not just in the liturgy but also in the invitations and banners welcoming compatriots, the to-go snacks, and even the displays of architectural blueprints for expanding temple complexes. By gathering in sangha not just in the formal ceremony but also along the edges, festivalgoers make Buddhism in the Gulf South, and likely elsewhere in the United States.

What was most striking were the performances of allegiance during the festival. In Louisiana and Mississippi, the congregations opened their ceremonies by displaying the US flag, the Buddhist flag, and the Vietnamese heritage flag and playing the respective anthems, "The Star-Spangled Banner," "Vietnamese Buddhism" (Phật giáo Việt Nam), and the "National Anthem of the Republic of Vietnam" (Quốc ca Việt Nam Cộng Hòa). Women dressed in Vietnamese aó dàis led the procession of monks, embodying the place of heritage in Vietnamese Buddhism. That the emphasis on heritage was strongest in Louisiana and Mississippi is not surprising, given how claims of heritage compensate for the entrenched racial formations that have marginalized Vietnamese residents in the region. In contrast, the symbolic repertoire of the Republic of Vietnam was not visible at the festivals of the monasteries located just outside Mobile, Alabama, and the popular Florida seaside area. The absence of these symbols may signal a stronger monastic role and reveal that both monasteries drew most of their financial support from elsewhere, not from the few lay Buddhists in the vicinity. And perhaps for this reason, the crowds were noticeably smaller as well.

Despite these differences, all the Vu Lan festivals I attended were conducted almost entirely in Vietnamese, even in Florida, where of the nearly fifty or so attendees, one-third were not Vietnamese. Even then, the nearly hour-long service included just a brief five-minute explanation in English about the legend of Mulian. These differences return us to the question raised by the contradictions concerning the mother figure. Does Vu Lan promote a vision of particular love that orients practitioners to their own family and homeland, or does Vu Lan offer a lesson in the boundless universal love expressed by the figure of Quan Âm?

RED ROSE AND PARTICULAR LOVE

The principal symbol of Vu Lan, both in Vietnam and along the US Gulf Coast, is the red rose. At the end of the formal ceremony, the senior monk blesses a basket of roses. Lay Buddhists then distribute a rose to each person. A red rose signifies that one's mother is still living, while a white rose symbolizes that one's mother is deceased. Sons and daughters, moved by a sense of filial piety, attend the Vu Lan ceremony, where their relationship to their mother is made public, and they then return home, having been reminded of their obligation to their mother, a "three-step circuit that moves from the private to the public and then back to the private again."[43] Yet the rose as a symbol exposes the conflicting views over how the mother figure is represented—as particular love, in which the parent-child bond is bounded and exclusionary, or as universal love, unbounded and expansive.

The legend of Mulian is centuries old, but the custom of distributing roses is decidedly modern. The Venerable Thích Nhất Hạnh introduced the tradition in his 1962 essay "A Rose for Your Pocket," in which he lauds a custom in Japan that symbolizes the mother-child relationship. He describes meeting Thích Thiên-Ân in front of a bookstore in Tokyo, where they were greeted by two young Japanese students. The students discreetly asked if Thích Nhất Hạnh's mother were still alive, before pinning a white carnation to his robes. After learning what the white signified, he reflected on his overwhelming grief at her death:

> The day my mother died, I made this entry in my journal: "The greatest misfortune of my life had come!" Even an old person doesn't feel ready when he loses his mother. He too has the impression that he is not yet ripe, that he is suddenly alone. He feels as abandoned and unhappy as a young orphan.[44]

In the essay, he proposed that people in Vietnam adopt the Japanese custom so they would be reminded to show appreciation for their mothers: "Only when she is no longer there do we realize that we have never been conscious of having a mother." Thích Nhất Hạnh's memory of his mother leads him to think of Vietnam: "Each night I pray for my mother, but it is no longer possible for me to savor the excellent *ba huang* banana, the best-quality *nep mot* sweet rice, and the delicious *mia lau* sugar cane."[45]

Thích Nhất Hạnh's essay inspired composer Phạm Thế Mỹ to write the song "A Rose for Your Pocket" (Bông hồng cài áo), which opens, "A red rose for you, sister / A red rose for you, brother / And a red rose for all those / whose mothers are still with us," and closes, "A red rose has been placed on your lapel / Please be happy."[46] During Vu Lan, the song is performed or broadcast over the audio system as women and girls distribute the roses, almost always artificial, with a label and a small adhesive backing or safety pin. Holding baskets filled with flowers, they wind their way through the rows of people seated on cushions, bending down to each person to ask in a whisper, "Is your mother still alive?" People take a white or red flower and then drop a dollar or two into the basket, underscoring the reciprocity of support that marks the relationship between parent and child, the monastic sangha and the laity, and the diaspora and the homeland.

Some temples elaborate on the distinction between those people whose mothers are still living and those whose mothers are not. At Hồng Ân Monastery, the head monk stood up and asked people to acknowledge their mothers or grandmothers in attendance by offering them a bouquet, sold as part of the temple's fund-raising activities. After each presentation of a bouquet, the audience applauded with appreciation. The resident monk then announced that the bouquets were not to sadden those people whose mothers had passed away, and so the temple would recognize them with a small gift. This time the women passed around blue-and-white checkered gift bags from a bath and beauty store to each person who was wearing a white rose. As they opened the bags, the women sitting around me cried out in delight at the bottle of scented body lotion they received. The roses and scented lotion are "divine gifts," or *lộc* in Vietnamese. But *lộc*, the material blessing, is not merit (*phước*), that basis of the spiritual economy linking monks and lay Buddhists. As the gifts were distributed, a senior monk from Dallas, Texas, reminded the audience that the custom of wearing a rose was not an ancient tradition but one introduced by Thích Nhất Hạnh after a visit to Japan. He turned the rose into an object of contemplation. "Don't think," he counseled, "that because you wear a red rose, it means you are happy because you still have a mother, or because you have a white rose that it means you are suffering because your mother has died." He then turned to the meaning of filial piety, or *hiếu*. "The lessons are quite clear," he expounded. "You have two Buddhas in your house—your mother is Buddha, your father is Buddha [*mẹ là Phật, cha là Phật*]," reminding those in attendance of how the parents were models of Buddhahood and should not be understood in terms of attachment, loss, and suffering. As he spoke, the audience engaged in low-level conversations, alternating their attention between the stage, where the senior monk stood, and their companions nearby.

For other monks, the red rose is problematic because it invokes the particular love that defines the mother-child bond, rather than the universal love cultivated within Mahayana Buddhism. At the monastery in Florida, only red roses were distributed. During the ceremony, a monk from Georgia stood up to give a short dharma talk by way of a parable. He recounted how a man in his forties met a young girl selling flowers by the roadside so she could earn enough money to visit her mother's gravesite. Upon seeing the girl's devotion to her mother, the man felt ashamed that he had intended only to send his mother a small present through the mail, and he vowed to visit his mother in person to tell her how much he loved her. He drove all night and all day to visit his mother to wish her well. The moral of the story, the monk explained, was that we should not ignore our mother while she is alive, a lesson imparted as well in Thích Nhất Hạnh's "A Rose for Your Pocket." The monk then described the custom of wearing a red rose to signify that one's mother was still living or a white rose to show that one's mother had passed away. When he glanced over at the basket of artificial roses sitting on the stage to be blessed and distributed, he stopped in midsentence. The basket contained nothing but red roses. The monk then corrected himself: "Dear guests, please remember the most important thing is to show respect and love for your parents by coming to the temple, keeping a vegetarian diet, studying meditation, not acting mean or stingy, and behaving well toward all people—that is what we call 'filial piety.'" The senior monk took the microphone to explain why at this particular monastery only red roses were distributed. "We are all mothers and fathers, and we are all children," he intoned, counseling the audience on the virtue of interdependence promoted by Buddhism that worked against the particular love expressed by the parent-child relationship and shown in whether one wore a white or a red rose. He explained that Buddhist ethics (*giáo lý*) taught that our parents in this lifetime might have been our children in previous lifetimes and that any-one around us might have been our parents in previous lifetimes, thus turning the particular parent-child relationship into a universal model encompassing all sentient beings.

Later that afternoon, after we had put away equipment and the remain-ing food, Master Deep Awakening mused, "Why should we make people sad by reminding them that their mothers passed away?" She then asked, "What about those people who feel closer to their fathers than to their mothers?" Implicit in her question was a critique of how the emphasis on maternal imagery may be inadequate to represent the variations in parent-child rela-tionships. Pointing to my own two children, she noted that they had physi-cal traits of both parents. "Even when you pass away," she reasoned, "we could say that your presence continues through the genetic makeup of your children." While her comments were intended to explain why she distrib-uted only red roses, her explanation pointed to a more significant problem at the heart of Buddhism—how our attachments lead to suffering.

Vu Lan as a Buddhist festival conveys contradictory messages. The occasion once inserted the monastic sangha into popular religious prac-tices and amplified popular representations of women as ritually impure but also deserving of gratitude through their gift of life. While the legend is part of a broad category of Chinese Buddhism, its meanings are plural, including the emphasis on distributing roses that come from a celebration of motherhood, the roots of which lie in modern nationalism. We have seen how the festival provides Buddhist temples on the Gulf Coast with an occa-sion to raise funds as they project their institutions as guardians of ances-tral time and toward the future through the presentation of architectural blueprints and expansion plans. Vu Lan effectively repackages filial piety as a celebration of both motherhood and homeland while simultaneously pro-moting the monastic sangha. Through this festival, we can see how Bud-dhist temples mediate people's long-distance separation from family members and especially their mothers, the traumatic crossings of the

Pacific, and their efforts to inhabit new landscapes by creating new forms of dwelling, a Pure Land in the making.

• • •

Promoting Vu Lan as a Vietnamese Mother's Day domesticates its meaning in terms familiar to its local context. This process, like the legend of Mulian, reflects the ongoing accommodation of Buddhism to new settings and societies. In medieval China, Buddhist scholars inserted the monastic sangha within the intimate sphere of family relations by ensuring their benefactors would fulfill their filial obligations toward their mothers. Along the US Gulf Coast, Buddhist monks present themselves as guardians of ancestral time by chanting prayers for deceased relatives while their twenty-first-century benefactors enjoy specialty vegetarian food and cultural performances and even wear the *áo dài* as a symbol of the nation.

Yet it is on the margins of the formal service that we see the plural negotiations underway. In some temples, performances of filial piety involve displays of the Vietnamese Freedom and Heritage Flag and processions of women and children dressed in *áo dài*s. Monks bless both red and white roses as people reflect on and remember their mothers. In other temples, the white rose disappears, and everyone receives a red one. At some festivals, the communal lunch is boisterous, and at others, people eat in silence. Despite variations in their performance, monks encourage reflection on the role of universal love—"We are all mothers, we are all fathers." Even at the festivals in Alabama and Florida, it is the sangha—monks, lay Buddhists, and compatriots—that transforms Buddhism, if only momentarily, into a moral community that honors ancestral time.[47]

Buddhist temples are fixtures in the infrastructure of remembrance. People entrust photographs of their loved ones to Buddhists monks, who perform a labor of care by lighting incense, summoning spirits for liberation, and converting material donations into otherworldly merit. The audience is a distinctly Vietnamese public, in which the cultural referents invoke transnational practices such as passing out roses by way of remembering one's mother. And these symbols include prominent markers of the Vietnamese diaspora such as the heritage flag and the anthem of the Republic of Vietnam. Various forms of identification—displays of the flag, the consumption of food and song, and the role of dress, whether in the *áo dài* or *áo tràng*—show Vu Lan both in its theological guise and as a distinctly Vietnamese version of the Buddhist observance Ullambana. As the senior monk intoned to the lay Buddhists in attendance, the moral lessons drawn from Vu Lan are clear: individual acts of piety and devotion are not enough; instead, it is through the collective ethics of care that the moral community, or sangha, memorializes ancestral time.

Still, while Vu Lan celebrates filial piety, its moral lessons are not easily transmitted to younger Vietnamese, whose subjective identifications with the homeland and ancestors are not the same as their parents'. Filial piety, as some Vietnamese American scholars have argued, is a disciplinary mandate that entrenches generational privilege at the expense of the vulnerability of youth.[48] During the Vu Lan celebrations I attended, children were few and far between, showcased in the procession that led from the monastic residence to the temple hall and in the cultural performances that followed the ceremony. Most children who attended sought other forms of refuge in smartphones, jumping castles, the air-conditioned monastic residence, and the companionship of other children (figure 4.2).

Let us return to Quán Thế Âm, whose image is installed both inside the worship hall on the right-hand side of Amitābha Buddha and outside on

4.2   Two children seek refuge in the worship hall, not to pray but to check their phones. Photo by the author.

the temple grounds, where her gaze is directed toward the street. The bodhisattva dissolves rather than consolidates territorial identities, manifested in her powers to rescue refugees on their perilous journeys. She is oriented not to the ancestors but to the world of the living, ready to respond to their suffering. Quán Thế Âm hears the cries of all living beings, and her powers are particularly resonant with many Vietnamese in the United States, as her powers come from the margins of structures—patrilineal kinship relations, the territorial state, and legal citizenship. Quán Thế Âm opens up a politics of recognition that is bound neither by the family nor by the nation, making her an especially important figure for liberating the souls of those people who died in war or were lost at sea.

CHAPTER FIVE

Preparing to Die Well

IN Vietnam, America is colloquially referred to as "the other side." During the American War, revolutionaries called themselves "our side" (*bên ta*) and US and South Vietnamese military forces the other side (*bên kia*), a language that drew its force from the Cold War, a protracted global struggle premised on an opposition between capitalism and communism.[1] In everyday conversations, people still refer to life in America (or Vietnam when in America) as "over there," highlighting the historical divide that engendered the diaspora.[2] Vietnamese in the United States try to overcome the lingering divide with gifts of money or remittances and trips to the homeland. For people who never left Vietnam, these gifts and visitors appear to reinforce America "not merely [as] a geographic and cultural outside, but [as] potentially divine: the vicissitudes of fate that allowed some to leave, some to return, and others to perish remain enigmatic."[3] While transpacific crossings now form a tighter and denser network connecting the US Gulf South and Vietnam, the success of those crossings is still never assured.[4]

After a formal service in New Orleans, the resident monk introduced two monks who had just arrived from Vietnam. The first monk received a visa to travel to the United States on his first try, but the second was interviewed four times at the US Consulate in Ho Chi Minh City before he was granted a visa. The thirty or so people gathered in the worship hall laughed, all too familiar with the capriciousness of who received a visa and who did not. With this opening gesture, the resident monk acknowledged what everyone knew to be true—the distance separating Vietnam and the United States was so vast and the journey so uncertain that even a monk could not be assured of a successful crossing.

Death marks a crossing of a different sort, the passage from this world into another world (*thế giới bên kia*) that lies beyond human comprehension. The Pure Land, as we have seen, is not a unified realm, but a prism reflecting the multiple perspectives of practitioners. For some, it is a celestial realm overseen by Amitābha Buddha, and they express their intention to be reborn in the Pure Land through embodied practices of chanting sutras, reciting the names of buddhas and bodhisattvas, and serving the sangha. For others, these practices purify their mind through concentration. Still others focus on attaining the Pure Land in the here and now. The Pure Land thus provides a rich terrain for Buddhist commentary on not just what it means to live well but also how to die well.

During the service, the visiting monk who received a visa after several attempts sat down to deliver a dharma talk. He opened with a simple question: "Dear fellow Buddhists, we live to do what?" A few people laughed. A woman in the front offered, "Repay our karmic debt" (Để trả nghiệp). Another woman replied, "We live to prepare to die" (Sống để chuẩn bi chết). He nodded approvingly. He then asked if anyone in attendance had ever seen a ghost, using the term *con mã*, a wilder version of "hungry ghosts" (*cô hồn*). The audience laughed hesitatingly. One man slowly raised his hand. The monk asked mischievously, "What color was the ghost?" and then leaned forward to ask, "And were you scared?" He then recounted several miracle tales in which monks quelled those ghosts. In one case, a dead soldier led a monk to the spot where he had died, so the monk could carry out rites to liberate the soldier's soul. In another tale, a monk etched lines from a sutra on small pebbles and then placed them around the monastery to ward off wrathful ghosts. The audience laughed as the monk recounted these ghost stories using menacing facial expressions. He did not mock the idea of ghosts, but neither did he exhibit dread. These stories served a purpose—to remind practitioners that they prepared for death through their actions in this lifetime.

In Buddhism, karmic foundations are built on ethical conduct, not external factors. In Vietnamese, these foundations of thought, speech, and action are known as "three karmic types" (*ba nghiệp*), which shape one's present circumstances, future actions, and the conditions for rebirth. The monk stressed how karma was a form of debt accumulated not only by an individual but also by the family (*gia nghiệp*), and not just in this lifetime (*kiếp*) but over several lifetimes, a form of conditioning that is both collective and transcendent. Just as the monk teased the congregation with his imitations of ghosts, he also acted out a caricature of devout lay Buddhists, loudly chanting "Homage to Amitābha Buddha" while pretending to pound on a wooden drum, as if the sound of the chanting and rhythmic beat alone would catapult him to the Pure Land. The audience laughed, familiar as well with such figures. He then reminded his audience that the strength of praying lies not in the volume but in the intent of their collective action. During the week, only a handful of lay Buddhists gathered to chant sutras to ensure their relatives would be reborn in the Pure Land. But their prayers, he counseled, would be more efficacious if they did so as a form of repentance (sám hối). By repenting, he did not mean the Catholic dispensation of guilt through the act of confessing to a priest.[5] Rather, by becoming mindful of their habits of thought, speech, and action, people could liberate themselves and, through such mindfulness, prepare themselves to die well. We should pray, he advised, not just for the safe crossing of the spirits of deceased family members but to become mindful of our own conditioning. Rituals for the dead, in other words, were lessons for the living.

TRANSGENERATIONAL OBLIGATIONS

The monk's model of karmic conditioning is a theory of the subject, one that is collective and intergenerational. It challenges the prevailing models of subjectivity in secular, liberal societies that emphasize the sovereignty of the individual, free from external constraints. In liberalism, the individual is conceptualized as ontologically prior to social groups and relations—the family, nation, and community. By way of accommodating beliefs understood to reside within the interior subject, liberal societies acknowledge religious pluralism and multiculturalism arise. Yet such recognition is "cunning," insofar as differences are acknowledged so long as they adhere to sociological categories such as culture, ethnicity, and religion.[6] What if we were to admit another possibility—that these differences are grounded instead in a different ethics around living and dying?[7]

Liberal societies have banished ghosts, relegating those beliefs to the primitive, cultural difference, or even trauma. These explanations foreclose the possibility in how ghosts upset dominant conceptions of subjectivity in societies like the United States.[8] They also marshal ritual action—prayers, offerings, and even elaborately staged ceremonies—as evidence for how the accrual of culture or heritage has contaminated Buddhism, thereby preserving an authoritative model that privileges the modern, liberal subject.[9] What if we instead framed these rituals as exemplifying an alternative ethics, one in which ghosts were no longer banished? What if practices addressing the spirit world were instead permitted to expose the limitations of the prevailing, and often unquestioned, tenets of liberal social theory?

Buddhist cosmologies posit not one world but three—the world of desire and suffering, the world of form, and the world of formlessness. Ghosts are formless, inhabiting the third world and standing in for the vast stores of consciousness accumulated over lifetimes. They signal disturbed elements of the past that cannot be seen, felt, or perceived but nevertheless condition how we act, speak, and think. When people address these spirits, they engage in collective action to repair fragments of the unspoken past—the legacies of US militarism, the journey of refugees, or even more distant events such as settler colonialism and contemporary conditions of state neglect and marginalization. Through these rituals, practitioners also cultivate an ethics of hospitality toward strangers and the displaced, thereby claiming their right to belong in particular places, as with the land blessing ceremony. While such rituals are overlooked in mainstream media and even academic scholarship, they tie together spiritual practices and political circumstances: How does one dwell in a new land? How should one acknowledge others? How does one address violence otherwise silenced in broader national culture?

Preoccupations with ghosts are not peculiar to Vietnamese religious practices. Nineteenth-century anthropologist Edward Burnett Tylor linked the soul to all forms of life through the Latin *anima*, for "breath." Souls that failed to complete their journey to a post-mortem existence were doomed to a liminal existence, no longer inhabiting the world of the living but not yet released to another world, lingering around the vicinity of the body's death, still attached to their material form. Such a slippage between the material body and its animating force produced ghosts. Tylor interpreted observed differences in funerary and mortuary rituals along a continuum of social evolution such that people would progress from a "primitive" stage marked by belief in ghosts and other spirits to a "civilized" or modern stage defined by the principles of science. As if not sure of his own model, Tylor admitted that the technical language of science itself banished souls and ghosts from the social landscape, where they remained preserved in the language of poets.[10]

The evolutionary models of the nineteenth century have since been dismantled, but two dominant frames explaining why people summon spirits still prevail. On the one hand, hauntings are said to evoke experiences otherwise excluded from public representations of history.[11] On the other hand, hauntings are attributed to ontological entities who can act upon the world.[12] This latter frame is evident in a model that distinguishes good deaths from bad deaths throughout Southeast Asia. The model of a good death is envisioned when an individual has fulfilled his or her obligations in this lifetime—a person at the end of life, who slips away peacefully at home, surrounded by children and grandchildren. In such cases, both the dying and their relatives have prepared for death, and so when the dying depart, it is without regrets or attachments. In contrast, the image of a bad death befalls someone who dies too young, unexpectedly, or even violently. The death is said to be bad not just because of its circumstances but also because the soul of the deceased, not having prepared to die, remains attached to its material body. These souls, having been neither ritually transformed into ancestors nor released to future rebirth, haunt the vicinity as ghosts.

The postwar landscape in Vietnam is especially haunted. Anthropologist Heonik Kwon, drawing on the slippage between ghosts as figures of history and ghosts as ontological actors, shows how villagers reckoned with "pressing moral and political issues in contemporary life" through rituals that address ghosts.[13] The Vietnamese state honors war heroes, or martyrs who sacrificed their lives for the fatherland. Not all the dead are recognized by state-sanctioned forms of commemoration. These ghostly figures— South Vietnamese soldiers, massacred villagers, and even civilians caught in the cross fire of war—are not represented by the official history of the Vietnamese state.[14] Villagers in central Vietnam who perform rituals acknowledge the grievances of these ghosts and therefore resolve an ethical dilemma in collective memory by attending to the deaths of those spirits who were otherwise forgotten.

Kwon's analysis is based on the structures of intergenerational belonging, namely, ceremonies performed for those deceased family members ritually transformed into ancestors "benevolently disposed" toward their living descendants. By making offerings and endeavoring not to offend their ancestors with moral transgressions, the living reinforce the values of intergenerational continuity and virtues such as filial piety. Such rituals, however, produce exclusions: ghosts are external to the structural relations of ancestor worship, what cannot be represented through ancestral rites but must still be acknowledged. Kwon spatializes the difference between ghosts and ancestors in the opposition of the house and the street: villagers first face the ancestral altar to acknowledge genealogical continuity, and they then turn to face outside shrines to recognize a solidarity based not on particular ties of genealogical continuity or nationhood but on place, through performing "act[s] of hospitality to the unknown and unrelated."[15] Will then these ghosts of war disappear over time? Some scholars suggest the grievance of these ghosts may eventually fade along with the stories of elders, but not all ghosts and spirits are so easily appeased.[16]

In Vietnam's largest cities, hungry ghosts remain external to ongoing cycles of obligation and reciprocity, standing in for desire and identified with money. People call upon the wildness of these spirits to bring both customers and profits. Ghosts even appear in the guise of living people, or *cô hồn sống*—idle teenagers in the urban streets of southern Vietnam who snatch people's handbags or socialist cadres who deploy their official status to harass market traders.[17] People carry out ceremonies to solicit the power associated with these ghosts, not simply to mollify them but also to draw on their wildness associated with profit and gain.

Along the Gulf Coast, sanghas also summon these ghosts for their power to attract donors. Congregations like the one at Hồng Ân Monastery carry out the ritual, as these unseen spirits are said to lead strangers to the temple to make unexpected donations. The donor is not a ghost, but through a hunch, a chance meeting, or a premonition, the donor is led to the temple. People also ask monks to bless their businesses, homes, and even new cars. One afternoon as I sat with several retreatants on the patio of a temple, two women drove up in a new Toyota SUV and asked the senior monk if he would bless the car. As he approached it, he exclaimed for all to hear, "So beautiful, so beautiful," and the two women then opened the doors of the car, including the rear hatch. He moved his hand as if shooing away those spirits that might otherwise jump into the car. "It's so the family will do well in business," one woman sitting next to me whispered, amused by the scene. Ghosts represent alienating and alienated forms of value, feared but desired, excluded yet acknowledged on the grounds of Buddhist temples.

While the distance between villages in central Vietnam and Buddhist temples along the US Gulf Coast is vast, preoccupations with ghosts point toward a common resolution for reckoning with the unsettling and unsettled aftermath of war. In Buddhist temples, lay leaders open ceremonies by asking for a moment of silence for those people who died for freedom, now lost in the streams of history. These moments of silence are also observed in churches and at community-wide events. In these ceremonies, however, monks also pray for the spirits of these dead to be "released," not as liberal but as liberated subjects, so they may be reborn in the Pure Land.

SPATIAL OPPOSITIONS

Buddhist temples acknowledge ghosts and ancestors in different locations, spatializing the relationship of the dead to the Pure Land. In the enclosed space of the worship hall, photographs of deceased family members are displayed on a memorial board (*khung thờ hương linh*), thereby singular-izing the identity of ancestral spirits by their image. These spirits are also acknowledged in a ritual (*lễ cầu siêu*) in which the monk incorporates the identity of the deceased into the service by reciting their dharma name and their year of birth and death, thus locating these individuals in his-torical time.[18] Attendees who request these prayers stand or kneel, bowing three times when they hear the name of their family member. The proxim-ity of the photographs to the main worship hall ensures these ancestral spirits partake of the merit produced by the sangha, ritual work that sanc-tifies the worship hall as the Pure Land, both through displaying photos of the deceased and by transmitting merit for their liberation.[19] This point was made by a Buddhist monk in a case heard by the California Supreme Court, in which he argued that services could not be held at another loca-tion, for doing so would require removing the photographs of deceased family members, tantamount to moving a grave.[20] The sangha cares for these spirits in a practical way as well. In the kitchen, monks and lay Bud-dhists set aside dishes for these spirits. Small dishes wrapped in cello-phane are placed on a table in front of the memorial tablet, demonstrating how these spirits partake in not just the merit produced by the sangha but the conviviality as well.

Maintaining an altar is a practice that encompasses, even transcends, religious differences. Many Vietnamese in the United States maintain an altar at home where they display photographs of deceased family members. These altars are colloquially referred to as "grandparent altars" (*bàn thờ ông bà*) rather than ancestral altars (*bàn thờ gia tiên*), emphasizing how these spirits are beloved family members.[21] While these altars appear to index a coherent and unified set of practices, in fact people ascribe different mean-ings within religious orientations. Vietnamese Catholics, for example, maintain home altars but do not engage in practices around making and transferring merit. Buddhists, in contrast, regard the absence of memorial boards in churches as a "refusal to acknowledge the Vietnamese ancestral identity."[22]

Even for Buddhists, the placement of ancestral altars becomes a source of disagreement and contention. For some practitioners, the worship hall is a manifestation of the Pure Land, where a statue of Amitābha Buddha is installed, the dharma is disseminated, and the sangha generates merit, so the ancestral spirit altar should be adjacent to, or even within, the hall. However, not all worship halls can easily incorporate this display. In one monastery housed in a three-bedroom ranch-style home, the worship hall itself was just wide enough for four seat cushions in each of the six rows.

The memorial tablet was located in the entryway, reflecting the architectural constraints of a house converted into a Buddhist temple. A lay Buddhist who had entrusted the image of her mother expressed her disappointment in the location of the altar. Moreover, she disapproved of the monk's focus on improving the temple's landscaping before renovating the worship hall so that the memorial board could be moved from the entryway, a public area where people gathered to chat. The monk, in contrast, saw the temple complex as a sanctuary where people escaped from the stress of everyday life. Because many people visited the grounds before they entered the worship hall, the sangha's efforts to improve the landscape was a form of dharma work that would guide people to experience the Pure Land in the present moment.

It is not just the care for ancestral spirits that sacralizes these spaces but the care extended to ghosts as well. During a retreat at a Buddhist monastery in Alabama, a man in his sixties, a devout Catholic, spoke about his restless sleep the night before. He had envisioned people walking across the grounds of the monastery and pausing directly in front of him. Their dress, he said, was from a previous epoch. He did not describe the grounds as haunted. Rather, the appearance of these spirits was evidence of how the sangha had sacralized the grounds of the temple, summoning these spirits so they could be released. In so doing, Buddhist sanghas constitute themselves as caretakers, not just of ancestral spirits but also of ghosts.

It is the bodhisattva Quán Thế Âm, not Amitābha Buddha, who oversees the world outside the worship hall. Her gaze is directed not toward a transcendental horizon of human existence but to the world of the living, reminding both monks and lay Buddhists of the importance of cultivating compassion toward their own family and strangers as well. Through these outdoor rituals to summon ghosts, Buddhist practitioners acknowledge the inclusive ties of residence by recognizing the moral right of these unseen beings to be in the vicinity, an act of both hospitality and compassion.[23]

THE ETHICS OF HOSPITALITY

Every afternoon, Sister Deep Justice prepared a simple offering of rice porridge, salt, and water. She opened a toolshed on the grounds in which was housed an image of Hộ Pháp, "Protector of the Dharma," a wrathful, even frightening, figure.[24] There she laid out the offerings and recited a mantra so the water might multiply and quench the thirst of the hungry spirits. The ritual was brief, only five or so minutes. By carrying out this simple ceremony, day in and day out, she recognized the presence of unseen beings on the grounds of the monastery and how the temple required protection from them as well. Nameless and restless, these ghosts serve an ambiguous role. They manifest themselves in nonhuman forms as well—wasps that build nests in the rafters over an outdoor dining room or a branch that collapses on a ladder at the very moment a tree is being trimmed. This simple ceremony stood in sharp contrast to a more elaborate ritual. Once a month, a feast was prepared that required the efforts of the monastic sangha and faraway lay practitioners, who donated money to finance the ritual. Unlike a small toolshed, the altar for this ritual was temporary and overseen by Quán Thế Âm.

On a late Saturday afternoon at the monastery in Florida, after people had dispersed from a retreat, I stayed behind to attend the ceremony. We first set up two folding tables and then on one placed an incense holder, a set of small musical instruments, and a portable statue of Quán Thế Âm, to create a makeshift altar. The handful of people in attendance brought out a steady stream of dishes from the kitchen—a large platter with a heaping pile of salt on one side and uncooked rice on the other, topped with a handful of pennies; a bowl of just-microwaved popcorn; bowls of milky coffee and small plates of sticky rice; a platter of boiled corn and sweet potatoes; piles of mangoes; tapioca dumplings wrapped in banana leaves; small servings of stir-fried greens with garlic; bowls of thick vegetable broth; and small servings of porridge made from mung beans (chè) and rice. The last items placed on the makeshift altar were a bowl filled with snack-size bags of tortilla chips and cheese puffs, a bag of cellophane-wrapped candy, and a package of store-bought chocolate-chip cookies (figure 5.1). The packaged treats beloved by children and the rustic fare associated with the Vietnamese countryside were not intended for us, at least not at first, but were for the hungry ghosts.

Buddhas and bodhisattvas are seen as exemplars of compassion, but other spirits are quickly dissatisfied.[25] Hungry ghosts are temperamental, which may explain why none of the four female monks appeared satisfied with the altar's arrangement that day. Sister Deep Justice, an older woman in her late sixties, grumbled that the vase of flowers should have been in the center, rather than a corner, of the table. "Why don't those who came after ask those who came first," she said, more to herself than to me, although I knew she was referring to Sister Deep Recitation, a novice who was decades younger. As she surveyed the arrangement, she noticed the lack of symmetry. "If one bowl of chè is on the edge of the table, then the other one should be too," she muttered and then shrugged, as if she remembered the presentation should not matter, at least not for ghosts. I quickly moved the plates

5.1

Preparations for feeding the hungry ghosts. The altar for the ceremony shows tables full of dishes. On the left is a plate of uncooked rice and salt with coins sprinkled on top. Photo by the author.

around, but the sheer number of dishes made it difficult to arrange them in a balanced presentation. As I was doing so, Sister Deep Blossom walked by and picked up one of the pieces of candy. "What is it?" she asked with surprise. "Oh, just wrapped candy, but not the kind I bought." Their concerns made visible the different forms of care. People also often arrange the altar in the main worship hall, with flowers, a statue of a young Buddha on Vesak, and even platters of fresh fruit. But the ceremonies for hungry ghosts indexed a different ethics of care—people draw the ghosts near to hear the teachings, but they do not liberate them.

Little fanfare marked the ceremony. The senior monk sat down in a folding chair in front of the altar and started ringing a bell with no discernible rhythm or beat, at least not to me, as other monks took their places at the table. Master Deep Awakening lit several sticks of incense and passed one to each lay Buddhist, including the three children in attendance, drawing ghosts near with the scent of incense, the sound of bells and chimes, and the aroma of fresh popcorn and ripened fruit. Their voices accelerated to a buzz of syllables as they punctuated their chants with chimes and gongs. Fifteen or so minutes into the ceremony, the senior monk ran his fingers through the uncooked rice, salt, and coins, mixing them by drawing a mudra, or ritual gesture, with his index finger. One of the lay Buddhists waved to the three children to follow her. She showed them how to take a fistful of the salt, pennies, rice, and popcorn and scatter it across the grounds of the monastery, as if feeding chickens.

When the chanting ended, and the incense had burned down, one of the monks looked indulgently at the three children and invited them to eat whatever they wanted. Children stand in for hungry ghosts, their eyes glued on the candy and chips, but their ears open to the chanting and the sound of bells and chimes intended to awaken their Buddha-nature. As the children ripped open the packaged cookies, their father urged them to eat "real food." I had often wondered why treats are dispensed so freely to children at these Buddhist sites, and I found my answer in these ritual offerings staged once a month to summon hungry ghosts. The lay Buddhists and monks then pulled up chairs to eat dinner, first offered to ghosts and now enjoyed by the sangha.

Ghosts that emerge with such vengeance on the postwar landscape of Vietnam are more challenging to discern along the US Gulf Coast because they have retreated from public life. The offerings that invoke their presence are made not in the streets but on the grounds of the temples. Seen in a different light, it is US liberalism that banishes these ghosts, as Vietnamese Americans must reckon with an unsettled past not fully incorporated into national culture, caught in between the unfinished history of the Republic of Vietnam and the relentless demands of cultural assimilation and economic integration.[26] The ritual of feeding hungry ghosts is likewise caught between two different kinds of hauntings, primary and secondary.[27] In primary hauntings, ghosts possess an ontological status, which is said to disrupt genealogical continuity, whereas secondary hauntings constitute a methodological approach, in which scholars search for cultural traces of traumatic experiences in disparate places—biographies maintained in digital archives, Vietnamese place-names in Little Saigons, and even statues banished to private property as unsanctioned for public display—to represent traces of social life that are otherwise in the shadows or silenced.[28] Yet the opposition between primary and secondary hauntings relies on a "sequential construction of experiencing and telling," which cannot account for ritual activities such as the ceremony of feeding hungry ghosts.[29] The ritual works at two levels—first, by invoking the presence of the ghosts through the lavish offerings and, second, by instructing participants to offer hospitality to strangers. Moreover, this form of ritual resolution is productive, as through these acts of radical hospitality Buddhists transform themselves into hosts. They acknowledge the right of these ghosts to exist and, by doing so, invert their status from refugees, migrants, and foreigners into hosts, staking their right to belong.[30]

The daily and monthly rituals of feeding hungry spirits are neighborly gestures, but their only traces are in scattered coins and grains of rice. While these rituals occur with regularity at Buddhist temples, sanghas, on occasion, sponsor even more elaborate ceremonies, with the intention not just to offer hospitality but to liberate these spirits. If primary hauntings like those of hungry ghosts are said to seek reparations for ritual failures or resolve the historical accidents that prevent them from peaceful afterlife, reparations for secondary hauntings are broader in scope and scale, often mobilizing a moral community to address past injustices, such as the enslavement of Africans or the sexual labor of Korean comfort women during World War II. What unifies these reparations is "serious and sympathetic awareness of the social lives of ghosts, of whatever sort, with a strategic use of their power to compel mourning, humility, and compassion among the living."[31] On occasion, a sangha sponsors a more elaborate rite that aims to liberate these aggrieved souls (giải oan) and bring peace to the survivors. These ceremonies seek to generate compassion and peace in the world by liberating the spirits of those who died from the violence of war, the neglect of the state, and even settler colonialism.

LIBERATING AGGRIEVED SOULS

In 2006, I witnessed a ceremony that sought to liberate the souls of those people who died during Hurricane Katrina. The hurricane's tremendous storm surge and the massive failure of the levee system in New Orleans killed more than eighteen hundred people in Louisiana and Mississippi and left hundreds of thousands more displaced from their homes. I arrived to carry out a project on new populations for Louisiana Folklife, a program under the Division of Culture, Recreation, and Tourism. What I found was a ceremony involving more than twenty monks, solemnly walking around the outdoor pavilion of the complex. The few lay Buddhists who stood outside the circle appeared mildly interested in what was happening. A woman explained to me that the monks came from Georgia and Texas to perform the ceremony, to address a central concern to everyone in the region, whether Buddhist or Catholic, Vietnamese or not—how to recover from the devastation and loss of life wrought by the storm.

The ceremony I observed at the Buddhist temple in New Orleans in 2006 was not the only ritual response to the social injustices exposed by Hurricane Katrina. Other groups, including Women of the Storm, presented a carnivalesque jazz funeral to reject the national media claims about the "death of New Orleans."[32] Participants used umbrellas, a symbol of the transitional moment during jazz funeral processions when brass bands burst into celebratory song. Followers fall in behind the "first line," or the brass band and the social club that sponsored the procession. These followers or "second lines" are associated with the city's working-class Black communities, thus the use of the umbrella ignited debates over who could speak for displaced residents.[33] Other groups such as the Congo Square Preservation Society gathered on Sundays for drumming to connect ancestral memories to the very ground where men, women, and children were auctioned as slaves, recognizing how the political violence of the past still shaped the present in the Gulf South. In contrast, the Buddhist ceremony of liberating souls is not about honoring ancestors, nor is it about national heritage; it is far broader in scope—a ceremony that redresses injustices in order to bring stability and peace to the region.

Despite its relevance to people living in the Gulf South, the ceremony in 2006, like the Hùng Kings' Death Anniversary, garnered no interest from the local press.[34] The lack of interest among other residents in the city was not because of the absence of memorials to those people who had died during the storm. In New Orleans, six small mausoleums hold the remains of the dead who were unclaimed or unidentified after the waters receded in 2005. For many Vietnamese, the tremendous force of Hurricane Katrina demonstrated anew both the power of the sea and the failure of the state. The Vietnamese word for country is *water* (*nước*), and if water sustains collective life, water can also destroy it.[35] Countless numbers of people perished fleeing the country by sea. Those who survived were caught in a liminal zone—many were refused entry and left adrift within sight of land, embodying the "violence of statelessness," caught between the threat of the sea and the neglect of nation-states.[36]

The ceremony I stumbled upon in 2006 links the Gulf South with the transpacific, as it is also carried out in Buddhist institutions across China, Hong Kong, and Singapore, a ritual enactment of how present circumstances are not easily liberated from past conditioning.[37] The Liberation Rites of Water and Land, or Lễ Trai Đàn Chẩn Tế, not only summon spirits, as do the monthly rituals for hungry ghosts, but release them as well. In

Hong Kong, performing these rites of liberation is seen as a way for monasteries to participate in society. For example, in 2003, the abbot of Baolian Chan Monastery dedicated the merit for the health of all the people of Hong Kong during the SARS scare, emphasizing the role of the monastery and monks in the community.[38] In 2007, the Venerable Thích Nhất Hạnh organized a ceremony at three different pagodas in Vietnam as a gesture of reconciliation, "[untying] the knots for all people dead in the war, including soldiers killed in battles, war victims, missing peoples, . . . regardless of their ethnicity, North-South, religion, political view, age, or gender," so that the conditioning of war would not be transferred to future generations.[39] Likewise, by performing ceremonies that called upon the souls of those who perished during Hurricane Katrina, Buddhist monks inserted themselves into the Gulf South (figure 5.2).

In Vietnam, these rites are often classified as popular religion, an expansive inventory of practices by which people assemble "diverse sources of

5.2   Prayer ceremony for the victims of Hurricane Katrina. The Liberation Rites of Water and Land (Lễ Trai Đàn Chẩn Tế) seek to free the souls of individuals who died because of a calamity. This ceremony was carried out by ritual specialists at Chùa Bồ Đề in New Orleans in summer 2006. Photo by the author.

power to aid their everyday survival."[40] Specialists attempt to liberate the spiritual remains of those who had an "untimely, violent, or unjust death" (*chết oan*), a social category that differs in intensity from hungry or homeless ghosts (*cô hồn*).[41] In Buddhist ethics, these figures signify how spirits are entrapped by the qualities of their particular incarnation—anger, greed, violence—and the power comes from their accumulated force, threatening the collective well-being of the living.[42] As I would learn, the spirits addressed by monks in Louisiana were also those unnamed refugees who died before they reached land, soldiers who never returned home, Indigenous peoples displaced by settlers, and enslaved peoples who tilled plantations in the Gulf South.

While the ceremonies may be held regularly in Taiwan and Hong Kong, Vietnamese Buddhist communities on the Gulf Coast sponsor the ceremony once, if ever at all, because of the expense. Ritual specialists are invited to oversee the construction of the ritual area, which is composed of seven different halls, each with a specific ritual, offering, design, and purpose. In spite of the costs, in 2013, Hồng Ân Monastery sponsored the liberation rites as part of its weeklong celebration of hosting the Jade Buddha. The day before the unveiling of the jade statue, monks and lay Buddhists prepared for the opening ceremony, decorating the stage with artificial flowers and building a platform with a small wading pool. When I asked Mr. Đức why he and other members of the community sponsored the ceremony, he responded with a palpable description: "I feel them," he said, "and my daughter does, too. They sometimes pull at her arm. She's very sensitive to spirits." A ceremony in the afternoon, he explained, would liberate the spirits of "Indian children" (a term he used in English) who had died in the vicinity. He paused before he added, "Don't be frightened, but I built my house over a gravesite. The man's name was Henry Patrick. He was a short, stocky man." He then pointed to a man working on the stage, an electric drill in his hand, as an example. "He was alive in 1789, and I felt his presence while I was meditating." Indian children were not the only spirits that Mr. Đức envisioned would be liberated. Others were the "unborn children," a category of beings never born, through either miscarriage or terminated pregnancies, underscoring how Buddhist ethics of care are unbound by patrilineal kinship structures or even national origins.

Mr. Đức's reference to "Indian children" took me aback, and I scanned the grounds of the monastery that stretched back into a large field. The area where we stood that day is now known as "Acadiana," an image carefully crafted by regional and state tourism campaigns to "exoticize the physical and cultural landscapes of Louisiana's French Triangle region once looked down upon for its very exoticism."[43] Less celebrated by the state's tourist industry is the archaeological evidence that suggests the area where we stood had first been occupied as long as thirty-five hundred years ago in a region known as the Prairie Terrace, which provided diverse food supplies along the great coastal marshes that stretched between what is today Texas and Mississippi. The arrival of Spanish colonists led to the enslavement of many native peoples.[44] Later, thousands of Acadian exiles settled in a new land that a diverse blend of people would call home—free persons of color, Isleños, Irish migrants, Laotians, and Vietnamese. By referring to the ghosts as Indian children, Mr. Đức identified just one of many hauntings on the social landscape in which ties to family, place, and racial identity had long been contested. He added, "These spirits don't know where to go, so this ceremony is to lead them to another place so that they may be reborn."

I was both puzzled and intrigued that the sangha would address this sense of history and the centuries-long processes of migration and settlement. Another lay Buddhist, Mr. Long, attributed the head monk's motivation for carrying out the ceremony to his conviction that the land now occupied by the temple had been occupied by "many generations of spirits." Thus the ceremony, cast in the Buddhist idiom of liberation, was understood as an ethical act in which participants recognized the accumulation of history, a sharp contrast with settler colonialism and its attendant paradigm of occupying uninhabited space.

Later, as I was helping a female monk prepare for the opening ceremony, I noticed a collection of plastic dolls, all about the size of an actual baby. The dolls varied in their coloring—some were peach-colored, others caffe-colored, representing the variety of the spirits of young humans to be released (figure 5.3). But the work of liberation is not easily accomplished. On the day of the opening ceremony, a cold front passed through, turning the skies gray and shaking the wooden frame of the altar with strong winds. People wrapped themselves up in scarves and pulled their jackets tightly around their bodies. Some people gathered around the kitchen, where steaming bowls of a vegetarian version of the spicy noodle soup *bún bò Huế* were offered for sale, while others hunkered down around the tables to enjoy their food and waited for the skies to clear. When the winds calmed down, a procession of older men dressed in ceremonial robes and holding parasols were followed by thirty or so monks. The master of ceremonies announced how the lay members of the Buddhist temple enjoyed the benefits of living in the United States, above all freedom. Recordings of "The Star-Spangled Banner" and the anthem of the Republic of Vietnam played

5.3

Plastic dolls used in a ceremony held at Hồng Ân Monastery to liberate the souls of the aggrieved dead. The ceremony is practiced in East Asia and, on occasion, by Vietnamese communities on the Gulf Coast. Photo by the author.

over the public address system. The monks then unveiled the Jade Buddha, pulling up a curtain that had concealed the statue and releasing balloons and several white doves. But the dolls, symbolizing the spirits of children, did not cooperate. Instead of floating in the water, they tipped over, as if they could not quite play their part in undoing the long history of settler colonialism, enslavement, and structural racism that had shaped southwestern Louisiana's cultural landscape.

Releasing the spirits of children was just one act in the elaborate ceremony that took place once the crowds at the opening-day celebration had dispersed. Several dozen monks gathered for three afternoons to chant for four hours, transmitting the merit they had accumulated to those who had died violent deaths. Lengthy, repetitive, and without the draw of accumulating merit for one's family members, the ceremony attracted only a few lay Buddhists. It addressed not only the children whose presence

Mr. Đức felt but also the conditions or consciousness arising from war and other disasters. The ritual specialists had set up altars connected by paper bridges, and as the monks pulled on these bridges, they called out, "Be released, be released" (Giải thoát, giải thoát), urging the spirits toward liberation. After the ceremony was over, Mr. Long observed that he had once regarded those ceremonies only as "good for business," for calling upon wild spirits associated with profit and money, not to stir compassion. This ceremony, however, left no doubt in his mind about its purpose in liberating those spirits, thus enacting an ethical orientation toward human existence caught in the stream of history.

The ceremony called up a long history of displacement and violence across the grassy plains of the Gulf South and the Mississippi Delta to enact the ethics not of liberalism but of liberation for centuries-old struggles over land and people—the Opelousa, the Spanish, the French, enslaved Africans, Anglo-Americans, and, finally, Southeast Asians fleeing the ruins of a failed US war. The dozens of monks from around the United States who gathered to witness the event staged the liberation of the souls of the grievous dead— refugees lost at sea, soldiers who died at war, even Indigenous children displaced by settler colonialism. In so doing, they also inscribed new meanings in the Gulf South by recognizing its long history of suffering that cannot be comprehended through Buddhist modernism or liberal social theory, which both locate meaning in the individual, not the collective.

BOWING TO REPENT

Buddhism places death front and center. And in the Mahayana tradition, preparing to die well is realized through the practice and discipline of repentance and requires kindness, above all, toward oneself. Master Pure Word counseled those of us who gathered, "Whoever knows how to take good care of themselves also knows to take care of other sentient beings, but whoever does not, may suffer and hurt sentient beings." The emphasis on caring for oneself appears at odds with the focus on non-self, but it is through repentance that practitioners cultivate a self-power rooted in right effort.

A key practice of repentance, or *sám hối* in Vietnamese, is bowing. On Sundays, people bow to take refuge in the Three Jewels—the Buddha, the Dharma, and the Sangha. And they bow to cultivate mindfulness of the conditioning that generates karmic debt, through words or speech (*khẩu nghiệp*), thoughts (*ý nghiệp*), and actions (*thân nghiệp*). In some ceremonies, people will bow five hundred times. Master Deep Awakening described her form of repentance: after reading a verse from the Lotus Sutra, she bowed once, a daily practice that took her three years to complete.

> In Buddhism, we do a practice we call repentance. All of us make mistakes in our past lives and in our present life that brought us right to this moment and [will bring us to] the future. There is a practice in Buddhism that every day we bow to the Buddha, we bow to the bodhisattva, and we also bow to our ancestors, to our friends, our good friends, so that we know that we have made mistakes, intentionally or unintentionally. We bow to remind ourselves not to make a mistake. We may make a mistake, but we don't even recognize it, so we just bow and repent for our mistake.

In the United States, many people see bowing as a sign of submission and devotion, rather than a practice of humility, an ethical disposition with little reinforcement in American culture. In the 1970s, the Buddhist practice of bowing captured the attention of the US media when an American Buddhist, Heng Sure, made a pilgrimage of eight hundred miles from the Gold Wheel Temple in Los Angeles to the City of Ten Thousand Buddhas near Ukiah, California, following the practice called "three steps, one bow." He and a novice, Heng Chau, walked along the side of a highway as they carried out their practice of repentance. Eventually, the monks published their journal and later the collection of letters to their master, Hsuan Hua, which provide an eye-opening account of how ordinary Americans they met along the way responded to their slow procession as they took three steps and then made a full prostration or bow. Heng Sure described a woman in Los Angeles who yelled at the two men, "Stop bowing! That's disgusting. This is America." He also confessed how hard it was for him to bow:

> Of all the doors of cultivation, bowing was last choice. It really makes you feel unimportant and humble. Bowing is the exact opposite of fighting for self and striving to be number one. Winners don't *kow tow*. That's for losers. Everybody wants to win. No one wants to lose. But winning is messing up the world. So we bow.[45]

Repentance, unlike merit-making and merit transference, cannot be carried out on someone else's behalf, even by a senior monk. Repentance is more akin to sweeping fallen leaves or pulling weeds on the grounds of the monastery, a task one never completes. In Vietnam, the image of a monk sweeping the grounds of a temple represents a practice for cultivating mindfulness, no different from sitting on a cushion, sipping tea, or walking while focusing on one's breath. At a monastery set on a property of forty wooded acres, the monks not only swept the leaves but also cleared away small twigs, branches, and even pinecones. The work of clearing the ground was no different from the work of clearing one's mind; both were done daily, reinforced by practicing repentance—not chores but "dharma work." During retreats, Master Deep Awakening would call everyone in residence to assign them a specific task, but even monks look for shortcuts. One of the young monks would strap a leaf blower to her back to clear the leaves more quickly, a sight that amused some older lay Buddhists, perhaps because of the juxtaposition of the speed and efficiency of carrying out daily chores in the United States with the slower tempo of monastic life in Vietnam or because of how and where one could cultivate mindfulness, if monks no longer swept the grounds of the monastery.

On the last day of the year in 2015, I returned with my family to the monastery in Florida for a celebration to honor Quan Âm and perform a ceremony of repentance. Master Deep Awakening admitted that she had invented the tradition for herself, and she opened the monastery so people would join her, if they so wished. Each participant donated money for a scented candle, set inside a lotus-shaped paper holder. We then each wrote down a wish for the New Year. Before the service began, she announced to the dozen or so attendees that she would lead us in a ritual of bowing five hundred times in front of the altar but cautioned us not to count the number of times we bowed; doing so would diminish the act of repentance. She would count for us. We only needed to bow for the sake of bowing, and through this ritual atonement, we would cultivate the capacity to reflect on our actions, words, and thoughts.

Bowing so many times was harder than I anticipated. As I bowed, I thought of her advice to bow for the sake of bowing; I felt the reed mat under my knees, my head spun from the motion of standing up and then bending down, and I eventually sat down as the people around me continued to bow. I looked at the statue of Quán Thế Âm, whose gentle gaze looked down at the small sangha, illuminated by the candles that flickered in the darkness. My secular perspective intruded on my thoughts—what could be gained by bowing so much? One answer is found in the letters of Heng Chau, the American novice, who describes his own practice:

Bow, bow, bow—all the time bow. I have so much arrogance I
don't even see it until I start bowing. Like breathing—so uncon-
scious, automatic. It's only when you stop breathing, you realize
how vital it is. Only when I start bowing do I realize how huge
my arrogance is.[46]

For Master Deep Awakening, bowing was not a sign of submission but a
condition of liberation. Bowing purifies existing karmic offenses and paves
the way to continue down the Eightfold Path of Buddhist practice. It is an
ethical practice that cultivates the practitioner's capacity for right effort, on
which mindfulness and concentration depend. While mindfulness as a
practice has gained widespread currency in the United States, it is detached
from the Eightfold Path and its three essential elements—moral conduct,
mental discipline, and wisdom. Mindfulness and concentration constitute
wisdom, but wisdom can only arise when one follows the right conduct and
right mental discipline through effort and livelihood. As one lay practitioner pointed out to me, anyone can bow, and anyone can bow five hundred times, but few people do. As I learned on that late evening in December,
to summon the intention and effort is not easy.

In Mahayana Buddhism, the expenditure of effort matters. People
gather to recite sutras and mantras and chant the names of buddhas and
bodhisattvas. They bow hundreds of times. They make donations and serve
the sangha. When these activities are described as devotionalism, we overlook the labor involved. It is not that these activities are difficult, but they
are also not "easy." Effort is required to recite Buddha names, chant the
Great Compassion Mantra twenty-one times, or bow five hundred times,
which is the point. People form the syllables of the mantra with their lips,
stand up and bow down, not just as devotion but as a form of repentance to
become aware of their condition in thought, word, and action, all folds
along the Eightfold Path.

"Easy practice" is often opposed to concentration said to be attainable
by religious specialists like monks. At the same time, magic is said to happen when a practitioner achieves concentration, the eighth branch of the
Eightfold Path, neither its culmination nor its end point but rather one
branch connected to all the other branches, a rhizomatic structure without
a single point of origin. On one occasion, Master Deep Awakening recalled
witnessing her own master expel the spirit of a young boy from the body of
a woman. After reciting the Great Compassion Mantra, her master spoke
compassionately to the boy, who had died after being given an injection

from a nurse. The monk told him it would do him no good to occupy the body of the woman, because she was old; he should allow himself to forgive the nurse and be reborn into another life. As the spirit of the young boy left the woman's body, the woman collapsed from relief. For Master Deep Awakening, the story conveyed the power in the mantra, but we also understood its power to emanate not from belief in the mantra but from lifelong practice. Concentration is possible not just for religious specialists but for everyone. But even what appears to be easy—chanting, reciting, bowing—requires effort.

Bowing as a practice associated with the Liberation Rites of Water and Land is often invoked as evidence of Buddhism's mingling with other ethical systems such as Daoism and Confucianism in East Asia. In Vietnam, a popular sutra is the Repentance Ritual of the Emperor of Liang (Lương Hoàng Sám), performed during the water and land liberation rites. The sutra is based on the legend of Emperor Wu, a great sponsor of Buddhism during the Liang dynasty (502–87). He is also reputed to have met the Bodhidharma, the first Chinese patriarch of Zen Buddhism, who dismissed the emperor's attempt to gain merit from having built numerous temples. In addition to this apocryphal tale of how one cannot buy merit with riches, he is attributed with sponsoring the first Liberation Rites of Water and Land. His wife was said to have died prematurely and been reborn as a snake. Today that repentance ceremony is regarded as a practice to save the spirits of the dead and bless the living. But it is also known for having promoted bowing as a form of repentance and self-cultivation.

The Repentance Ritual of the Emperor of Liang was translated into Vietnamese by the Venerable Thích Viên Giác (1912–1976), and an English version was made available only in 2016.[47] The Vietnamese translation is beloved today for its rendering in a style familiar and accessible to ordinary people. His translation can be said to have accumulated an immense store of merit (phước báo). The sutra and its practices have now spread across the Pacific Ocean to the Gulf Coast, even if only a dozen or so people carried them out on that night in 2015. Bowing as an act of repentance is part of a long chain of transmission, preserved in Chinese texts and disseminated in Vietnamese as part of the Buddhist reform movement spurred by nationalist monks and now part of the repentance rituals practiced by Vietnamese Buddhists along the Gulf Coast. It is a practice through which Buddhists repent their thoughts, actions, and speech, not for forgiveness but to prepare to die well, thus performing an ethics of life and death that cannot be comprehended from the standpoint of liberalism. Likewise, we may miss the ethics at play when we dismiss these practices as "ethnic" or "heritage."

Certainly, we overlook the labor involved in the making of the Pure Land and the efforts required to liberate us all from the regional and continental histories of displacement and dispossession.

♦ ♦ ♦

Rituals for spirits and aggrieved souls are lessons for the living, reminders of the difficulty of crossing to the celestial realm of the Pure Land and escaping the consciousness accumulated by generations of human existence. Buddhist communities in the Gulf South have sponsored ceremonies to liberate spirits, bringing in ritual specialists and gathering vast stores of merit through the virtuous bodies of assembled monks. Through these rituals, Vietnamese Buddhists have inscribed a supernatural geography on the Gulf South to redress the deaths of those people who died in the floodwaters after Hurricane Katrina, in distant wars, and in the passages from Africa and Asia to the Americas.

These Mahayana teachings of compassion are not part of the dominant discourses of Buddhism that circulate in the United States. It is small wonder that scholars have often seen these activities through the lens of cultural accretions or heritage that Vietnamese refugees and immigrants carried with them to the United States. Activities such as tossing uncooked grains of rice risk amplifying the perception of the foreignness of spiritual practices. Ceremonies of feeding hungry spirits or bowing as a form of repentance are dismissed as either corrupt forms of Buddhism or as un-American, as one woman shouted at the two men slowly proceeding with three steps and one bow on a California highway.

Within these rituals is an ethical lesson. What does it mean to live so we may prepare to die well? The freedom that is produced by these activities is not the freedom of liberalism, cultural assimilation, and economic integration but liberation that begins by acknowledging suffering. Hungry ghosts and aggrieved spirits are both real and figurative—they stand in for conditioning and indebtedness accumulated across generations and over continents. These stories are American stories, and their ghosts are as well.

Conclusion

Regenerating Buddhism

I N a 1998 essay, religion scholars Cuong Tu Nguyen and A. W. Barber proclaimed Vietnamese Buddhism "relevant only for a small number of people isolated within an ethnic ghetto."[1] More than twenty years later, Vietnamese Buddhist temples in the United States number in the hundreds, and these numbers continue to grow, especially in regions such as the Gulf Coast, where Buddhism had made few inroads before the arrival of Southeast Asian refugees in the 1970s.[2] Profiling temples from southwestern Louisiana to the Florida Panhandle, this book has delineated practices of the Pure Land tradition of Mahayana Buddhism that are located not in the liturgy or spaces of worship but in networks of temples, monks, and lay practitioners. Like rhizomes, these networks spread new spiritualities and express otherwise silenced geopolitical histories across the region. Still, it is important to ask, as Nguyen and Barber did, whether the story of these institutions is a first-generation one.

The typology of generation is one that haunts Asian American communities. Generation as a category is invoked to measure the sequential distance of migrants from their homeland or, alternatively, a process of assimilation into American society whereby each generation is more integrated than the preceding one. The ritual of lighting incense neatly encapsulates the dilemmas posed by the Asian immigrant narrative. First-generation migrants invoke an extraordinary array of ghosts, ancestors, and gods, reaffirming relations binding the living to the dead. Transferring the meanings of those practices to their children and grandchildren (e.g., the second and third generations) is not so easy, as Vietnamese American journalist Andrew Lam describes through his mother's worries about her own mortality.[3] When his mother asks her sister-in-law who will pray to their dead ancestors when they are gone, his aunt replies, "None of my children will do it, and we can forget the grandchildren. They don't even understand what we are doing when we pray to the dead. I guess when we're gone, the ritual ends."[4] Sheepishly, Lam admits they are right; he cannot even imagine what to say to his long-departed ancestors.

Lighting incense is not just a private act, one that takes place only inside the home and toward one's family altar. It can also be a public act, one in which Buddhist monks and lay Buddhists recognize geopolitical histories that have been rendered silent in the United States, and one by which these practitioners also engage in dwelling or home-making. Through lighting incense and other acts described in this book, such as transmitting merit and praying for ancestors, practitioners maintain transpacific ties, navigating their own marginalization in a region long structured in terms of racial segregation. The category of generation, much like the assimilation myth, reinforces perspectives that these practices are instances of heritage, preserved by first-generation Buddhists whose practices are tainted by culture and therefore less authoritative.

What the typology ignores are factors such as the temporalities of migration, the role of the state and mandates of citizenship, and the persistence of a color line.[5] The generational typology further fails because of the impossibility of the full incorporation of minorities into the national body, evident in exclusion acts, the incarceration of Japanese Americans, and the construction of the "model minority." Observed differences across generations, such as those distinguishing the Japanese immigrant generation (Issei) from their US-born children (Nisei), arose in response to US internment policies and the mandates of cultural assimilation, which have influenced how Japanese Buddhists present the public face of their religious expressions. "Asian American," a category that arose in the 1960s to harness the political energies of diverse groups, glosses over vastly different experiences and pathways of integration. While Japanese American Buddhists may express pride at having "a white pastor, whose Buddhism augments their American identity" and confers the legitimacy of their religion, Southeast Asian refugees express their pride through the rhetoric of "freedom," and even Buddhist congregations invoke slogans of anticommunism and display the Vietnamese Freedom and Heritage Flag as they collectively make themselves into Vietnamese Americans.[6] Yet the still-fraught relationship between the diaspora and the Socialist Republic of Vietnam itself has amplified generational differences. Filial piety, a virtue reenacted in the legend of Mulian and celebrated during Vu Lan, exerts a disciplinary force on many young Vietnamese scholars and artists who seek new forms of representing their identities and their homelands and are sometimes met with protests.[7] These tensions are visible in temples, confounding the Buddhist soteriological goal of liberation with the US imperative of liberalism even as these tensions also contribute to the ongoing process of regenerating Vietnamese Buddhism.

Despite these limitations, the typology of generation is still productive for understanding the ongoing negotiations of spirituality, especially as second-generation Asian Americans adopt and transform spiritual practices in relation to their status as minorities.[8] Asian migrants established collective spaces of worship not just to maintain the comfort of familiar practices but also to buffer against their marginalization and poverty. Their children confront a sprawling spiritual marketplace, resulting in a plethora of different strategies. Second-generation Korean Americans imagine themselves as Christian first and Korean second, prioritizing their religious identities over their racialized ones.[9] Similarly, Christian South Asians see the immigrant religious organizations of their parents as "social gathering[s]," not as "faith communit[ies]," and like Korean Americans, they see their Asianness as an obstacle to their spiritual growth.[10] Even when young Japanese Americans participate in a festival held at a Buddhist temple in downtown Los Angeles, they do not attend regular services, performing their ethnicity as "episodic," to be expressed on some occasions and not on others.[11] Other tactics emphasize "familistic traditioning," as evident in "Chinese popular religion, Vietnamese ancestral veneration, and even Indian American Hinduism."[12] Young Hindu Americans associate their faith not with a global church but with the family and material culture, above all food.[13] Not all practitioners have the leeway to engage in experimentation, because they are subject to surveillance, detention, and even deportation, a dynamic especially prevalent for Muslims in the post-9/11 context.[14]

Such strategies appear in *Pure Land in the Making* as well. Ethnoreligious hybridization seems to explain why people attend temples, not as disciples but as compatriot Buddhists, where they express their affiliation as both Vietnamese *and* Buddhist, while "familistic traditioning" brings people to festivals such as Vu Lan, where they express their devotion on Vietnamese Mother's Day. However, this book has also emphasized the limitations of categorizing these practices as "ethnic" or "heritage," variants of a more authentic and authoritative version of Buddhism, which itself arose in response to the provocations of modernity. While heritage presumes an unambiguous relationship between the "right here" of the Gulf Coast and the "over there" of Vietnam, Buddhism has long exhibited plasticity, bending and accommodating to the societies in which it has spread. Many Vietnamese experience their religious life in terms of both crossing and dwelling, through their investments in building temples and praying to the bodhisattva Quán Thế Âm, but also behind the scenes in cooking and preparing food, organizing fund-raisers, and rebuilding temples after Hurricane Katrina. Ethnicity likewise fails to address the aspirations of practitioners who negotiate multiple tensions—asserting their religious freedom, maintaining spiritual connections with Vietnam, and praying for the liberation of all sentient beings, not just fellow Vietnamese, an ethical and collective project that works against race, nation, and empire. How can we comprehend the conditions for regenerating Vietnamese Buddhism that does not rely on the typology of generations or the immigration narrative?

VIETNAMESE BUDDHISM AS RHIZOME

Since the early 2000s, the number of monks in the Gulf Coast region has grown, contributing to the spread of Buddhism. Newly arrived monks recruited to reside in temples administered by lay associations eventually leave and establish temples elsewhere. While monks and lay Buddhists expend considerable time, labor, and money to establish new temples, their departures are the hidden rhizomes that spread new spiritual practices across the social landscape of the United States. Vietnamese Buddhism itself is also "regenerated" through novel ownership structures, in which administration is in the hands, no longer of lay Buddhists, but of monks themselves, many ordained and trained under the Socialist Republic of Vietnam and some raised in the United States and trained in Taiwan, India, and even France, thereby ensuring that Vietnamese Buddhism has not ossified but is instead pluralizing, as evident in the variations of the Vu Lan celebration. Still, the legacy of the Cold War and the preferences of older Vietnamese shapes these institutions, particularly in people's concern with the sincerity of monks, whether educated and ordained in contemporary Vietnam or trained in cosmopolitan versions of Buddhism in the United States and elsewhere.

Not all Vietnamese Buddhist centers or monks follow the Mahayana tradition, nor do all people who identify as both Vietnamese and Buddhist attend these temples. People experiment with other spiritual practices, including those of Tibetan Buddhism or groups like Soka Gakkai. Some monks self-consciously fashion themselves as Zen masters, drawing on the teachings of Thích Thanh Từ and Thích Nhất Hạnh. Other monks promote the dharma through Facebook, distributing CDs, touring different temples, and even broadcasting their prayer sessions over satellite television as large groups of people chant in unison "Homage to Amitābha Buddha," a form of revivalism where lay Buddhists fill high school stadiums in California and occasionally temples in Louisiana.

What is at stake is the plasticity or regeneration of Buddhism itself. New Orleans is now home to five Vietnamese temples, a Thai temple under the jurisdiction of the Royal Thai Embassy, a Soka Gakkai center, and numerous meditation centers. In southwestern Louisiana, Cambodian Americans carry out prayers for the New Year's Festival at the Cambodian Fishermen's Community Center.[15] Meditation groups convene at universities and other community centers, attesting to how Buddhism has pluralized in the region. New spiritual networks are created; several of the people interviewed in this book also attended temples across the United States, Vietnam, and India. The teachings of Thích Thanh Từ, once circulated on cassette tapes in the 1990s, are now institutionalized in meditation centers around the United States, while Thích Nhất Hạnh's Order of Interbeing now has four monasteries in the United States, including one that is a five-hour drive from New Orleans. Vietnamese Buddhism is thus part of a broader regeneration of Buddhism underway in the United States.

Given these processes of regeneration—the making, unmaking, and remaking of Buddhism—does it make sense to think of these temples as distinctly Vietnamese? Consider the Venerable Thích Nhất Hạnh, a Vietnamese monk who now has a global following and practice centers around the world. His teachings infuse practices associated with Pure Land into Zen, making these practices available to people who stand outside those traditions. Monks, however, see his teachings as standing within a long tradition of "Pure Mind" over "Pure Land,"[16] and those associated with the Order of Interbeing have shaped the activities of some of the temples described in this book, in which retreats are held that attract racially diverse participants (figure C.1).

Despite the international following of Thích Nhất Hạnh, Vietnamese Buddhism has not gained global recognition, unlike Tibetan Buddhism, which fuses Buddhism with the compelling claim of a potentially lost heritage through the appeal of its charismatic leader in exile, or even academic interest as with Chinese Buddhism.[17] In the case of Tibet, national identity and Buddhism are entwined, so the government in exile and especially the Dalai Lama are popularly seen as authentic representatives of "Tibetanness," a nation without a state.[18] In 2013, His Holiness the Fourteenth Dalai Lama arrived in New Orleans, where residents visibly embraced his visit. Prayer flags adorned front porches across the city. Tibetan monks fanned

C.1 Day of Mindfulness retreat. These retreats, often styled after those held at monasteries and practice centers affiliated with Thích Nhất Hạnh, include dharma sharing in which participants discuss their experiences and gather in a circle to sing in English and Vietnamese. Photo by Quang Huynh.

out to local temples, where they drew elaborate sand paintings, only to destroy them to teach the idea of impermanence. The Dalai Lama gave lectures at not one but three of the largest venues in New Orleans—the New Orleans Theater; the Superdome, for Tulane University's commencement ceremony; and the University of New Orleans Lakefront Arena. While the Dalai Lama is recognized as the spiritual leader of Tibetan Buddhism, it is not easy to see Buddhism in the figure of a refugee, a shrimper, a restaurant worker, an accountant, or a social worker, even though it is their labor that has transformed commercial stores, ranch houses, and fishing camps along the Gulf Coast into the Pure Land.

The tradition of academic scholarship poses a different problem for understanding the practices described in this book. On the one hand, liturgical traditions have long been privileged over contemporary practices and formal worship over the myriad activities that happen behind the scenes. Vietnamese Buddhist traditions of practice are also integrated with other systems of meaning such as Daoism and Confucianism, or the "three teachings" (*tam giáo*). Their integration is often encompassed within an even broader frame of inquiry, Chinese popular religion. The designation of popular religion contributes to why the practices of diasporic groups are seen as corrupted versions of Buddhism. Even Chinese Pure Land is measured against Japanese Pure Land, despite the significant differences in these traditions.[19]

Vietnamese Americanist scholars, in contrast, emphasize facets of collective life, including family structures, political activism, and the entertainment industry. "Staying Vietnamese" is not an individual project but one of collective formation. Activities to bring people together in diaspora require a place, a dwelling to support gatherings, as sociologist Karin Aguilar–San Juan shows in her comparisons of Little Saigons in Boston and Orange County, California.[20] Yet these collective spaces of worship both bring people together and sometimes contribute to their dispersal. Religious pluralism is a common element of people's biographies, even among monks—people raised Catholic took refuge in Buddhism, or those raised Buddhist found sanctuary in evangelical churches. Yet Vietnamese churches and temples provide visibility for people to gather and celebrate their common origins on the Hùng Kings' Death Anniversary, in which people reenact the myth that otherwise irreconcilable differences such as religious affiliations can be contained by common origins, bound both by place and by descent as we have seen in the call to compatriots. These dynamics are not extraneous to Vietnamese Buddhism; they are intimately related to people's expressions of spirituality.

BETWEEN LIBERALISM AND LIBERATION

Pure Land in the Making is also a story of the tensions between the American ideals of liberalism and the Buddhist goals of liberation. The changing US religious landscape reflects a "de-Christianization of American religion" through the shift toward multiculturalism, yet spirituality is still constructed as a source of interior expression and thus consistent with the focus on the sovereignty of the individual.[21] Popular interest in mindfulness in the United States has repackaged Buddhist practices in ways amenable to the dominant models of personhood and neoliberal assumptions such that "everyone is free to choose their responses, manage negative emotions, and 'flourish' through various modes of self-care."[22] Consequently, many Americans are surprised when they learn that even Buddhism casts shadows, since religious institutions, including monastic sanghas, are deeply entwined with nationalist aspirations.[23] Even Vietnamese Buddhists recognize that the dharma requires protection, not just by Hộ Pháp, but by the legal regimes that recognize minority religious institutions. Some threats come from within: while gossip and legal disputes may threaten the harmony of sanghas, practitioners can still establish new temples across the Gulf South, regenerating Buddhism.

Yet liberalism provides a narrow scope in which these practices are recognized, which in turn reinforces perspectives of these religious practices as ethnic or heritage. Another perspective would admit that these practices convey alternative relational ethics, evident in how practitioners entrust the care of the spirits of their deceased family to the sangha and how the sangha, in turn, prays not just for the liberation of these ancestral spirits but also for the unresolved remnants of history, the hungry ghosts and aggrieved spirits. Vietnamese Buddhists enact an ethical system that stretches across the Pacific from the Gulf South to Vietnam as monks ritually liberate those unassimilated fragments of the past that US society silences. Buddhist temples house not just "the soul of the people" but a tradition of practice organized around liberation as a collective, even humanistic project, not just for the deceased kin and the sometimes wayward spirits in the vicinity but for the stores of deep consciousness arising from centuries of human migration, enslavement, warfare, and disasters. The rituals invoke an ethical relation with the dead, voiced in a minority language and premised on a notion of social debt that cannot be discharged.

Buddhism in the making is not a prepackaged religion or an age-old philosophy but a mode of dwelling. Through blessing the land, installing statues, welcoming compatriot Buddhists, reciting sutras, transmitting the merit, preparing the food, and lighting the incense, practitioners make a place not only for Buddha but also for themselves, connecting the Gulf Coast to the transpacific as a vast expanse of people and ideas that cannot be contained by territorial nation-states.[24] Still, even those Buddhists who have dedicated their time and donated their hard-earned cash, prepped and cooked for days at a time, cleaned and scrubbed, felled trees, and repaired buildings may retreat to their houses, where they practice in private or not at all. If Vietnamese Buddhism is made along the Gulf Coast, it can also be unmade. In Vietnamese, the expression "as deserted as Bà Đanh Pagoda" (*vắng như chùa Bà Đanh*) refers to an actual pagoda in northern Vietnam that is rarely visited despite the beauty of its architectural features. Some people attribute its abandonment to its location, far from populated areas and accessible by only one road. Others tell stories of ghosts that haunt the vicinity. The temple's desertion, however, is a reminder that the meanings are not in the built structure but in how people embody those spaces. Along the Gulf Coast, Vietnamese practitioners inhabit vacated spaces, consecrating them with new meanings and forms of sociality. Yet the specter of abandonment is possible: the making of Buddhism can also be its unmaking, a point that Cuong Tu Nguyen and A. W. Barber recognized as well.

In unmaking lies the possibility of regeneration, or the doctrine of "expedient means," alluding to plasticity in both the forms and teachings of Buddhism, changing shape to address the needs of its audiences. Expedient means explains why Avalokiteśvara, once depicted as a male attendant of Buddha, converted into a female form, Guanyin or Quan Âm. Expedient means explains why monks trained in Zen practice also chant the names of buddhas and bodhisattvas, thus ensuring the dharma is made available to all. And expedient means is why monks welcome Vietnamese American pop stars or offer their services to bless new cars and businesses. The accommodations of Buddhism to East Asian contexts is well documented, and scholars are now exploring how Buddhism in the twentieth and twenty-first centuries is accommodating colonialism, US imperialism, refugee camps, capitalism, and outposts such as the US South. In the 1970s, people recited the name of the bodhisattva Quán Thế Âm, clutched amulets as they fled the country, and drew strength from mantras they believed held a protective force. Today monks use their hands to bless platters heaped with grains of rice or a newly purchased Toyota SUV, they roll prayer beads and recite mantras before blessing lay Buddhists with a bracelet as a talisman against illness or bad luck. From a secularized perspective, these practices are "devotional," but they are also the very making of Buddhism, the expedient means by which monks adapt their practices to attract more followers. Monks refer to this skill as "miraculousness" (*huyền diệu*), but it is also "skillfulness," cultivated through the union of compassion and knowledge that leads to wisdom.

High in the Santa Cruz Mountains, Thích Tịnh Từ was overseeing the construction of a 30,000-square-foot worship hall when I visited in January 2020. The roof of the monastery was almost complete, its red tiles glimmering in the sun to welcome visitors for the lunar New Year. As he often does with visitors, he recounted the story of how he founded the monastery. One day, while meditating, he had a vision of climbing on the back of a white tiger, which soared through the sky and led him to the summit of a mountain. For a year, he searched for that very spot of land, until he found the property high on Mount Madonna. With only five thousand dollars in cash, he convinced the owner to offer him a steep discount. To listen to his story is to hear a miracle tale, one that blesses the land with supernatural qualities, no longer a real estate transaction but divine intervention.

My purpose in making the trip was to deliver a copy of the essay Thích Tịnh Từ had written for the Fort Chaffee newsletter in 1975. He described how over ten thousand times, he guided refugees who declared themselves Buddhist by vowing to maintain the five precepts, and ten thousand times he wrote out a piece of paper affirming that the man, woman, or child had taken refuge: "I gave them five rules, five precepts to practice, and three things to be like an island. Take refuge in the Buddha because Buddha is not only Shakyamuni Buddha but is inside ourselves." True dwelling, he explained, was to find refuge in oneself, the island of one's self. He then spoke of his own life. "I became a monk when I was fourteen years old, and I wanted to do something like that bodhisattva, with many arms, many eyes, many hearts," he said. "When I went to the Fort Chaffee camp, I vowed to build monasteries for Vietnamese refugees. They left Vietnam, without anything, just as when you pass away or die, you cannot bring anything with you. When they left, they left with nothing, just two empty hands, and one mind and one body." Since then, people have returned with the piece of paper they received from him, offering cash and support to his monastic sangha.

Like hidden rhizomes spreading from nodes in Vietnam, Fort Chaffee, and California, Buddhism is now visible on the US Gulf Coast. Its shoots have spread not from the transmission of patriarchs to disciples but through the horizontally networked aspirations of lay associations and monks who reckon with the aftermath of war, maintain transpacific ties, and navigate their marginalization as racialized minorities. In these temples, people enact a relational ethics of collective well-being. Although Vietnamese Buddhism is a minority practice, it deserves a much more prominent place in how people in the United States understand Buddhism today.

NOTES

PREFACE

1 Masquelier, "Why Katrina's Victims Aren't Refugees."

INTRODUCTION: MAKING VIETNAMESE BUDDHISM

1 Thích Thiên-Ân founded the first Buddhist university in Saigon. He arrived in the United States in 1968 and, at the behest of his students, established a center for teaching Zen meditation.

2 Operations and Readiness Directorate, *After Action Report: Operations New Life/New Arrivals, US Army Support to the Indochinese Refugee Program, 1 April 1975–1 June 1976* (Washington, DC: Department of the Army, Office of the Deputy Chief of Staff for Operations and Plans, January 25, 1977), ix, http://cgsc.cdmhost.com/cdm/ref/collection/p4013coll11/id/1278.

3 Thích Tịnh Từ, "Như một phép lạ nhiệm mầu," 21.

4 Before April 1975, there were few Vietnamese Buddhist monks in the United States outside of those who had been sponsored to study at Thích Thiên-Ân's center. At Fort Pendleton, California, Catholic priests and Protestant pastors were among those who had fled Vietnam as refugees. See Richard Chandler, "Religion Vital to Vietnam Refugees," *Los Angeles Times*, May 19, 1975, sec. B.

5 During World War II, an estimated seventeen thousand Japanese Americans were incarcerated at Fort Chaffee, attesting to the legacy of the camp in the "ongoing power of military structures in the American landscape." See Lipman, "A Refugee Camp in America," 60; Smith, "The Response of Arkansans," 340.

6 Buddhists around the world seek refuge in the Three Jewels: the Buddha; the Dharma, or rules for right conduct; and the Sangha, or community. People make a vow to take refuge during the close of services, and many

people take part in a formal initiation ceremony (*quy y*) in which adults and children vow to uphold the five precepts. The presiding monk then gives them a dharma name (*pháp danh*).

7 Thích Tịnh Từ, "Như một phép lạ nhiệm mầu," 22.

8 Rev. Thích Tịnh Từ, "Hã nắm lấy cơ hội" [Let's grasp the opportunity], *Tân dân* [New people], no. 192 (December 10, 1975).

9 The Vietnamese version reads, "Cánh cửa huyền nhiêm dễ được mở rộng cho chúng ta, khi chúng ta biết can-đảm nhìn thắng vào cuộc-đời, nhìn thắng vào con đường dài trước mất của chủng ta và không tin-tưởng phó thác đời mình vào một nơi nào khác."

10 US institutions, including schools, hospitals, and social work agencies, were instrumental in conveying these models of personhood. See Ong, *Buddha Is Hiding*.

11 In the essay, Thích Tịnh Từ uses the phrase "trú xứ tính thần," which could be translated as a "refuge in oneself" or "an island of the self," in which the practitioner focuses within, not on an external agent. See Suzuki, *Selected Works*, 2:12.

12 Refugees were not allowed to leave the camp until a sponsor was identified, either an individual or a nongovernmental organization (NGO) that would agree to receive the refugees and their families and provide for their material needs, including assistance in finding jobs and enrolling children in school.

13 Goldstein, *One Dharma*.

14 Soucy, "Vietnamese Buddhism's Status as 'Ethnic,'" 41.

15 Thích Thiên-Ân, *Buddhism and Zen in Vietnam*. For a discussion of the importance of Theravada practices in southern Vietnam, see Philip Taylor, *The Khmer Lands of Vietnam*.

16 Anthropologists emphasize how ethical subjectivity is shaped by awareness of how our speech and actions have consequences toward others. In Buddhism, these ethics are well developed and practiced through collective action within these spaces. See Lambek, *Ordinary Ethics*.

17 See Jeff Wilson, *Dixie Dharma*, 3.

18 See Zhou and Bankston, *Growing Up American*; VanLandingham, *Weathering Katrina*.

19 In Vietnam, a paradox is evident—despite the visible and often spectacular manifestations of spiritual life, many people declare themselves as "not religious." This paradox can be partly explained by the historic antagonism of the Communist Party toward organized religions and a population who often designated their religious affiliation as "none." Today people engage in self-fashioning through religion, which means that affiliation becomes difficult, if not impossible, to measure. The Pew-Templeton Global Religious Futures Project estimates that in 2010,

16 percent of the population were Buddhist and 6.5 percent were Catholic, while nearly 30 percent declared themselves unaffiliated and 45 percent identified with Indigenous religions. What is important for the purposes of this book is that the religious affiliation of Vietnamese on the Gulf Coast has long been different than in Vietnam as a whole, which makes designators such as "ethnic" or even "heritage" suspect. See Pew-Templeton Global Religious Futures Project, "Vietnam," accessed February 27, 2020, www.globalreligiousfutures.org/countries/vietnam.

20 Hurd, "Believing in Religious Freedom"; Lambek, *Ordinary Ethics.*

21 Aguilar–San Juan, *Little Saigons.*

22 Aguilar–San Juan, xxviii, 61.

23 Nguyen and Barber, "Vietnamese Buddhism in North America," 146.

24 Tweed, *Crossing and Dwelling*, 83.

25 T'an-Luan (ca. 488–554) is said to have taught, "The way of easy practice means that simply by faith in the Buddha one aspires to be born in the Pure Land, and by riding on the Buddha's vow-power one attains birth in that Pure land." Andrews, "Pure Land Devotionalism," 23.

26 Thích Thiên-Ân, *Buddhism and Zen in Vietnam*, 102. Unlike Japanese Pure Land, Chinese Pure Land is better understood as a "tradition of practice," a "dharma-gate" rather than an institution, a sect, or a set of master-discipline lineages. Most significantly, "it offered a chance for non-elite or even morally evil people to attain a goal that was tantamount to the attainment of buddhahood itself: rebirth in the Pure land of the Buddha Amitābha." See Charles B. Jones, *Chinese Pure Land Buddhism*, 31.

27 Mainland Southeast Asia is predominantly Buddhist, but this designation obscures the great diversity in religious orientations as well as significant divides in Buddhist traditions. Today Theravada Buddhism is the dominant form in Thailand, Laos, Cambodia, and Myanmar, while Mahayana Buddhism prevails in Vietnam as well as in China and Japan. Theravada Buddhism is often regarded as more authoritative than Mahayana because of its adherence to the Pali Canon and the influence of the monastic sangha. Monks are required to follow a stricter reading of the precepts, or Vinaya, that govern their moral behavior.

28 In Thailand, Cambodia, and Myanmar, ancient and modern kings legitimated their power through patronage of the monastic sangha, and in these countries today, Theravada Buddhism is the dominant tradition. In the southeastern part of the Mekong Delta in Vietnam, the Theravada sangha is strong, reflecting how the region was once part of the expansive Khmer kingdoms, a connection preserved by its recognition as an important center for Theravada teachings. See Philip Taylor, *The Khmer Lands of Vietnam.*

29 Soucy, "Vietnamese Buddhism's Status as 'Ethnic.'"

30 The liturgy draws heavily from Sino-Vietnamese, or words and morphemes borrowed from Chinese, not colloquial Vietnamese.

31 Goscha, *Vietnam*, 171; Hansen, *How to Behave*; Turner, *Saving Buddhism*.

32 See McHale, *Print and Power*. For instance, Master Taixu (1890–1947), the Chinese monk who emphasized "Buddhism for the world," may have inspired leading reformers such as the Venerable Thích Trí Hải, who established the Tonkin Buddhist Association and the Quán Sứ Pagoda in Hanoi as the center for Buddhist teaching in the country. See DeVido, "Master Taixu," 413–58.

33 Hoskins, *The Divine Eye and the Diaspora*.

34 McHale, *Print and Power*, 145.

35 McHale, 145.

36 Rozenberg, *The Immortals*, 37.

37 Tweed, *The American Encounter with Buddhism*.

38 These designations were invoked first as capturing what appeared to be empirical differences. Ethnic communities, for example, are multigenerational, and their activities focus on imparting cultural and family values and sponsoring activities like language lessons that appear marginal to Buddhism proper. These congregations also invoke a set of cosmological and soteriological views that many so-called Western Buddhists reject. Instead, these congregations emphasize individual practitioners over families and eschew concepts such as transmitting merit to the spirits of deceased relatives.

39 Hickey, "Two Buddhisms"; Cheah, *Race and Religion*; Williams, *American Sutra*.

40 Goldstein, *One Dharma*.

41 Goldstein.

42 Payne, "Pure Land or Pure Mind?," 22.

43 Payne.

44 The Chinese Exclusion Act was renewed in 1892 and 1902 and made permanent in 1904. By 1917, the peoples excluded encompassed the vast majority of Asia—inhabitants of China, India, Burma, Siam (then Thailand), part of Russia, all of Arabia and Afghanistan, and the Malay states, as well as most of the Polynesian islands. In 1921, Congress imposed national-origins quotas, a strategy intended to maintain the racial demographics of the country prior to the influx of migrants from outside northwestern Europe. These quotas were formalized by the 1924 Immigration Act, which effectively closed the door on further Asian immigration by denying admission to all aliens who were "ineligible for citizenship," a clause specifically aimed at Japanese. See Lee, *The Making of Asian America*, 171.

45 Williams, *American Sutra*.

46 Williams, 121.

47   Clifford, "Looking Several Ways."
48   Kim, Warner, and Kwon, "Korean American Religion," 4.
49   Chen, *Getting Saved in America*, 98.
50   Aguilar–San Juan, *Little Saigons*.
51   La. Rev. Stat. Ann. § 49:153.3 (2004), cited in Nami Kim, "Letting Bayous Be Bygones," 129–30.
52   See Brettell and Reed-Danahay, *Civic Engagements*.
53   Võ Văn Tường, "Vietnamese Buddhist Temples in America—the New Tourist Destination," Trang Nhà Quảng Đức, accessed June 16, 2019, https://quangduc.com/a30465/vietnamese-buddhist-temples-in-america-the-new-tourist-destination.
54   Võ, *108 danh lam cổ tự Việt Nam*; Võ, *Danh lam nước Việt*.
55   Singh, *Black Is a Country*.
56   Singh, 42–43.
57   Iwamura, *Virtual Orientalism*.
58   See Klein, *Cold War Orientalism*, 16. In 1943, the US Congress repealed the Chinese Exclusion Act in order to counter Japanese war propaganda. Japan roundly criticized US policies, a move seen by some policy makers as an attempt to weaken ties between the United States and its ally, the Republic of China.
59   The first revision of immigration law eliminated the racial bar to citizenship, which allowed Japanese, Koreans, Chinese, Indians, and Filipinos to become citizens. But it also created an "Asian-Pacific Triangle," which established race-based quotas to restrict Asian immigration to the United States. Persons of Asian descent born or residing anywhere in the world could only immigrate under the Asia-Pacific quotas of one hundred per country. See Ngai, *Impossible Subjects*, 238.
60   See Ngai, 262.
61   See Kwon, *The Other Cold War*.
62   Viet Thanh Nguyen, *Nothing Ever Dies*; Kwon, *The Other Cold War*.
63   Kwon, *Ghosts of War*.
64   Malarney, "The Exceptional Dead"; Kwon, *Ghosts of War*.
65   Soucy, "Contemporary Vietnamese Buddhism," 181.
66   Phi-Vân Nguyen, "A Secular State."
67   Ford, *Cold War Monks*.
68   Scholars still debate the origins of the conflict, some pointing to the role of Buddhist nationalists and others emphasizing the privileged role of Catholics under President Ngô Đình Diệm. In 1963, Buddhist monks were forbidden from flying the Buddhist flag during Vesak, the celebration of the historical Buddha's birthday, even though just days before the Vatican flag had been flown over the city of Da Nang. Hundreds of Buddhist monks marched through city centers in Hue and Saigon, and a leading monk, Thích Quảng Đức, immolated himself to protest

restrictions on Buddhist practices. A year later, the crisis still roiled through the monastic sangha; some monks supported the regime, while others saw anticommunist laws as pro-Catholic. The Unified Buddhist Sangha of Vietnam was founded to unite the increasingly fractured ordained-Buddhist clergy. In Buddhist prayer books printed in Vietnam, he is regarded as a bodhisattva, and the day of his immolation is included in the ritual calendar for the fourth lunar month. See Thích Minh Thời, *Kinh nhật tụng*, 520.

69 Preston, "Introduction: The Religious Cold War," xvi.

70 Although the initial resettlement program ended in 1975, people continued to flee Vietnam, many in small boats that drifted for days until officials in neighboring countries permitted them to come ashore. By 1979, more than 350,000 people languished in camps throughout Southeast Asia and Hong Kong as they awaited sponsorship for permanent resettlement in a country like the United States. The United Nations declared the situation a humanitarian crisis and attempted to resolve it through the enactment of the Orderly Departure Program, a multilateral agreement that legalized migration directly from Vietnam for humanitarian reasons and family unification. Under the program, nearly half a million people migrated to the United States, including military veterans of South Vietnam who had been imprisoned in reeducation camps and Amerasians—the children of US servicemen—as well as their families.

71 Espiritu, "Toward a Critical Refugee Study."

72 Klein, *Cold War Orientalism*; Kwon, *The Other Cold War*.

73 Mimi Thi Nguyen, *The Gift of Freedom*.

74 Ong, *Buddha Is Hiding*.

75 Espiritu, *Body Counts*, 11.

76 Phuong Tran Nguyen, *Becoming Refugee American*.

77 Singh, *Black Is a Country*.

78 Parikh, "Minority," 163.

79 Aguilar–San Juan, *Little Saigons*, 44.

80 See Iwamura, *Virtual Orientalism*.

81 Rudrappa, *Ethnic Routes*, 178.

82 Agamben, *The Highest Poverty*.

CHAPTER ONE: SEEKING REFUGE IN THE GULF SOUTH

1 This claim is often cited in newspaper articles at the time, although the original source is not mentioned. See Benjamin Morrison, "From Vietnam to Marrero," *Times-Picayune*, March 5, 1978, 21.

2 While the population of Vietnamese in the United States had grown by 37.9 percent since 2000, in Louisiana the growth rate was less than half that rate, or 16 percent. See US Census Bureau, "The Vietnamese

Population in the United States: 2010," accessed March 21, 2020, www
.vasummit2011.org/docs/research/The%20Vietnamese%20Population%20
2010_July%202.2011.pdf.

3 Stephen Hiltner, "Vietnamese Forged a Community in New Orleans.
Now It May Be Fading," *New York Times*, May 5, 2018; Park, Miller, and
Van, "Everything Has Changed," 79.

4 The Mississippi River runs through the metropolitan area. The East Bank
includes the city of New Orleans, and the West Bank is largely made up
of smaller municipalities in Jefferson Parish. Because of how the river
bends as it flows to the Gulf, the area known as the West Bank lies *east* of
downtown New Orleans. Federal highway signs combined the words
West Bank into Westbank to ensure that travelers did not use the name
as a cardinal direction. The area is integral to greater New Orleans, home
to diverse demographics, including many immigrants, and more amenable to inscribing new meanings on the built environment. See Campanella, *The West Bank of Greater New Orleans*, 2020.

5 In keeping with the conventions of ethnographic writing, I use pseud-
onyms to provide individuals some veil of anonymity.

6 By the time of this writing, a fifth temple in metropolitan New Orleans
had celebrated its grand opening.

7 Anthropologist Alexander Soucy describes a similar pattern in which
disputes have accelerated the "spread of Vietnamese Buddhism" across
Canada. See Soucy, "Outpost Buddhism," 113.

8 The Venerable Thích Nhất Hạnh asks why the Four Noble Truths begin
with suffering, and he then likens suffering to mud: "If you know how to
make good use of the mud, you can grow beautiful lotuses. If you know
how to make good use of suffering, you can produce happiness." See
Thich Nhat Hanh, *No Mud, No Lotus*, 14.

9 Deleuze and Guattari, *A Thousand Plateaus*, 21.

10 Studies of Japanese American internment during World War II often
neglected the role of Buddhism, an oversight that reinforced the "prevailing narratives of what makes a person American. In short, Buddhism
disappears from view, paradoxically, due to the same underlying pre-
sumption of America as a white and Christian nation that contributed to
the wartime incarceration of Japanese Americans in the first place." See
Williams, *American Sutra*, 4.

11 Cartwright and Salvaggio, "Introduction: Gulf Souths, Gulf Streams," 8.

12 Clifford, "Diasporas," 303.

13 Mintz, "The Localization of Anthropological Practice," 119.

14 Campanella, "Gulf Souths, Gulf Streams."

15 Nguyen and Hoskins, "Introduction: Transpacific Studies," 2.

16 Espina, *Filipinos in Louisiana*.

17 Yun, *The Coolie Speaks*.

18 Campanella, *Cityscapes of New Orleans*, 52. The *Times-Picayune* reported that Chinese in New Orleans had worked under contracts in Cuba, suggesting how the presence of Asian Americans in New Orleans has long been part of the making of the circum-Caribbean world.

19 "Food for the Dead: A Curious Chinese Custom and Ceremony," *Daily Picayune*, August 31, 1895, Saturday edition.

20 Jun, *Race for Citizenship*.

21 Jun, 17.

22 Mia Tuan, *Forever Foreigners or Honorary Whites?* In his study of Chinese in Mississippi, James W. Loewen describes how the Chinese were essentially "white," a status he marks in doubt through the use of scare quotes. Loewen, *The Mississippi Chinese*, 2.

23 Bow, *Partly Colored*, 2.

24 Claire Jean Kim, "Racial Triangulation," 107.

25 Klein, *Cold War Orientalism*; Kwon, *The Other Cold War*.

26 Nonini, "Critique: Creating the Transnational South."

27 Elliott and Ionescu, "The Deep South Triad," 164.

28 Woods, *Development Arrested*.

29 Mintz, "The Localization of Anthropological Practice," 119; Yi-Fu Tuan, "Humanistic Geography," 269.

30 "50,000-Plus Refugees on Way," *Times-Picayune*, May 1, 1975, sec. 5, 27.

31 See Edgar Poe, "Viet Evacuees Are Being Screened," *Times-Picayune*, May 1, 1975, sec. 5, 27.

32 "Viet Center Here Denied," *Times-Picayune*, May 1, 1975, New Orleans edition, sec. 1, 3.

33 Millie Ball, "Viets Coming to N.O. Area," *Times-Picayune*, May 7, 1975, sec. 1, 6.

34 Joan Treadway, "'Shoe Box' Resettlement: It's Working," *Times-Picayune*, May 16, 1975, sec. 1, 6.

35 "Clergy Urges Refugees Aid," *Times-Picayune*, May 29, 1975, Thursday morning edition, sec. 1, 10.

36 "Collection for Viets," *Times-Picayune*, July 12, 1975, Saturday morning edition, sec. 2, 3.

37 "Refugees' Rally Seeks N.O. Move," *Times-Picayune*, July 17, 1975, sec. 1, 26.

38 Bankston, "Vietnamese-American Catholicism," 46. The estimates of how many refugees were resettled by the ACC vary. According to the Archdiocese of New Orleans, ten thousand Vietnamese were resettled in New Orleans by Archbishop Hannan and the ACC. See "Catholic Charities Remembers Archbishop Hannan," *Clarion Herald*, September 29, 2011, https://clarionherald.org/news/catholic-charities-remembers-archbishop-hannan.

39 Phuong Tran Nguyen, *Becoming Refugee American*, 35.

40 Operations New Life/New Arrivals was the official name of the refugee processing program. In early April 1975, the US Army developed a plan, tentatively called Operation Compassion, to establish safe havens for evacuees to be medically screened and reunited with their families before they were relocated to the continental United States. This plan was eventually named Operation New Life. See Operations and Readiness Directorate, *After Action Report: Operations New Life/New Arrivals, US Army Support to the Indochinese Refugee Program, 1 April 1975–1 June 1976* (Washington, DC: Department of the Army, Office of the Deputy Chief of Staff for Operations and Plans, January 25, 1977), http://cgsc.cdmhost.com/cdm/ref/collection/p4013coll11/id/1278.

41 "Letter from Vietnamese in Louisiana," *Đất mới* [New land], June 6, 1975, 6.

42 Bill Crider, "Viet Fishermen Lead Tough Life in Louisiana," *Mobile Press Register*, July 23, 1978, Sunday edition, sec. D, 14.

43 Crider.

44 Crider.

45 Crider.

46 Warren Brown, "Vietnamese Refugees Caught in Black-White Friction in New Orleans: A Different War," *Washington Post*, July 18, 1978, sec. A, 3.

47 Brown.

48 "Catholic Body Raps Galmon Nomination," *Times-Picayune*, August 17, 1978, Thursday edition, sec. 7, 20.

49 "Refugee Aid May Be Sought," *Times-Picayune*, June 3, 1978, sec., 1, 3. For an extended and insightful analysis of this debate, see Marguerite Nguyen, "'Like We Lost our Citizenship.'"

50 Brown, "Vietnamese Refugees," 3.

51 Arden, "Troubled Odyssey," 378.

52 Arden, 386.

53 Arden, 386. See Starr, "Troubled Waters," for an extended analysis.

54 Crider, "Viet Fishermen."

55 Ong, *Buddha Is Hiding*.

56 Ong, 2.

57 David McQueen, "Catholic Refugees Honor Statue," *Helping Hand*, December 12, 1975.

58 Airriess, "Creating Vietnamese Landscapes and Place," 238.

59 Airriess.

60 Parishioners raised $750,000 to build a new church consecrated by Archbishop Hannan on November 29, 1986.

61 Sociologist Thien-Huong T. Ninh reports that Bishop Dominic Mai Luong, when asked why Vietnamese Catholics in Orange County, California, were not given a personal parish, explained: "We are all Catholics under one God. If we remain ethnically separated, we will go

astray from God." Ninh notes that the large numbers of Vietnamese Catholics, clerical participation, and financial contributions in the county constituted a "racial threat," which led the Diocese of Orange County to restrict their influence. Ninh, "Colored Faith," 81–82.

62 Airriess, "Creating Vietnamese Landscapes and Place," 346.

63 Tweed, *Crossing and Dwelling*, 82.

64 Aguilar–San Juan, *Little Saigons*; Wood, "Vietnamese American Place Making."

65 "Talk Slated by Buddhist," *Times-Picayune*, March 26, 1977, sec., 2, 2.

66 Ong, *Buddha Is Hiding*.

67 "Ceremony Will Launch New Temple," *Times-Picayune*, April 1, 1983, West Bank edition, sec. 1.

68 Tweed, *Crossing and Dwelling*.

69 This congregation emphasized the global aspects of Buddhism, hosting sacred relic tours in 2004, 2008, and 2010. The relics were of Buddhist saints and masters from Tibetan, Chinese, and Indian traditions and were on view as part of a fund-raising effort to build a 500-foot Buddha statue in northern India.

70 These kinds of outbursts could still be heard in the Gulf South, even as late as 2016. That year I attended a retreat in Mobile with a sangha of twenty or so monks from Magnolia Grove, in Mississippi. The retreat was held in a large antique store located within a suburban complex of one-story office buildings. During the retreat, participants slowly walked in the store's empty parking lot. A group of men shouted, "Don't drink the Kool-Aid," invoking a phrase associated with the Jonestown massacre, which occurred on November 18, 1978, when a cult leader called on his followers to drink cyanide-laced Flavor Aid.

71 "Baptist Neighbors Oppose Texas Buddhist Temple," *New York Times*, February 3, 1984.

72 Tom Frazer, "Work on Buddhist Temple Delayed," *Times-Picayune*, July 21, 1984, sec. A, 20.

73 Judi Russell, "Buddhists Gather in Algiers Temple," *Times-Picayune*, September 26, 1989, sec. B, 1.

74 Valerie Faciane, "Buddhists Flock to Bo De Temple," *Times-Picayune*, June 22, 1991, sec. A, 21.

75 A root temple usually refers to where a monk became ordained or a lay Buddhist took refuge; thus the root temple represents that dharma lineage. Religion scholar Charles B. Jones suggests that Chinese Pure Land is not a denomination-style institution, and therefore there is no emphasis on direct transmission, a characteristic of Zen and Japanese Pure Land dharma communities. See Jones, *Chinese Pure Land Buddhism*, 11.

76 Cedric Johnson, *The Neoliberal Deluge*, xxxviii.

77 Lipsitz, "Learning from New Orleans," 460.

78 Adams, *Markets of Sorrow, Labors of Faith*, 7.

79 Vincanne Adams is ultimately critical of these organizations because of how they absolve both federal and state agencies of their responsibility in addressing the social well-being of residents. Moreover, as the vast majority of these organizations were Christian, their assistance raises questions of which populations and what forms of suffering are seen as deserving help. See Adams, *Markets of Sorrow, Labors of Faith*, 130.

80 Uyen Phan, "Cause for Celebration," *Times-Picayune*, June 25, 2006, sec. Algiers Picayune.

81 Tang, "A Gulf Unites Us."

82 Airriess et al., "Church-Based Social Capital"; Marguerite Nguyen, "'Like We Lost Our Citizenship'"; Tang, "A Gulf Unites Us"; VanLandingham, *Weathering Katrina*.

83 Bruce Hamilton, "'Home' Has New Meaning—Vietnamese Vow to Rebuild," *Times-Picayune*, October 22, 2005, 1.

84 Tang, "A Gulf Unites Us," 123.

85 Aguilar–San Juan, *Little Saigons*, xxii.

86 Park, Miller, and Van, "Everything Has Changed," 89–93.

87 Katherine Bergeron, "Buddhists Believe You Are Totally Responsible for Your Actions," *Biloxi Sun Herald*, August 26, 2005, sec. B.

88 Bankston, "New People in the New South," 39–40.

89 Gaillard, "After the Storms," 860.

90 Gaillard, 858.

91 Lowe and Shaw, "After Katrina," 809.

92 Russ Henderson, "Temple of Hope," *Mobile Press-Register*, May 14, 2006, sec. A.

93 The Vietnamese term *bào thai* means "fetus," so the compound *đồng bào* conveys common biological origins that are symbolically represented by the legend of this union.

94 Keith Weller Taylor, *The Birth of Vietnam*.

95 Dang, "The Cultural Work of Anticommunism," 66.

96 Malarney, "The Exceptional Dead."

97 Nami Kim, "Letting Bayous Be Bygones," 129.

98 Aguilar–San Juan, *Little Saigons*, 66.

99 Viet Thanh Nguyen, "Speak of the Dead."

CHAPTER TWO: RECRUITING MONKS

1 Tom Wilemon, "Buddha Bides Time in Garage," *Biloxi Sun Herald*, February 1, 2001, sec. B1.

2 Reggie Beehner, "Buddhists Now Have Room for Worship," *Biloxi Sun Herald*, November 18, 2002, sec. A2.

3 Katherine Bergeron, "Followers Celebrate Spiritual, Physical Growth on Mississippi Coast," *Biloxi Sun Herald*, August 26, 2005, sec. B.

4 Queen and Williams, *American Buddhism*, xix.

5 See Quli, "Buddhist Temples in Northern California"; Cadge, *De Facto Congregationalism.*

6 The precepts govern behavior and thought and are sometimes defined as a basic code of ethics. Some lay practitioners undergo a formal ceremony of taking refuge (*quy y*) in the Three Jewels, in which they accept the five precepts. These precepts are traditionally framed in terms of constraints in order to acknowledge their voluntary nature: refrain from harming others (i.e., killing); refrain from taking what is not freely given (i.e., stealing); refrain from sexual misconduct; refrain from false speech; and refrain from using intoxicants that cloud the mind.

7 Sparham, "Saṅgha," 740.

8 Sparham, 744.

9 See Mitchell, *Buddhism in America*, 104. American audiences are familiar with how the Catholic Church has been exposed for its spectacular failure to uphold vows of celibacy among its religious specialists.

10 Klein, *Cold War Orientalism.*

11 Iwamura, *Virtual Orientalism.*

12 My husband, children, and I were given dharma names, and the first part of the names is the same, whereas the second part is intended to designate a feature of our personality.

13 Bảo and Lê, *Tu tại gia.*

14 John Kuo Wei Tchen traces American Orientalism to the late eighteenth century and argues that while its contours have changed over time, it contributed to the production of a "white" identity. See Tchen, *New York before Chinatown.*

15 Iwamura, *Virtual Orientalism*, 4.

16 Iwamura, 21.

17 For example, Suzuki popularized Japanese Zen as a mystical experience that conveyed the essence of all religions, and thus no religion at all. Cheah, *Race and Religion.*

18 Cheah.

19 Braun, *The Birth of Insight.*

20 McMahan, *The Making of Buddhist Modernism*, 185.

21 Jeff Wilson, *Mindful America.*

22 Goldstein, *One Dharma*, 2.

23 McMahan, *The Making of Buddhist Modernism*, 196.

24 Cadge, *Heartwood*, 138.

25 Numrich, *Old Wisdom in the New World*, 119.

26 Sandra Bell found that in Britain, Thai monks relied on Buddhists in Thailand for monetary donations, although British lay followers chipped in with labor and expertise. See Bell, "British Theravada Buddhism," 155.

27 McMahan, *The Making of Buddhist Modernism*, 184.

28 Tanabe, "Merit and Merit-Making."

29 Walsh, *Sacred Economies*.

30 Sihlé, "The Buddhist Gift."

31 Gombrich, "'Merit Transference' in Sinhalese Buddhism," 204.

32 Keyes, "Merit-Transference," 274.

33 Carl L. Bankston III found that in southwestern Louisiana, young Lao men were reluctant to be ordained. By refusing to enter, even temporarily, the monastic sangha, they contributed to professionalizing monkhood as a vocation, thus loosening the bonds between the monastic sangha and family life. See Bankston, "Bayou Lotus," 465.

34 Bourdieu, *Theory of Practice*, 171.

35 Tambiah, "The Renouncer," 305.

36 Sponberg, "Women and the Feminine."

37 Tanabe, "Merit and Merit-Making," 532.

38 Cook, *Meditation in Modern Buddhism*, 152.

39 Cook, 6.

40 Gross, *Buddhism after Patriarchy*, 10.

41 Gross, 37.

42 Out of nine temples that I visited (2013–17), female monks were in residence at four, although two of those temples were affiliated with a monastery in California overseen by a male abbot. In two temples, the abbot was a male monk, but there were female monks in residence as well. In one temple, the board of directors had recruited both male and female monks, and at one time both a female and a male monk were in residence. Finally, at two temples, only male monks were in residence. Those temples that had both male and female monks, however, were often scrutinized for whether the monks were adhering to their precepts of celibacy.

43 Religion scholar Jeffrey Samuels shows that in Sri Lanka, fathers described how the ordination of sons would bring status to the family and educational opportunity for those sons, but the mothers only expressed regret, even anger. See Samuels, "Families Matter."

44 Soucy, *The Buddha Side*.

45 Soucy, "Outpost Buddhism."

46 Shorn hair symbolizes social control, evident in the highly regulated lives of both monks and soldiers. See Douglas, *Natural Symbols*, 72.

47 Lang, "Shaven Heads and Loose Hair," 34.

48 Masquelier, "Dirt, Undress, and Difference," 2.

49 Agamben, *The Highest Poverty*, 13.

50 Hansen, *How to Behave.*

51 One monk explained that the color gray signaled a blending of black and white.

52 People also distinguish between Theravada and Mahayana monks by referring to the color of their robes.

53 Luong, *Discursive Practices and Linguistic Meanings*; Sidnell and Shohet, "Peers in Vietnamese Interaction," 633.

54 Ryan LaFontaine, "Police Break Up Fight at Buddhist Temple," *Biloxi Sun Herald*, December 7, 2007, sec. A.

55 Christopher Mele, "The Fake Monks Are Back, Aggressively Begging," *New York Times*, July 1, 2016; Joseph Goldstein and Jeffrey E. Singer, "If He Walks and Talks like a Monk, but Has His Hand Out . . . Panhandlers Dressed as Monks Confound New Yorkers," *New York Times*, July 5, 2014.

56 The discourse of fake monks presupposes a model of an authentic Buddhism that shuns materialism. Gregory Schopen argues that scholarly presuppositions of Buddhism have led archaeologists to disregard findings such as hoards of coins that would suggest some monks were "men of considerable wealth." See Schopen, "Archaeology and Protestant Presuppositions," 7.

57 See Kitiarsa, "Buddha-izing a Global City-State." Other stories of fake monks abound, but money can transform even real monks. Dawn Starin recounts how the morning alms offering in Luang Prabang, Laos, appeared to be transformed into a "sideshow orchestrated for tourists." See Starin, "World Heritage Designation," 642.

58 For a discussion of how these dynamics play out in a Thai monastery in California, see Bao, *Creating a Buddhist Community*, 77–78.

59 Lieu, "Performing Culture in Diaspora," 197.

60 Iwamura, *Virtual Orientalism*, 6.

61 Philip Taylor, *The Khmer Lands of Vietnam*, 241–48.

62 See Numrich, *Old Wisdom in the New World*, 68.

63 Bell, "British Theravada Buddhism."

CHAPTER THREE: BUILDING A HALL FOR BUDDHA

1 Ong, *Buddha Is Hiding*, xvi.

2 The reconstruction of San Francisco's Chinatown after the 1906 earthquake and fire invoked a manufactured aesthetic with similarities to the architectural styles featured on Vietnamese temples. See Upton, *Architecture in the United States*, 84.

3 For the lyrics of the poem in Vietnamese, see Huyen Khong Monastery, "Nhớ chùa," accessed May 27, 2020, www.huyenkhong.org /ThoHuyenKhong/NhoChua.php.html.

4 Reverend Chan Tu, "Thoughts on My Teacher: No Hair in Your Mind," *Tricycle: The Buddhist Review*, accessed May 24, 2019, https://tricycle.org /magazine/thoughts-my-teacher-no-hair-your-mind.

5 The Venerable Thích Mãn Giác was born in Hue in 1929 and later studied at the University of Tokyo, where he received a doctorate degree in 1965. Upon his return to Vietnam, he served as vice president of Vạn Hạnh University, the leading Buddhist university in the Republic of Vietnam, better known as South Vietnam. After the collapse of the regime in 1975, he worked as a liaison between the Unified Buddhist Church of Vietnam and the Communist government in Vietnam. Two years later, he fled the country in a fishing boat crammed with nearly eighty people. The boat drifted for eight days before it reached Malaysia. After three months, the Venerable Thích Nhất Hạnh arranged for him to go to Paris, and he eventually resettled in Los Angeles, where he served as president of the Vietnamese United Buddhist Churches of America, an umbrella association for the growing number of Vietnamese temples across the United States, and abbot of the Vietnamese Buddhist Temple in Los Angeles, founded by Thích Thiên-Ân. Quang Duc Monastery, "Thành kính tưởng niệm cố Hòa thượng Thích Mãn Giác" [Memorial to the late Most Venerable Thích Mãn Giác], November 14, 2006, www.tuvienquangduc .com.au/Danhnhanvn/htmangiac/htmangiac.html.

6 Huyen Khong Monastery, "Nhớ chùa."

7 Ong, *Buddha Is Hiding*, 5.

8 As taught by Buddha, the steps of the Noble Eightfold Path lead to liberation. The Four Noble Truths are encompassed in the first part, right understanding, followed by right thought, right speech, right action, right livelihood, right effort, right mindfulness, and, finally, right concentration. These parts are not sequential, such that one part must be mastered before attempting the next; rather, each part assists in the cultivation of the others. See Walpola Sri Rahula, "The Noble Eightfold Path," *Tricycle*, accessed May 24, 2020, https://tricycle.org/magazine /noble-eightfold-path.

9 Charles B. Jones, *Chinese Pure Land Buddhism*, 63.

10 The idea of Pure Land in the human realm is associated with the Buddhist leader Taixu, who proposed that Buddhism needed to be redirected to this world, not the afterlife. See Jones, 55.

11 Thiền sư Hư Vân, "Chia sẻ về Thiền Tịnh song tu" [Sharing about Zen and Pure Land parallel practices], Phật Giáo [Buddhism], December 26, 2015, https://phatgiao.org.vn/chia-se-ve-thien-tinh-song-tu-d20638.html; translation by the author.

12 Luhrmann, *When God Talks Back*.

13 Amstutz, "The Politics Pure Land Buddhism," 75.

14 Charles B. Jones, *Chinese Pure Land Buddhism*, 51.

15 Second-generation Vietnamese Americans see these aesthetic practices as distractions. See Peché, "'I Would Pay Homage.'"

16 *Bát nhã* is a Vietnamese term for "wisdom." The Heart Sutra in Vietnamese is called Kinh Bát Nhã. The sounds from the bell and the drum are not simply to incite excitement but also to penetrate the body and bring about understanding and compassion that lead to wisdom.

17 Haleigh Atwood, "Giant Jade Buddha Arrives Home in Australia after 9-Year World Tour," *Lion's Roar* (blog), May 23, 2018, www.lionsroar.com /giant-jade-buddha-arrives-home-in-australia-after-9-year-world-tour.

18 McMahan, "The Jade Buddha."

19 Linh, a Vietnamese woman in her fifties, eagerly told me that after viewing the Jade Buddha, she and her friends planned to see a well-known statue of Buddha located on Avery Island, home of the famous Tabasco sauce, on their way back to New Orleans. In Asia, excursions to different Buddhist temples is a common pastime, even, and perhaps especially, among those who regard themselves as Buddhist. "Leisure Buddhism," in which people admire the art, statuary, and architecture, does not diminish the role of these places as collective spaces of worship and even enhances their appeal. See McDaniel, *Architects of Buddhist Leisure.*

20 See Bankston, "Bayou Lotus."

21 The head monk was accused of using up to $250,000 from the temple to gamble at Baton Rouge's L'Auberge Casino. Richard Burgess, "Buddhist Monk with Blackjack Habit Accused of Embezzling at Least $150,000 from Lafayette Temple," *Advocate* (Baton Rouge), accessed July 29, 2016, www.theadvocate.com/acadiana/news/article_780a522e-9560-572d-87fa -8ed11ce53335.html. The monk had withdrawn cash from the bank accounts of the temple between 2010 and 2014. He later admitted to embezzling more than $263,000 from the temple and was sentenced to thirty months in a federal prison.

22 See Bao, *Creating a Buddhist Community,* 67.

23 The monk had presided over two other Buddhist sites along the Gulf Coast, one in Alabama and the other in Florida, both located outside metropolitan areas, on spacious grounds with long walking paths that led through wooded country.

24 One of the neighboring properties was listed for $170,000 and the other for $75,000.

25 In Vietnamese, people use the phrase "old ghosts" (*mã cũ*), a reference to authorities whose power is challenged by newcomers.

26 Pérez, *Religion in the Kitchen.*

27 Scott, *Nirvana for Sale?*

28 Petra Kuppinger has examined Muslim urban spaces in Stuttgart, Germany. While her primary interest is in how people create and

maintain an urban Muslim public sphere, her analysis is suggestive of how religious practitioners can creatively negotiate the meaning of spaces. See Kuppinger, "Flexible Topographies."

29 The arrest of Việt Khang in Vietnam was motivated by two songs he composed to draw attention to crackdowns on protests against the Chinese military maneuvers in the South China Sea.

30 Lieu, *The American Dream in Vietnamese*, 81.

CHAPTER FOUR: HONORING MOTHERS

1 The idea of setting aside one day a year to honor mothers was first proposed by Anna Jarvis in 1908 and later taken up by Protestant churches to combat the threat they perceived to motherhood in the Progressive Era. Since then, the holiday has served to define the often contested meanings accruing to motherhood in US society. See Kathleen W. Jones, "Mother's Day"; Antolini, *Memorializing Motherhood*.

2 Grant and Idema, *Escape from Blood Pond Hell*, 5.

3 Ullambana is thought to have originated in India, but it was in China, during the Tang dynasty (618–907), that the texts about the legend of the monk Mulian and the fate of his mother circulated.

4 Grant and Idema, *Escape from Blood Pond Hell*, 5.

5 Ohnuma, *Ties That Bind*.

6 Ohnuma, 15.

7 Buddhist monks sanctioned weddings in refugee camps in 1975. My own wedding was performed at a Buddhist pagoda near Ho Chi Minh City, in part as a strategy to ensure that my partner would obtain a visa to the United States, after having failed several times.

8 Liz Wilson, *Family in Buddhism*.

9 Jamieson, *Understanding Vietnam*, 17; Kelley, "'Confucianism' in Vietnam," 314.

10 Ikels, *Filial Piety*, 2.

11 Fong, "Filial Nationalism," 632.

12 Teiser, *The Ghost Festival*; Cole, *Mothers and Sons*.

13 Teiser, *The Ghost Festival*, 197.

14 Cole, "The Passion of Mulian's Mother," 120.

15 Grant and Idema, *Escape from Blood Pond Hell*, 17.

16 Cole, "The Passion of Mulian's Mother," 127.

17 Grant and Idema, *Escape from Blood Pond Hell*, 6.

18 Truitt, *Dreaming of Money*, 101.

19 Luong, "Vietnamese Kinship."

20 Harms, *Saigon's Edge*, 30.

21 Kwon, *Ghosts of War*, 90.

22 Paul C. Johnson, *Diaspora Conversions*, 33.

23 Johnson, 36. One of the characteristics of diasporas is the "nostalgic idealization of the homeland and ancestral time." In contrast to African diaspora religions, where few people return to live in Africa, Vietnamese maintain a different relationship to the homeland, one that is steeped in nostalgia among many first-generation migrants who reject the current state as a legitimate successor to the Republic of Vietnam. Given these tensions, the fatherland becomes resignified in terms of maternal imagery. See Johnson, 33, 36.

24 Yü, *Kuan-Yin*.

25 Yü.

26 Truitt, "Quán Thế Âm of the Transpacific."

27 Yü, *Kuan-Yin*, 389.

28 See Bingenheimer, *Island of Guanyin*, 2.

29 Watson, *The Lotus Sutra*, 304.

30 Tweed, *Crossing and Dwelling*, 82.

31 Luhrmann, *When God Talks Back*.

32 Paul and Wilson, *Women in Buddhism*, 66.

33 Karetzky, *Guanyin*, 21.

34 Dror, *Cult, Culture, and Authority*.

35 Shao-Yun Chang (anthropologist), personal communication.

36 Philip Taylor, *Goddess on the Rise*.

37 Duong, *Treacherous Subjects*.

38 Teiser, *The Ghost Festival*.

39 These requests are not limited to the Vu Lan festival. They can be made during the other ceremonies held year-round, including Buddha's birthday and the Tet holiday.

40 *Kinh Vu Lan và Báo Hiếu*, 34.

41 Paul C. Johnson, *Diaspora Conversions*, 37.

42 Lieu, *The American Dream in Vietnamese*.

43 Alan Cole describes a process in which debt is incurred within the private sphere of the family is then discharged by the son's patronage of public institutions, Buddhist monasteries. In this Buddhist version of filial piety, the duty of sons is reoriented from performing rites to the father and patrilineal ancestors to ensuring their mothers' salvation, which also reinforced the mother as an impure and defiled figure. See Cole, *Mothers and Sons*, 3.

44 Thich Nhat Hanh, *A Rose for Your Pocket*, 27–28.

45 Thich Nhat Hanh, 36; italics in the original.

46 For the Vietnamese lyrics and the English translation, see "Vườn Nhạc: Bông hồng cài áo—A Rose for Your Pocket (Nhất Hạnh / Phạm Thế Mỹ; Duy Khánh)," *Việt Nam ăn chay* [Vegetarian Vietnam] (blog), May 6, 2011, www.vietnamanchay.com/2011/05/vuon-nhac-bong-hong-cai-ao -rose-for.html.

47 Aguilar–San Juan, *Little Saigons*, ix.

48 Duong, *Treacherous Subjects*.

CHAPTER FIVE: PREPARING TO DIE WELL

1 See Kwon, *Ghosts of War*, 50.

2 Regional variations of the phrase "over there" include *ở bên kia, bên bển,* and *bên nớ*.

3 Small, *Currencies of the Imagination*, 50.

4 Truitt, "Quán Thế Âm of the Transpacific."

5 Voyce, *Foucault, Buddhism and Disciplinary Rules*.

6 Povinelli, *The Cunning of Recognition*; Rudrappa, *Ethnic Routes*.

7 Jean M. Langford poses this question, demonstrating how Cambodians and Laotians in the United States invoked stories to make sense not just of their past experiences of war and displacement but also of their encounters with the US medical system. See Langford, *Consoling Ghosts*.

8 Langford.

9 Jeff Wilson describes a "slave trade meditation vigil" that was carried out by a racially diverse group of Buddhists in Virginia. He examines reasons both for its success and for its failure. See Wilson, *Dixie Dharma*, 185–217.

10 Tylor, *Primitive Culture*, 1:284.

11 Kwon, *Ghosts of War*; Teiser, *The Ghost Festival*.

12 Viveiros de Castro, "Cosmological Deixis and Amerindian Perspectivism."

13 Kwon, *Ghosts of War*, 18.

14 Kwon argues that the problem of ghosts is in part their proximity to the violence of war. In the US South following the Civil War, people also described how ghosts haunted the landscape. See Kwon, 18.

15 Kwon, 87–88.

16 Gustafsson, *War and Shadows*, 137.

17 Truitt, *Dreaming of Money*, 100; Leshkowich, *Essential Trade*, 129.

18 McLellan, *Many Petals of the Lotus*, 121.

19 Photographs of the deceased are also displayed in funeral services and later hung or displayed on household altars. These images represent the deceased and mobilize the gathering of descendants by thus reaffirming

the moral community of the family. Lozada, "Framing Globalization"; Avieli, *Rice Talks*.

20 Breyer, "Religious Liberty," 367.

21 Dorais, "Politics, Kinship, and Ancestors."

22 McLellan, *Many Petals of the Lotus*, 123.

23 At one Buddhist temple, an elaborate gate marked the entrance. On several occasions, as lay Buddhists cut down tree limbs or hung banners to welcome people to a festival, they were stung by bees or even fell from the ladder. The monks attributed the fall to these place-based spirits, which both reinforced the role of the sangha in resolving this danger and justified why people suffer even while doing meritorious activities.

24 Hộ Pháp is a name often given to men who regularly volunteer, repairing and maintaining the temple complex buildings. The idea of protecting the dharma, however, also underscores the violence of protector deities in regular and special ceremonies. See Makley, *The Violence of Liberation*, 54.

25 Soucy, *The Buddha Side*, 30.

26 Espiritu, *Body Counts*, 130.

27 Lincoln and Lincoln, "Toward a Critical Hauntology."

28 Lincoln and Lincoln, 196.

29 McDowell, "Chunnilal's Hauntology," 508.

30 Benhabib, *The Rights of Others*, 177.

31 See Lincoln and Lincoln, "Toward a Critical Hauntology," 211.

32 David, "Gendered Collective Action," 141.

33 Regis, "Blackness and the Politics of Memory," 755.

34 A similar ceremony was carried out at Quang Minh Temple in Chicago on October 22, 1989, and covered by the *Chicago Tribune*. On that day, the Water and Land Incantation ceremony took place on the shore of Lake Michigan and was intended to liberate the spirits of those people who had drowned while swimming in the lake. The monks carrying out the ceremony went by boat out onto the waters of the lake in order to lead the spirits of the deceased back to land. After the ceremony, no one else was said to have drowned that year. See Thich Quang Minh, "Vietnamese Buddhism in America," 337.

35 The word for country is the compound *đất nước*, or "land and water," but in everyday conversations, people drop the first element in the compound phrase, so *country* is also *water*.

36 Patricia Nguyễn, "*salt | water*," 96.

37 While it is seen as a spectacular and popular ceremony in Hong Kong today, for most of the twentieth century it was seldom performed because few monks knew the special chanting techniques, and the economic resources needed to sponsor the ceremonies and the appropriate venues were lacking. See Chan, "Popular Buddhist Ritual."

38 Chan, 99.

39 Quoted in Trần Hữu Quang, "The Question of Reconciliation in Vietnam," 419–20.

40 Philip Taylor, "Modernity and Re-enchantment," 15.

41 These ceremonies differ in importance from the monthly ceremonies by mobilizing support by outsiders, a dynamic that Đỗ Thiện argues was especially prevalent in migratory regions, where the ties of kinship and place were looser. Whereas hungry or homeless ghosts signal what lies external to genealogical continuity—beggars found dead by the side of a road, young women who died unmarried, older women who died childless—spirits of violent deaths signal "death in strange places" and therefore may be elevated as tutelary deities through such rituals. Độ, "Unjust-Death Deification," 166.

42 Kwon, "Can the Dead Suffer Trauma?," 212.

43 Brasseaux, *Acadiana*, 1.

44 Webre, "Indian Slavery in Spanish Louisiana," 127.

45 Heng and Heng, *News from True Cultivators*, 235.

46 Heng and Heng, 19.

47 Buddhist Text Translation Society, *Repentance Ritual*.

CONCLUSION: REGENERATING BUDDHISM

1 Nguyen and Barber, "Vietnamese Buddhism in North America," 146.

2 Thich Quang Minh, "Vietnamese Buddhism in America," 225.

3 Lam, "Who Will Light the Incense?" The question of who will light the incense is not only a generational dilemma but also a gendered one. It is Lam's mother and her sister-in-law who discuss these practices and express a sense of resignation about the rituals. Much of the ritual labor of praying for ancestral spirits falls to women, just as women ensure the well-being of the family, a point that Alexander Soucy develops in *The Buddha Side*.

4 Lam, "Who Will Light the Incense?," 69.

5 Espiritu, *Asian American Panethnicity*.

6 Tsing, *The Mushroom*, 104.

7 An important institution is the Vietnamese Buddhist Youth Association (Gia Đình Phật Tử Việt Nam), a lay organization that was established in Vietnam before 1975 and has active chapters in the United States and elsewhere in the diaspora. These chapters sponsor retreats and camping trips. The organization came up in interviews, and its history merits further treatment.

8 Chen and Jeung, *Sustaining Faith Traditions*.

9 See Min, *Preserving Ethnicity*.

10 Kurien, "Decoupling Religion and Ethnicity," 456.

11 Le, "Episodic Ethnicity."

12 Jeung, Chen, and Park, "Introduction: Religious, Racial, and Ethnic Identities," 3.

13 Min, *Preserving Ethnicity.*

14 Rana, *Terrifying Muslims.*

15 Sara Sneath, "Tiny, Unique Sliver of Louisiana's Coast Clings to Culture as Threat Rises," *Times-Picayune*, April 13, 2017.

16 Payne, "Pure Land or Pure Mind?"

17 Hess, *Immigrant Ambassadors.*

18 Hess.

19 Charles B. Jones argues that Western academics first encountered Chinese Pure Land through the writings of Japanese scholars, often drawing on the distinct practices of the latter tradition to inform the former. See Jones, *Chinese Pure Land Buddhism*, 6.

20 Aguilar–San Juan, *Little Saigons.*

21 Jeung, Chen, and Park, "Introduction: Religious, Racial, and Ethnic Identities," 9.

22 Purser, *McMindfulness*, 11.

23 In Asia, Buddhism is now a symbol of the body politic and nationalism. In Japan, Zen Buddhism was not a sword against rising nationalism and militarism but a sword through which those discourses were carried out. In Southeast Asia, the rage of Buddhists, stirred by the United States as a force against communism, has since turned against Muslims in southern Thailand and Myanmar.

24 Hoskins and Nguyen, *Transpacific Studies.*

BIBLIOGRAPHY

Adams, Vincanne. *Markets of Sorrow, Labors of Faith: New Orleans in the Wake of Katrina.* Durham, NC: Duke University Press, 2013.

Agamben, Giorgio. *The Highest Poverty: Monastic Rules and Form-of-Life.* Translated by Adam Kotsko. Stanford, CA: Stanford University Press, 2013.

Aguilar–San Juan, Karin. *Little Saigons: Staying Vietnamese in America.* Minneapolis: University of Minnesota Press, 2009.

Airriess, Christopher A. "Creating Vietnamese Landscapes and Place in New Orleans." In *Geographical Identities of Ethnic America: Race, Space, and Place,* edited by Kate A. Berry and Martha L. Henderson, 228–54. Reno: University of Nevada Press, 2002.

Airriess, Christopher A., Wei Li, Karen J. Leong, Angela Chen, and Verna M. Keith. "Church-Based Social Capital, Networks and Geographical Scale: Katrina Evacuation, Relocation, and Recovery in a New Orleans Vietnamese American Community." *Geoforum* 39, no. 3 (2008): 1333–46.

Amstutz, Galen. "The Politics of Pure Land Buddhism in India." *Numen* 45, no. 1 (1998): 69–96.

Andrews, Allan A. "Lay and Monastic Forms of Pure Land Devotionalism: Typology and History." *Numen* 40, no. 1 (1993): 16–37.

Antolini, Katharine Lane. *Memorializing Motherhood: Anna Jarvis and the Struggle for Control of Mother's Day.* Morgantown: West Virginia University Press, 2014.

Arden, Harvey. "Troubled Odyssey of Vietnamese Fishermen." *National Geographic* 160, no. 3 (1981): 378–94.

Avieli, Nir. *Rice Talks: Food and Community in a Vietnamese Town.* Bloomington: Indiana University Press, 2012.

Bankston, Carl L., III. "Bayou Lotus: Theravada Buddhism in Southwestern Louisiana: Sociological Spectrum." *Sociological Spectrum* 17, no. 4 (1997): 453–72.

———. "Gender Roles and Scholastic Performance among Adolescent Vietnamese Women: The Paradox of Ethnic Patriarchy." *Sociological Focus* 28, no. 2 (1995): 161–76.

———. "New People in the New South: An Overview of Southern Immigration." *Southern Cultures* 13, no. 4 (2007): 24–44.

———. "Vietnamese-American Catholicism: Transplanted and Flourishing." *U.S. Catholic Historian* 18, no. 1 (Winter 2000): 36–53.

Bao, Jiemin. *Creating a Buddhist Community: A Thai Temple in Silicon Valley.* Philadelphia: Temple University Press, 2015.

Bảo Thông and Lê Thái Ất. *Tu tại gia* [Practicing as a householder]. Westminster, CA: Cát Tiên, 2010.

Bell, Sandra. "British Theravada Buddhism: Otherworldly Theories, and the Theory of Exchange." *Journal of Contemporary Religion* 13, no. 2 (1998): 149–70.

Benhabib, Seyla. *The Rights of Others: Aliens, Residents, and Citizens.* Cambridge: Cambridge University Press, 2004.

Bingenheimer, Marcus. *Island of Guanyin: Mount Putuo and Its Gazetteers.* New York: Oxford University Press, 2016.

Bourdieu, Pierre. *Outline of a Theory of Practice.* Translated by Richard Nice. Cambridge Studies in Cultural Anthropology 16. Cambridge: Cambridge University Press, 1977.

Bow, Leslie. *Partly Colored: Asian Americans and Racial Anomaly in the Segregated South.* New York: New York University Press, 2010.

Brasseaux, Carl A. *Acadiana: Louisiana's Historic Cajun Country.* Baton Rouge: Louisiana State University Press, 2011.

Braun, Erik. *The Birth of Insight: Meditation, Modern Buddhism, and the Burmese Monk Ledi Sayadaw.* Chicago: University of Chicago Press, 2016.

Brettell, Caroline B., and Deborah Reed-Danahay. *Civic Engagements: The Citizenship Practices of Indian and Vietnamese Immigrants.* Stanford, CA: Stanford University Press, 2012.

Breyer, Chloe Anne. "Religious Liberty in Law and Practice: Vietnamese Home Temples and the First Amendment." *Journal of Church and State* 35, no. 2 (1993): 367–401.

Buddhist Text Translation Society. *Repentance Ritual of the Emperor of Liang.* Ukiah, CA: Buddhist Text Translation Society, 2016.

Cadge, Wendy. "De Facto Congregationalism and the Religious Organizations of Post-1965 Immigrants to the United States: A Revised Approach." *Journal of the American Academy of Religion* 76, no. 2 (2008): 344–74.

———. *Heartwood: The First Generation of Theravada Buddhism in America.* Chicago: University of Chicago Press, 2005.

Campanella, Richard. *Cityscapes of New Orleans*. Baton Rouge: Louisiana State University Press, 2017.

———. "Gulf Souths, Gulf Streams, and Their Dispersions: A Geographer's Take." *Southern Literary Journal* 46, no. 2 (2014): 17–32.

———. *The West Bank of Greater New Orleans: A Historical Geography*. Baton Rouge: Louisiana State University Press, 2020.

Cartwright, Keith, and Ruth Salvaggio. "Introduction: Gulf Souths, Gulf Streams, and Their Dispersions." *Southern Literary Journal* 46, no. 2 (2014): 1–16.

Chan, Yiu Kwan. "Popular Buddhist Ritual in Contemporary Hong Kong: Shuilu Fahui, a Buddhist Rite for Saving All Sentient Beings of Water and Land." *Buddhist Studies Review* 25, no. 1 (2008): 90–105.

Cheah, Joseph. *Race and Religion in American Buddhism: White Supremacy and Immigrant Adaptation*. New York: Oxford University Press, 2011.

Chen, Carolyn. *Getting Saved in America: Taiwanese Immigration and Religious Experience*. Princeton, NJ: Princeton University Press, 2008.

Chen, Carolyn, and Russell Jeung, eds. *Sustaining Faith Traditions: Race, Ethnicity, and Religion among the Latino and Asian American Second Generation*. New York: New York University Press, 2012.

Clifford, James. "Diasporas." *Cultural Anthropology* 9, no. 3 (1994): 302–38.

———. "Looking Several Ways: Anthropology and Native Heritage in Alaska." *Current Anthropology* 45, no. 1 (2004): 5–30.

Cole, Alan. *Mothers and Sons in Chinese Buddhism*. Stanford, CA: Stanford University Press, 1998.

———. "The Passion of Mulian's Mother: Narrative Blood and Maternal Sacrifices in Chinese Buddhism." In *Family in Buddhism*, edited by Liz Wilson, 119–46. Albany: State University of New York Press, 2013.

Cook, Joanna. *Meditation in Modern Buddhism: Renunciation and Change in Thai Monastic Life*. Cambridge: Cambridge University Press, 2010.

Dang, Thuy Vo. "The Cultural Work of Anticommunism in the San Diego Vietnamese American Community." *Amerasia Journal* 31, no. 2 (2005): 65–86.

David, Emmanuel. "Cultural Trauma, Memory, and Gendered Collective Action: The Case of Women of the Storm following Hurricane Katrina." *NWSA Journal* 20, no. 3 (2008): 138–62.

Deleuze, Gilles, and Félix Guattari. *A Thousand Plateaus: Capitalism and Schizophrenia*. Translated by Brian Massumi. Minneapolis: University of Minnesota Press, 1987.

DeVido, Elise A. "The Influence of Chinese Master Taixu on Buddhism in Vietnam." *Journal of Global Buddhism* 10 (2009): 413–58.

Đỗ Thiện. "Unjust-Death Deification and Burnt Offering: Towards an Integrative View of Popular Religion in Contemporary Southern Vietnam." In *Modernity and Re-enchantment: Religion in Post-revolutionary Vietnam*, edited by Philip Taylor, 161–93. Singapore: Institute of Southeast Asian Studies, 2007.

Dorais, Louis-Jacques. "Politics, Kinship, and Ancestors: Some Diasporic Dimensions of the Vietnamese Experience in North America." *Journal of Vietnamese Studies* 5, no. 2 (2010): 91–132.

Douglas, Mary. *Natural Symbols*. London: Routledge, 1996.

Dror, Olga. *Cult, Culture, and Authority: Princess Liễu Hạnh in Vietnamese History*. Honolulu: University of Hawai'i Press, 2007.

Duong, Lan P. *Treacherous Subjects: Gender, Culture, and Trans-Vietnamese Feminism*. Philadelphia: Temple University Press, 2012.

Durkheim, Émile. *The Elementary Forms of the Religious Life*. Translated by Joseph Ward Swain. London: Allen and Unwin, 1957.

Elliott, James R., and Marcel Ionescu. "Postwar Immigration to the Deep South Triad: What Can a Peripheral Region Tell Us about Immigrant Settlement and Employment?" *Sociological Spectrum* 23, no. 2 (April 2003): 159–80.

Espina, Marina E. *Filipinos in Louisiana*. New Orleans: A. F. Laborde, 1988.

Espiritu, Yến Lê. *Asian American Panethnicity: Bridging Institutions and Identities*. Philadelphia: Temple University Press, 1992.

———. *Body Counts: The Vietnam War and Militarized Refugees*. Berkeley: University of California Press, 2014.

———. "Toward a Critical Refugee Study: The Vietnamese Refugee Subject in US Scholarship." *Journal of Vietnamese Studies* 1, no. 1–2 (2006): 410–33.

Faure, Bernard. *The Rhetoric of Immediacy: A Cultural Critique of Chan/Zen Buddhism*. Princeton, NJ: Princeton University Press, 1994.

Fong, Vanessa. "Filial Nationalism among Chinese Teenagers with Global Identities." *American Ethnologist* 31, no. 4 (2004): 631–48.

Ford, Eugene. *Cold War Monks: Buddhism and America's Secret Strategy in Southeast Asia*. New Haven, CT: Yale University Press, 2017.

Gaillard, Frye. "After the Storms: Tradition and Change in Bayou La Batre." *Journal of American History* 94, no. 3 (2007): 856–62.

Gleig, Ann. *American Dharma: Buddhism beyond Modernity*. New Haven, CT: Yale University Press, 2019.

Goldstein, Joseph. *One Dharma: The Emerging Western Buddhism*. Reprint, New York: HarperOne, 2003.

Gombrich, Richard. "'Merit Transference' in Sinhalese Buddhism: A Case Study of the Interaction between Doctrine and Practice." *History of Religions* 11, no. 2 (November 1971): 203–19.

Goscha, Christopher. *Vietnam: A New History*. New York: Basic Books, 2016.

Grant, Beata, and Wilt L. Idema, trans. *Escape from Blood Pond Hell: The Tales of Mulian and Woman Huang*. Seattle: University of Washington Press, 2011.

Gross, Rita M. *Buddhism after Patriarchy: A Feminist History, Analysis, and Reconstruction of Buddhism*. Albany: State University of New York Press, 1993.

Gustafsson, Mai Lan. *War and Shadows: The Haunting of Vietnam*. Ithaca, NY: Cornell University Press, 2010.

Hansen, Anne Ruth. *How to Behave: Buddhism and Modernity in Colonial Cambodia, 1860–1930*. Honolulu: University of Hawai'i Press, 2007.

Hardacre, Helen. *Marketing the Menacing Fetus in Japan*. Berkeley: University of California Press, 1997.

Harms, Erik. *Saigon's Edge: On the Margins of Ho Chi Minh City*. Minneapolis: University of Minnesota Press, 2011.

Heng Sure and Heng Chau. *News from True Cultivators—Letters to the Venerable Abbot Hua*. 2nd ed. Burlingame, CA: Buddhist Text Translation Society, 2002.

Hess, Julia Meredith. *Immigrant Ambassadors: Citizenship and Belonging in the Tibetan Diaspora*. Stanford, CA: Stanford University Press, 2009.

Hickey, Wakoh Shannon. "Two Buddhisms, Three Buddhisms, and Racism." *Journal of Global Buddhism* 11 (2010): 1–25.

Hoskins, Janet. *The Divine Eye and the Diaspora: Vietnamese Syncretism Becomes Transpacific Caodaism*. Honolulu: University of Hawai'i Press, 2015.

Hoskins, Janet, and Viet Thanh Nguyen, eds. *Transpacific Studies: Framing an Emerging Field*. Honolulu: University of Hawai'i Press, 2014.

Hurd, Elizabeth Shakman. "Believing in Religious Freedom." In *Politics of Religious Freedom*, edited by Winnifred Fallers Sullivan, Elizabeth Shakman Hurd, Saba Mahmood, and Peter G. Danchin, 45–56. Chicago: University of Chicago Press, 2015.

Ikels, Charlotte, ed. *Filial Piety: Practice and Discourse in Contemporary East Asia*. Stanford, CA: Stanford University Press, 2004.

Iwamura, Jane. *Virtual Orientalism: Asian Religions and American Popular Culture*. New York: Oxford University Press, 2011.

Jamieson, Neil L. *Understanding Vietnam*. Berkeley: University of California Press, 1995.

Jeung, Russell, Carolyn Chen, and Jerry Z. Park. "Introduction: Religious, Racial, and Ethnic Identities of the New Second Generation." In *Sustaining Faith Traditions: Race, Ethnicity, and Religion among the Latino and Asian*

American Second Generation, edited by Carolyn Chen and Russell Jeung, 1–22. New York: New York University Press, 2012.

Johnson, Cedric. *The Neoliberal Deluge: Hurricane Katrina, Late Capitalism, and the Remaking of New Orleans*. Minneapolis: University of Minnesota Press, 2011.

Johnson, Paul C. *Diaspora Conversions: Black Carib Religion and the Recovery of Africa*. Berkeley: University of California Press, 2007.

Jones, Charles B. *Chinese Pure Land Buddhism: Understanding a Tradition of Practice*. Honolulu: University of Hawai'i Press, 2019.

Jones, Kathleen W. "Mother's Day: The Creation, Promotion and Meaning of a New Holiday in the Progressive Era." *Texas Studies in Literature and Language* 22, no. 2 (1980): 175–96.

Jun, Helen Heran. *Race for Citizenship: Black Orientalism and Asian Uplift from Pre-emancipation to Neoliberal America*. New York: New York University Press, 2011.

Karetzky, Patricia Eichenbaum. *Guanyin*. Oxford: Oxford University Press, 2004.

Kelley, Liam C. "'Confucianism' in Vietnam: A State of the Field Essay." *Journal of Vietnamese Studies* 1, no. 1–2 (2006): 314–70.

Keyes, Charles F. "Merit-Transference in the Kammic Theory of Popular Theravada Buddhism." In *Karma: An Anthropological Inquiry*, edited by Charles F. Keyes and E. Valentine Daniel, 261–86. Berkeley: University of California Press, 1983.

Kim, Claire Jean. "The Racial Triangulation of Asian Americans." *Politics and Society* 27, no. 1 (1999): 105–38.

Kim, Kwang Chung, R. Stephen Warner, and Ho-Youn Kwon. "Korean American Religion in International Perspective." In *Korean Americans and Their Religions: Pilgrims and Missionaries from a Different Shore*, edited by Ho-Youn Kwon, Kwang Chung Kim, and R. Stephen Warner, 3–24. University Park: Pennsylvania State University Press, 2001.

Kim, Nami. "Letting Bayous Be Bygones: Should Louisiana Be Allowed to Mandate Use of the Pre-Socialist Vietnam Flag?" Comments. *Pacific Rim Law and Policy Journal* 14, no. 1 (2005): 129–58.

Kinh Vu Lan và Báo Hiếu [Vu Lan and Filial Piety Sutras]. Hanoi: Nhà xuất bản Tôn giáo, 2012.

Kitiarsa, Pattana. "Buddha-izing a Global City-State: Transnational Religious Mobilities, Spiritual Marketplace, and Thai Migrant Monks in Singapore." *Mobilities* 5, no. 2 (2010): 257–75.

Klein, Christina. *Cold War Orientalism: Asia in the Middlebrow Imagination, 1945–1961*. Berkeley: University of California Press, 2003.

Kuppinger, Petra. "Flexible Topographies: Muslim Spaces in a German Cityscape." *Social and Cultural Geography* 15, no. 6 (2014): 627–44.

Kurien, Prema. "Decoupling Religion and Ethnicity: Second-Generation Indian American Christians." *Qualitative Sociology* 35, no. 4 (December 2012): 447–68.

Kwon, Heonik. "Can the Dead Suffer Trauma? Religion and Science after the Vietnam War." In *Religion and Science as Forms of Life: Anthropological Insights into Reason and Unreason*, edited by Carles Salazar and Joan Bestard, 207–20. New York: Berghahn Books, 2015.

———. *Ghosts of War in Vietnam*. Cambridge: Cambridge University Press, 2008.

———. *The Other Cold War*. New York: Columbia University Press, 2010.

Lam, Andrew. "Who Will Light the Incense?" In *East Eats West: Writing in Two Hemispheres*, 69–71. Berkeley, CA: Heyday, 2010.

Lambek, Michael. *Ordinary Ethics: Anthropology, Language, and Action*. New York: Fordham University Press, 2010.

Lang, Karen. "Shaven Heads and Loose Hair: Buddhist Attitudes toward Hair and Sexuality." In *Off with Her Head! The Denial of Women's Identity in Myth, Religion, and Culture*, edited by Howard Eilberg-Schwartz and Wendy Doniger, 32–52. Berkeley: University of California Press, 1995.

Langford, Jean M. *Consoling Ghosts: Stories of Medicine and Mourning from Southeast Asians in Exile*. Minneapolis: University of Minnesota Press, 2013.

Le, Andrew Nova. "Episodic Ethnicity: A Case Study of a Japanese Buddhist Temple." *Journal of Ethnic and Migration Studies* 45, no. 15 (2018): 2989–3006.

Lee, Erika. *The Making of Asian America: A History*. New York: Simon and Schuster, 2015.

Leshkowich, Ann Marie. *Essential Trade: Vietnamese Women in a Changing Marketplace*. Honolulu: University of Hawai'i Press, 2014.

Lieu, Nhi T. *The American Dream in Vietnamese*. Minneapolis: University of Minnesota Press, 2011.

———. "Performing Culture in Diaspora: Assimilation and Hybridity in *Paris by Night* Videos and Vietnamese American Niche Media." In *Alien Encounters: Popular Culture in Asian America*, edited by Mimi Thi Nguyen and Thuy Linh Nguyen Tu, 194–220. Durham, NC: Duke University Press, 2007.

Lincoln, Martha, and Bruce Lincoln. "Toward a Critical Hauntology: Bare Afterlife and the Ghosts of Ba Chúc." *Comparative Studies in Society and History* 57, no. 1 (2015): 191–220.

Lipman, Jana K. "A Refugee Camp in America: Fort Chaffee and Vietnamese and Cuban Refugees, 1975–1982." *Journal of American Ethnic History* 33, no. 2 (2014): 57–87.

Lipsitz, George. "Learning from New Orleans: The Social Warrant of Hostile Privatism and Competitive Consumer Citizenship." *Cultural Anthropology* 21, no. 3 (2006): 451–68.

Loewen, James W. *The Mississippi Chinese: Between Black and White.* 2nd ed. Long Grove, IL: Waveland Press, 1988.

Lowe, Jeffrey S., and Todd C. Shaw. "After Katrina: Racial Regimes and Human Development Barriers in the Gulf Coast Region." *American Quarterly* 61, no. 3 (2009): 803–27.

Lowe, Lisa. *The Intimacies of Four Continents.* Durham, NC: Duke University Press, 2015.

Lozada, Eriberto P., Jr. "Framing Globalization: Wedding Pictures, Funeral Photography, and Family Snapshots in Rural China." *Visual Anthropology* 19, no. 1 (2006): 87–103.

Luhrmann, T. M. *When God Talks Back: Understanding the American Evangelical Relationship with God.* New York: Alfred A. Knopf, 2012.

Luong, Hy Van. *Discursive Practices and Linguistic Meanings: The Vietnamese System of Person Reference.* Amsterdam: John Benjamins, 1990.

———. "Vietnamese Kinship: Structural Principles and the Socialist Transformation in Northern Vietnam." *Journal of Asian Studies* 48, no. 4 (1989): 741–56.

Mahmood, Saba. "Feminist Theory, Embodiment, and the Docile Agent: Some Reflections on the Egyptian Islamic Revival." *Cultural Anthropology* 16, no. 2 (2001): 202–36.

Makley, Charlene E. *The Violence of Liberation: Gender and Tibetan Buddhist Revival in Post-Mao China.* Berkeley: University of California Press, 2007.

Malarney, Shaun Kingsley. "Festivals and the Dynamics of the Exceptional Dead in Northern Vietnam." *Journal of Southeast Asian Studies* 38, no. 3 (2007): 515–40.

Masquelier, Adeline. "Dirt, Undress, and Difference: An Introduction." In *Dirt, Undress, and Difference: Critical Perspectives on the Body's Surface,* edited by Adeline Masquelier, 1–33. Bloomington: Indiana University Press, 2005.

———. "Why Katrina's Victims Aren't Refugees: Musings on a 'Dirty' Word." *American Anthropology* 108, no. 4 (2006): 735–43.

McDaniel, Justin Thomas. *Architects of Buddhist Leisure: Socially Disengaged Buddhism in Asia's Museums, Monuments, and Amusement Parks.* Honolulu: University of Hawai'i Press, 2017.

McDowell, Andrew J. "Chunnilal's Hauntology: Rajasthan's Ghosts, Time Going Badly, and Anthropological Voice." *Ethos* 47, no. 4 (2019): 501–18.

McHale, Shawn Frederick. *Print and Power: Confucianism, Communism, and Buddhism in the Making of Modern Vietnam*. Honolulu: University of Hawai'i Press, 2004.

McLellan, Janet. *Many Petals of the Lotus: Five Asian Buddhist Communities in Toronto*. Toronto: University of Toronto Press, 1999.

McMahan, David L. "The Jade Buddha for Universal Peace." Object Narrative. *Conversations: An Online Journal of the Center for the Study of Material and Visual Cultures of Religion*, 2014. https://mavcor.yale.edu /conversations/object-narratives/jade-buddha-universal-peace.

———. *The Making of Buddhist Modernism*. Oxford: Oxford University Press, 2008.

Min, Pyong Gap. *Preserving Ethnicity through Religion in America: Korean Protestants and Indian Hindus across Generations*. New York: New York University Press, 2010.

Mintz, Sidney W. "The Localization of Anthropological Practice: From Area Studies to Transnationalism." *Critique of Anthropology* 18, no. 2 (1998): 117–33.

Mitchell, Scott A. *Buddhism in America: Global Religion, Local Contexts*. London: Bloomsbury Academic, 2016.

Ngai, Mae M. *Impossible Subjects: Illegal Aliens and the Making of Modern America*. Princeton, NJ: Princeton University Press, 2004.

Nguyen, Cuong Tu, and A. W. Barber. "Vietnamese Buddhism in North America: Tradition and Acculturation." In *The Faces of Buddhism in America*, edited by Charles S. Prebish and Kenneth K. Tanaka, 129–46. Berkeley: University of California Press, 1998.

Nguyen, Marguerite. "'Like We Lost Our Citizenship': Vietnamese Americans, African Americans, and Hurricane Katrina." In *Asian Americans in Dixie: Race and Migration in the South*, edited by Khyati Y. Joshi and Jigna Desai, 264–88. Urbana: University of Illinois Press, 2013.

Nguyen, Mimi Thi. *The Gift of Freedom: War, Debt, and Other Refugee Passages*. Durham, NC: Duke University Press, 2012.

Nguyễn, Patricia. "*salt | water*: Vietnamese Refugee Passages, Memory, and Statelessness at Sea." *WSQ: Women's Studies Quarterly* 45, nos. 1–2 (2017): 94–111.

Nguyen, Phi-Vân. "A Secular State for a Religious Nation: The Republic of Vietnam and Religious Nationalism, 1946–1963." *Journal of Asian Studies* 77, no. 3 (2018): 741–71.

Nguyen, Phuong Tran. *Becoming Refugee American: The Politics of Rescue in Little Saigon*. Urbana: University of Illinois Press, 2017.

Nguyen, Viet Thanh. *Nothing Ever Dies: Vietnam and the Memory of War.* Cambridge, MA: Harvard University Press, 2016.

———. "Speak of the Dead, Speak of Viet Nam: The Ethics and Aesthetics of Minority Discourse." *CR: The New Centennial Review* 6, no. 2 (2006): 7–37.

Nguyen, Viet Thanh, and Janet Hoskins. "Introduction: Transpacific Studies: Critical Perspectives on an Emerging Field." In *Transpacific Studies: Framing an Emerging Field*, edited by Janet Hoskins and Viet Thanh Nguyen, 1–38. Honolulu: University of Hawai'i Press, 2014.

Ninh, Thien-Huong T. "Colored Faith: Vietnamese American Catholics Struggle for Equality within Their Multicultural Church." *Amerasia Journal* 40, no. 1 (2014): 80–96.

———. *Race, Gender, and Religion in the Vietnamese Diaspora: The New Chosen People.* Cham, Switzerland: Springer, 2017.

Nonini, Donald M. "Critique: Creating the Transnational South." In *The American South in a Global World*, edited by James L. Peacock, Harry L. Watson, and Carrie R. Matthews, 247–64. Chapel Hill: University of North Carolina Press, 2005.

Numrich, Paul D. *Old Wisdom in the New World: Americanization in Two Immigrant Theravada Buddhist Temples.* Knoxville: University of Tennessee Press, 1996.

Ohnuma, Reiko. *Ties That Bind: Maternal Imagery and Discourse in Indian Buddhism.* New York: Oxford University Press, 2012.

Ong, Aihwa. *Buddha Is Hiding: Refugees, Citizenship, the New America.* Berkeley: University of California Press, 2003.

Parikh, Crystal. "Minority." In *Keywords for Asian American Studies*, edited by Cathy J. Schlund-Vials, Linda Trinh Võ, and K. Scott Wong, 161–64. New York: New York University Press, 2015.

Park, Yoosun, Joshua Miller, and Bao Chau Van. "Everything Has Changed: Narratives of the Vietnamese American Community in Post-Katrina Mississippi." *Journal of Sociology and Social Welfare* 37, no. 3 (2010): 79–106.

Paul, Diana Y., and Frances Wilson. *Women in Buddhism: Images of the Feminine in the Mahayana Tradition.* Berkeley: University of California Press, 1985.

Payne, Richard K. "Pure Land or Pure Mind? Locus of Awakening and American Popular Religious Culture." *Journal of Global Buddhism* 16 (2015): 16–32.

Peché, Linda Ho. "'I Would Pay Homage, Not Go All "Bling"': Vietnamese American Youth Reflect on Family and Religious Life." In *Sustaining Faith Traditions: Race, Ethnicity, and Religion among the Latino and Asian*

American Second Generation, edited by Carolyn Chen and Russell Jeung, 222–40. New York: New York University Press, 2012.

Pérez, Elizabeth. *Religion in the Kitchen: Cooking, Talking, and the Making of Black Atlantic Traditions*. New York: New York University Press, 2016.

Povinelli, Elizabeth A. *The Cunning of Recognition: Indigenous Alterities and the Making of Australian Multiculturalism*. Durham, NC: Duke University Press, 2002.

Preston, Andrew. "Introduction: The Religious Cold War." In *Religion and the Cold War: A Global Perspective*, edited by Philip E. Muehlenbeck, xi–xxii. Nashville: Vanderbilt University Press, 2012.

Purser, Ronald. *McMindfulness: How Mindfulness Became the New Capitalist Spirituality*. London: Watkins Media, 2019.

Queen, Christopher, and Duncan Ryūken Williams. *American Buddhism: Methods and Findings in Recent Scholarship*. Abingdon, Oxon: Routledge, 2013.

Quli, Nathalie E. F. "Laicization in Four Sri Lankan Buddhist Temples in Northern California." PhD diss., Graduate Theological Union, Berkeley, CA, 2010.

Rana, Junaid Akram. *Terrifying Muslims: Race and Labor in the South Asian Diaspora*. Durham, NC: Duke University Press, 2011.

Regis, Helen. "Blackness and the Politics of Memory in the New Orleans Second Line." *American Ethnologist* 28, no. 4 (2001): 752–77.

Rozenberg, Guillaume. *The Immortals: Faces of the Incredible in Buddhist Burma*. Translated by Ward Keeler. Topics in Contemporary Buddhism. Honolulu: University of Hawai'i Press, 2015.

Rudrappa, Sharmila. *Ethnic Routes to Becoming American: Indian Immigrants and the Cultures of Citizenship*. New Brunswick, NJ: Rutgers University Press, 2004.

Samuels, Jeffrey. "Families Matter: Ambiguous Attitudes toward Child Ordination in Contemporary Sri Lanka." In *Family in Buddhism*, edited by Liz Wilson, 89–115. Albany: State University of New York Press, 2013.

Scheper-Hughes, Nancy, and Margaret M. Lock. "The Mindful Body: A Prolegomenon to Future Work in Medical Anthropology." *Medical Anthropology Quarterly* 1, no. 1 (1987): 6–41.

Schopen, Gregory. "Archaeology and Protestant Presuppositions in the Study of Indian Buddhism." *History of Religions* 31, no. 1 (1991): 1–23.

Scott, Rachelle M. *Nirvana for Sale? Buddhism, Wealth, and the Dhammakāya Temple in Contemporary Thailand*. Albany: State University of New York Press, 2009.

Sidnell, Jack, and Merav Shohet. "The Problem of Peers in Vietnamese Interaction." *Journal of the Royal Anthropological Institute* 19, no. 3 (2013): 618–38.

Sihlé, Nicolas. "Towards a Comparative Anthropology of the Buddhist Gift (and Other Transfers)." *Religion Compass* 9, no. 11 (2015): 352–85.

Singh, Nikhil Pal. *Black Is a Country: Race and the Unfinished Struggle for Democracy*. Cambridge, MA: Harvard University Press, 2004.

Small, Ivan V. *Currencies of Imagination: Channeling Money and Chasing Mobility in Vietnam*. Ithaca, NY: Cornell University Press, 2019.

Smith, C. Calvin. "The Response of Arkansans to Prisoners of War and Japanese Americans in Arkansas, 1942–1945." *Arkansas Historical Quarterly* 53, no. 3 (1994): 340–66.

Soucy, Alexander. *The Buddha Side: Gender, Power, and Buddhist Practice in Vietnam*. Honolulu: University of Hawai'i Press, 2012.

———. "Contemporary Vietnamese Buddhism." In *The Oxford Handbook of Contemporary Buddhism*, edited by Michael K. Jerryson, 177–95. New York: Oxford University Press, 2017.

———. "Outpost Buddhism: Vietnamese Buddhists in Halifax." *Canadian Journal of Buddhist Studies* 9 (2013): 106–28.

———. "A Reappraisal of Vietnamese Buddhism's Status as 'Ethnic.'" *Journal of Vietnamese Studies* 12, no. 2 (2017): 20–48.

Sparham, Gareth. "Saṅgha." In *Encyclopedia of Buddhism*, edited by Robert E. Buswell Jr., 2:740–44. New York: Macmillan Reference USA, 2003.

Sponberg, Alan. "Attitudes toward Women and the Feminine in Early Buddhism." In *Buddhism, Sexuality, and Gender*, edited by José Ignacio Cabezón, 3–36. Albany: State University of New York Press, 1992.

Starin, Dawn. "World Heritage Designation: Blessing or Threat?" *Critical Asian Studies* 40, no. 4 (2008): 639–52.

Starr, Paul D. "Troubled Waters: Vietnamese Fisherfolk on America's Gulf Coast." *International Migration Review* 15, no. 1–2 (1981): 226–38.

Suzuki, Daisetsu Teitaro. *Selected Works of D. T. Suzuki*. Vol. 2, *Pure Land*, edited by James C. Dobbins. Oakland: University of California Press, 2015.

Tambiah, S. J. "The Renouncer: His Individuality and His Community." *Contributions to Indian Sociology* 15, no. 1–2 (1981): 299–320.

Tanabe, George J., Jr. "Merit and Merit-Making." In *Encyclopedia of Buddhism*, edited by Robert E. Buswell Jr., 2:532–34. New York: Macmillan Reference USA, 2003.

Tang, Eric. "A Gulf Unites Us: The Vietnamese Americans of Black New Orleans East." *American Quarterly* 63, no. 1 (2011): 117–49.

Taylor, Keith Weller. *The Birth of Vietnam*. Berkeley: University of California Press, 1991.

Taylor, Philip. *Goddess on the Rise: Pilgrimage and Popular Religion in Vietnam*. Honolulu: University of Hawai'i Press, 2004.

———. *The Khmer Lands of Vietnam: Environment, Cosmology and Sovereignty*. Singapore: National University of Singapore Press, 2014.

———. "Modernity and Re-enchantment in Post-revolutionary Vietnam." In *Modernity and Re-enchantment: Religion in Post-revolutionary Vietnam*, edited by Philip Taylor, 1–56. Singapore: Institute of Southeast Asian Studies, 2007.

Tchen, John Kuo Wei. *New York before Chinatown: Orientalism and the Shaping of American Culture, 1776–1882*. Baltimore: Johns Hopkins University Press, 1999.

Teiser, Stephen F. *The Ghost Festival in Medieval China*. Princeton, NJ: Princeton University Press, 1998.

Thích Minh Thời, ed. *Kinh nhật tụng* [Daily chants]. 7th printing. Hanoi: Nhà xuất bản Tôn giáo, 2008.

Thich Nhat Hanh [Thích Nhất Hạnh]. *No Mud, No Lotus: The Art of Transforming Suffering*. Berkeley, CA: Parallax Press, 2014.

———. *A Rose for Your Pocket: An Appreciation of Motherhood*. Berkeley, CA: Parallax Press, 2008.

Thich Quang Minh. "Vietnamese Buddhism in America." PhD diss., Florida State University, 2007.

Thích Thiên-Ân. *Buddhism and Zen in Vietnam in Relation to the Development of Buddhism in Asia*. Rutland, VT: Charles E. Tuttle, 1975.

Thích Tịnh Từ. "Như một phép lạ nhiệm mầu" [Like a miracle]. In *Những Mẩu Chuyện Linh Ứng Quán Thế Âm* [Miracle tales of Quán Thế Âm], 3:20–26. Watsonville, CA: Tu viện Kim Sơn, n.d.

Trần Hữu Quang. "The Question of Reconciliation in Vietnam: A Relevant Social Issue." *Peace and Change* 38, no. 4 (2013): 411–25.

Truitt, Allison J. *Dreaming of Money in Ho Chi Minh City*. Seattle: University of Washington Press, 2013.

———. "Quán Thế Âm of the Transpacific." *Journal of Vietnamese Studies* 12, no. 2 (2017): 83–107.

Tsing, Anna. *The Mushroom at the End of the World: On the Possibility of Life in Capitalist Ruins*. Princeton, NJ: Princeton University Press, 2015.

Tuan, Mia. *Forever Foreigners or Honorary Whites? The Asian Ethnic Experience Today*. New Brunswick, NJ: Rutgers University Press, 1999.

Tuan, Yi-Fu. "Humanistic Geography." *Annals of the Association of American Geographers* 66, no. 2 (1976): 266–76.

Turner, Alicia Marie. *Saving Buddhism: The Impermanence of Religion in Colonial Burma*. Honolulu: University of Hawai'i Press, 2014.

Tweed, Thomas A. *The American Encounter with Buddhism, 1844–1912: Victorian Culture and the Limits of Dissent*. Bloomington: Indiana University Press, 1992.

———. *Crossing and Dwelling: A Theory of Religion*. Cambridge, MA: Harvard University Press, 2006.

Tylor, Edward Burnett. *Primitive Culture: Researches into the Development of Mythology, Philosophy, Religion, Art, and Custom*. 2 vols. Cambridge: Cambridge University Press, 2010.

Upton, Dell. *Architecture in the United States*. Oxford: Oxford University Press, 1998.

VanLandingham, Mark. *Weathering Katrina: Culture and Recovery among Vietnamese Americans*. New York: Russell Sage Foundation, 2017.

Viveiros de Castro, Eduardo. "Cosmological Deixis and Amerindian Perspectivism." *Journal of the Royal Anthropological Institute* 4, no. 3 (1998): 469–88.

Võ Văn Tường. *Danh lam nước Việt* [Vietnam's famous pagodas]. Hanoi: Nhà xuất bản Mỹ thuật, 1995.

———. *108 danh lam cổ tự Việt Nam* [108 famous and ancient Buddhist temples and pagodas in Vietnam]. Hue: Nhà xuất bản Thuận hóa, 2007.

Voyce, Malcolm. *Foucault, Buddhism and Disciplinary Rules*. London: Routledge, 2017.

Walsh, Michael J. *Sacred Economies: Buddhist Monasticism and Territoriality in Medieval China*. New York: Columbia University Press, 2010.

Watson, Burton, trans. *The Lotus Sutra*. New York: Columbia University Press, 1993.

Webre, Stephen. "The Problem of Indian Slavery in Spanish Louisiana, 1769–1803." *Louisiana History: The Journal of the Louisiana Historical Association* 25, no. 2 (1984): 117–35.

Williams, Duncan Ryūken. *American Sutra: A Story of Faith and Freedom in the Second World War*. Cambridge, MA: Belknap Press of Harvard University Press, 2019.

Wilson, Jeff. *Dixie Dharma: Inside a Buddhist Temple in the American South*. Chapel Hill: University of North Carolina Press, 2012.

———. *Mindful America: The Mutual Transformation of Buddhist Meditation and American Culture*. New York: Oxford University Press, 2014.

Wilson, Liz, ed. *Family in Buddhism*. Albany: State University of New York Press, 2013.

Wood, Joseph. "Vietnamese American Place Making in Northern Virginia."
Geographical Review 87, no. 1 (1997): 59–72.

Woods, Clyde Adrian. *Development Arrested: The Blues and Plantation Power in the Mississippi Delta*. New York: Verso, 1998.

Yü, Chün-fang. *Kuan-Yin: The Chinese Transformation of Avalokiteśvara*. New York: Columbia University Press, 2001.

Yun, Lisa. *The Coolie Speaks: Chinese Indentured Laborers and African Slaves in Cuba*. Philadelphia: Temple University Press, 2009.

Zhou, Min, and Carl L. Bankston III. *Growing Up American: How Vietnamese Children Adapt to Life in the United States*. New York: Russell Sage Foundation, 1998.

INDEX

A

"A Rose for Your Pocket," 116–18

Acadiana, 137

accumulating merit: money-like qualities, 52; Mulian, 104; offsetting karmic conditioning, 52–53; purification, 87; store of, 82, 144

Aguilar-San Juan, Karin, 152

American War, 104, 123. *See also* Vietnam War

Americanizing Buddhism, 11

Amitābha Buddha: bodhisattva attendant to, 105–6, 121; celestial realm of, 75, 124; enlightenment, 7; "Homage to Amitābha Buddha," 124, 150; image of, 66; Pure Land overseen by, 7, 10; reciting the name of, 74–75; statues, 51, 78, 85, 92, 129

ancestral spirits: care for, 130; identity of, 129; liberation of, 153; merit-making, 52; offerings, 103; praying for, 177n3; releasing, 112. *See also* Pure Land

ancestral time: evoking, 81; guardians of, 104, 119–20; idealization of, 174n23; maternal figure, 105; memorialization and, 121; temporality, 73

Associated Catholic Charities (ACC) of New Orleans, 6, 26, 27–28

Avalokiteśvara. *See* Quán Thế Âm

B

Bà Đanh Pagoda, 153

Bao, Jiemin, 87

Baolian Chan Monastery, 136

Barber, A. W., 6, 146, 154

Bayou La Batre, Alabama, 40

Bell Drum of Wisdom, 79

Biloxi, Mississippi, 12*fig*, 22, 24, 39, 65–66

Blessing Bell, 56

Bồ Đề, Thích, 32

Bodhidharma, 7, 51, 56, 78, 144

bodhisattva: bow to, 141; incarnation of, 110; name-recitation, 79; path, 61; Thích Tịnh Từ monkhood, 155; vows, 8, 63. *See also* Quán Thế Âm

bowing: altar, 94; bless the land, 90*fig*; Buddhist practice of, 141; Liberation Rites of Water and Land, 144; Master Deep Awakening, 143; repentance, 140, 144, 145; ritual of, 142; three times, 66, 79, 129 breaking the ground, 86–87

Bright Awakening, Brother, 68

Buddha: birthday, 81, 94; blessings, 91; counseling of Mulian by, 101, 104, 113; gold robes signal closer to, 63; historical, 7–8, 48, 56, 61, 85; "in hiding," 31, 72; Jade Buddha, 83–84, 85, 91, 137, 139, 172n19; models of Buddhahood, 118; monastic precepts as handed down by, 61; statues, 97–98; teachings of, 7, 115; Three Jewels, 4, 7, 47, 62, 79, 140

Buddha Hall: donations to, 83; formal ceremonies, 55, 78; Master Pure Word counseled, 87; raising funds, 84, 99; sanctioning the requests, 82; spatial dilemma, 92; worship hall, 89–91

Buddha name-recitation: Amitābha Buddha, 74, 75; bell chime, 79; collective power, 66; "easy path," 7, 74; effort of, 76, 143; embodied practices, 124; formal services, 75; merit-making activities, 52; practice at home, 99

"Buddhist crisis," 16

Buddhist flags, 14, 72, 114

Buddhist Social Service Organization, 32

Buddist practices: adapted to internment camps, 11; broad appeal, 75; corrupted versions, 152; filial piety, 104; Mahayana Buddhism, 69; repentance, 144; wealth and, 92. *See also* practices

Burma, 8, 49, 51, 159n28, 160n44. *See also* Myanmar

C

Caine, Kwai Chang, 49

California Supreme Court, 129

Cambodian Fishermen's Community Center, 150

Cambodians, 26, 40, 175n7

Caodaism, 9, 30, 32, 33

Catholics: division with Buddhists, 16, 42; do not engage in merit practices, 129; privileged role of, 161n68; Vietnamese in New Orleans, 6, 26, 30, 35; Vietnamese in the Gulf South, 30, 38, 44

chanting: calming effects, 76; effort of, 76, 77, 144; form of concentration, 75; prayers, 8, 120; resonant voice to lead, 68; sutras, 8, 111, 113, 124; at temple ground-breaking, 32

Chinese Buddhism, 119, 120, 144, 150

Chinese Exclusion Act of 1882, 10, 24, 160n44, 161n58

Chinese laborers, 23–24

Chinese Pure Land, 152

Chùa Bồ Đề: built by lay Buddhists, 34; Hurricane Katrina response, 37; political importance, 33; prominence on the Gulf Coast, 32, 36*fig*; ritual specialists at, 136*fig*; root temple, 35

Chùa Chánh Giác, 40

citizenship: 1924 Immigration Act, 160n44; contours changing, 21, 25, 29; debates over, 23, 24; exclusion of Chinese laborers from, 24; mandates of, 21, 147; racial bar to, 161n59; rights and resources of, 28; status, 21; Vietnamese Buddhism shaped by modes of, 7; Vietnamese in the United States, 43, 122; warrant of, 36. *See also* racialization

Cold War: anticommunism, 43, 16; end of, 14; immigration policies, 17, 29; legacies of, 5; moral vocabulary of, 16, 43; opposition between capitalism and communism, 123; the "Oriental Monk" and US audiences, 18, 48; Orientalism, 15, 47; refugee policies, 16; scholars of, 16; shaping Vietnamese Buddhism, 7; sincerity of monks, 67, 149; social mandates of, 29; and temples, 5; United States–Asia integration, 14–15; Vietnamese in Louisiana, 13. *See also* Orientalism

collective spaces of worship: consecrated, 11; creating, 19; gatherings and dispersals, 152; strategic memory projects, 43; transformed into, 82. *See also* spaces of worship

colonialism: accommodating, 154; promotion of Christianity, 8; settler colonialism, 126, 134, 138, 139, 140

communism: capitalism and, 123; containment of, 14, 15–16, 24, 48; did not threaten Buddhism, 67; fleeing, 26; force against, 15, 178n23; renunciation of, 68

compassion, 36, 108, 130, 145. *See also* Quán Thế Âm

compatriot Buddhists: attending temples, 148; banner welcoming, 13*fig*, 113, 114; call to, 5, 13, 42; discourse around, 13; non-members of temple, 113; place-based origins, 42; as welcoming, 152

compatriots: bridge the distance through maternal imagery, 105; Buddhism shaped by religious pluralism, 11; Buddhist, 97, 105, 115; calling upon, 42, 44; camp newsletter assured resettled families well, 27; fund capital

projects, 105; Khmer, 69; possible donors, 105, 112; as the sangha, 97, 112, 120; Vietnamese gathered as, 41

Confucianism, 102, 103, 152

creolization, 22–23, 25

cultural assimilation: demands of, 133, 146; as expressed by immigration narrative, 147

Cuong Tu Nguyen. *See* Nguyen, Cuong Tu

D

Dalai Lama, 150–51

Đan Nguyên, 96

Đạo Quang, Thích, 39

Daoism, 152

death: after, 101; bad deaths, 127; dying well, 124, 140, 144; forgotten spirits, 127; ghosts, 126; good deaths, 126–27; violent, 127, 137, 139, 177n41

debt: filial piety, 101, 102, 174n43; intergenerational, 5, 145; to mothers, 102, 104, 108; social, 153. *See also* karmic debt

Deep Awakening, Master: definition of sangha, 61; female monks as dedicated as male monks, 57; at Florida monastery, 119, 132, 142; instructed the laity, 114; lay Buddhists acknowledge teacher, 64; liberation, 143; monastery in Northern California, 77; monastic sangha, 46–47; parents' request, 59–60; practice of accumulating merit, 52–53; prayed for statue donation, 109; Pure Land attainable in the present moment, 77–78; renunciation (leaving the family), 60; repentance, 140–41; responsibility to serve Gulf South, 60–61

prepared foods, 82, 113; sponsorship of singer performances, 94

137; Liberation Rites of Water and
Land, 135; monks, 19, 124; Mulian's
mother, 101, 103, 110, 113; people
who died in war, 15; soldier's soul,
124; untimely, violent, or unjust
death, 137

Liberation Rites of Water and Land,
135, 136*fig*, 144

Liễu Hạnh, 109

lighting incense, 94, 120, 146, 147

lotus flower, 21, 163n8

Lotus Sutra, 51, 107–8, 141

M

Magnolia Grove, xii, 91, 166n70.
See also Nhất Hạnh, Thích

Mahayana Buddhism: bodhisattvas,
61, 106; effort, 143; ethics of, 66; as
inclusive of laypeople, 57; magical
practices of, 69; Pure Land, 146;
split with Theravada Buddhism,
7–8; universal love, 118

Mãn Giác, Thích, 72, 105, 171n5

Manilamen, 23

maternal imagery: ancestral time, 105;
appealing to, 104; bodhisattva, 109;
conflicting, 19; filial piety, 101–2;
sangha linked to the homeland, 102,
105, 174n23

Mazu, 110

merit: attempt to gain, 144; cultivation
of, 18, 52; dedication of, 66, 136;
donations, 112, 120; entering
monastic life, 58; generating, 76–77,
83, 129; how money flows, 54; merit-
making activities, 50–51, 52, 129,
141; offsetting negative karma, 51;
and the relic tour, 53; of the sangha,
110, 114, 129; spiritual economy

around, 50; work transformed into,
86. *See also* accumulating merit

merit transference: ceremonies, 8; form
of spirit insurance, 52; liberation,
129; prayers, 53, 56; and repentance,
141; transpacific practices, 147; to
violent deaths, 139

mindfulness: cultivation of, 140, 142;
Eightfold Path, 171n8; practices of,
78, 114, 125, 143, 152; retreat, 151,
151*fig*; secular variant of meditation,
4, 50; walking meditation, 88*fig*

Mobile, Alabama, 22, 24, 40, 116,
166n70

model minorities, 17, 24, 147

moments of silence, 128

monastic robes, 57, 62–64

monastic sangha: in California, 41;
de-emphasized, 47; food and, 101,
131, 133, 134; in the Gulf South, 61,
83; "invisible merit economy," 50;
and merit, 51–53; monastic rules,
8, 9, 46–47; Oriental Monk, 18, 50;
representations of women, 119–20;
in Southeast Asia, 8, 15; support for,
83, 111, 155; tensions between lay
Buddhists and, 34, 65, 68, 70

monk-lay relations, 34, 48, 60, 64, 65,
66, 68–69, 70, 71

Mother Goddess religion, 110

mothers: gentle mother (Quán Thế Âm),
102, 105, 108; particular love, 102,
110, 111, 116, 118, 119; universal love,
102, 110, 116, 118, 120; Vietnamese
Mother's Day, 101, 115, 120, 148

Mulian, 101, 116, 120, 147, 173n3

Mulian's mother: figure of, 110;
liberation, 101, 103, 115; role of
sangha saving, 112; Vu Lan, 19, 104,
113

grandparent altars, 129; at home, 99, 129; home-making, 6; liberation, 48, 153; line between lay and monastic, 76; Mahayana traditions of, 46; male and female monastics, 57; material comforts threats to sincerity of, 68; meditation, 50, 79; merit-making activities, 52; of mindfulness, 78, 88*fig*, 91, 114, 142, 143; multiple lineages, 5; never complete, 22; pluralism, 5, 6; Pure Land, 124, 146; relying on other-power, 74–75; transnational, 120; vernacular, 9. *See also* Buddhist practices; repentance; spiritual practices

Prairie Terrace, 138

precepts, 8

Pure Diamond, Brother, 55

Pure Land: absence from Western Buddhism, 10; attainable through practices of mindfulness, 78; Chinese Pure Land vs. Japanese Pure Land, 152, 159n26; cosmic realm, 7, 22, 77, 78, 124, 145; Mahayana Buddhism, 146; merit and, 129; monastery in Northern California, 77; other-power, 7, 74, 75; in the present moment, 78, 87, 124, 130; Pure Mind, 150; robes and, 62; sanctuary from society, 18; sidelined by Zen, 4; transform Gulf South into, 85, 87, 98, 151; whose labor transforms into, 74, 77, 85, 145; Zen-Pure Land union, 4, 7, 9, 75, 79, 150. *See also* Amitābha Buddha; rebirth into Pure Land

Pure Land in the making: Buddhist clergy, 45; forms of dwelling, 120; Gulf South, 17–19; monasticism

and merit, 50; monk-lay relations, 47; politics of, 98; practicing, 22

Pure Word, Master, 87, 89–90, 91, 140

Q

Quan Âm. *See* Quán Thế Âm

Quan Âm Nam Hải. *See* Quán Thế Âm

Quán Thế Âm: altar overseen by, 131; Buddhist celebration honoring, 94–96; digitized image of, 96; efficacious figure, 40; embodiment of compassion, 19, 109; as figure of universal love, 116; form of a female goddess and a male householder, 57; gaze directed to the living, 130; gentle mother, 102, 105, 108; invokes the transpacific, 107, 108; invoking the name of, 75, 107, 110, 122, 154; male converted into female, 154; other-power, 107; politics of recognition, 122; polymorphic nature of, 109; powers come from the margins of structures, 122; praying to, 149; resembles the Virgin Mary, 10; supernatural figure, 9, 109; unbound by hierarchical orderings, 110. *See also* bodhisattva; Eightfold Path; Kuan-Yin

Quán Thế Âm statues: Chùa Bồ Đề, 35–36*fig*; Florida monastery, 108–9, 131, 142; in the Gulf South, 72; Gulf South temples, 112; Hồng Ân Monastery, 101; Louisiana temple, 108; main altar usually features, 78; Mississippi temple, 107; monastery in Alabama, 71; outdoors and in the worship hall,

Quán Thế Âm statues (*continued*) 105–6, 121–22; portable, 131; Vạn Minh Pagoda, 92, 95; Vietnamese spaces, 14

R

racial segregation, 5, 23, 24, 28
racial triangulation, 24
racialization, 6, 14. *See also* citizenship
rebirth into Pure Land: celestial realm, 77; chanting sutras, 125; intention, 74, 124; liberation, 128; released from hell, 100; samsara, 51; transferring merit, 52. *See also* Pure Land
recruitment of monks: board members, 65, 169n42; challenges, 46; for Chùa Bồ Đề, 33; from Houston, 20; by lay Buddhists, 45, 47–48, 149; sincerity, 47; from Vietnam, 69–70
refuge: bowing, 140; ceremony, 109; intention, 4, 66, 79; lay followers, 46, 48; Sangha, 7, 47; taking, 4, 46, 48, 62, 66, 79, 140
refugee: as "freedom fighters," 16; identity, 17; origins, 22; settlement of, 26, 29
regeneration, 19, 148–50, 153, 154
religious freedom, 30, 33, 149
religious pluralism, 6, 11, 14, 16, 125, 152
renunciation, 48, 58, 60, 102
renunciation of communism, 68
repentance: bowing, 140–41, 142, 143, 144, 145; ceremony, 142, 144; harnessing, 5; practices, 19, 140–42, 144; prayers, 125; Repentance Ritual of the Emperor of Liang, 144; rituals, 144; services, 79. *See also* practices

Repentance Ritual of the Emperor of Liang, 144
rhizomes: hidden, 149, 155; lotus, 21; spread of Buddhism, 34–35, 44, 146; structure, 143
rituals: acquiring merit, 51; action, 50, 51, 52, 125; activities, 14, 51, 133, 145; for addressing ghosts, 127, 128, 130, 133–34, 135; of bowing, 142; ethics of hospitality, 126; gesture (mudra), 133; honor those lost, 43; items, 3, 82; legend of Mulian, 19; liberation, 19, 84, 111, 113, 153; of lighting incense, 146–47, 177n3; of purification, 87; purity of women, 19, 119; purposes, 57; renunciation, 102; repentance, 19, 144; ritual labor of liberation, 5, 113; settings, 65; specialists, 62, 136*fig*, 137, 140, 145; in temples, 31, 32; transformation, 62, 127; work, 129
roses, 116, 117–19, 120

S

sangha: caretakers of ancestral spirits and ghosts, 130, 153; collective body of, 56, 62, 65; collective efforts of, 103, 104, 110, 113, 115; collective power of, 66, 112; definition of, 61; dharma work, 130; females in, 56–57; in the Gulf South, 46, 66, 67, 115, 128; harmony, 46, 47, 54, 66, 79, 153; honors ancestral time, 120, 121; importance of food in gathering, 86; laymen and laywomen, 46, 61, 65, 66; material threat to, 55; maternal imagery links, 102; meditation detached from, 50; and merit, 18, 114, 129; monk-lay relations, 60, 66, 70, 71; monks leaving to pursue education, 69; official, 87; Oriental Monk, 71; rites to liberate spirits, 134, 153; the role of, 176n23; service to, 124, 143; sincerity of monks, 67; social body of, 79; support for, 105

Sangha (bowing), 62

Sangha (intention), 4, 79

Sangha (refuge), 7, 47, 140

self-power, 7, 9, 74, 75, 108

setting the cornerstone, 86–87

settler colonialism, 126, 134, 138, 139, 140

Shakyamuni Buddha, 7, 48, 85, 101, 115, 155. *See also* Buddha, historical

shaving the head, 47, 57, 61–62, 66

Soka Gakkai, 149, 150

souvenirs, 84, 101

spaces of worship: formal, 5, 6; Pure Land tradition located in networks, 146; sites of sociability and memory, 5. *See also* collective spaces of worship

spiritual labor: activities, 91; copying lines from the sutra, 51; different ideals, 58; forms of, 75, 77; Hurricane Katrina, 35–41; institutionalization of Buddhism, 54; merit, 76, 77; of ordained monks, 89; valuing, 78

spiritual practices: are mobilized, 7; ethnic, 10; foreignness of, 145; mindfulness, 91; and political circumstances, 126; refugee identity, 17; rhizomes, 149; superstitious, 8; transforming, 148. *See also* practices

staying Vietnamese, 6, 44, 152

support for temples: invisible merit economy, 50; jeopardizes, 67; merit, 52, 53, 55; in New Orleans, 99; sangha, 112

Suzuki, D. T., 49

T

temples: attended by compatriot Buddhists, 148; building of, 149; communal cooking and eating, 65; donations, 82, 105, 112; establishment of, 149, 153; expenses for maintaining, 68; Freedom and Heritage Flag, 14; ghosts and, 128, 133–34; and Hurricane Katrina relief, 40, 43; labor in tending to, 71, 77; and living and deceased mothers, 117; money flows through, 54, 82; monk's temple, 45–46; more temples than monks, 45, 69; in New Orleans, 20, 34, 99, 150; organizational structures of, 34; people made themselves into American citizens, 33; performances of filial piety, 120; political sites, 5; practice Buddhism at home, 99; practice organized around liberation, 153; racial safety zones, 18; "sitting around" in meditation, 76; spread of, 44; worship, 5, 6. *See also* worship halls

temples in the Gulf South: Chùa Bồ Đề, 36*fig*; few temples and Vietnamese Buddhists, 60; Quán Thế Âm statues, 106; spread of, 17, 21, 44, 146; support for, 67; Vietnamese Freedom and Heritage Flag, 11; Vu Lan in, 119

terms of address, 64

Thailand: Buddhist merit, 51, 52; Muslims in, 178n23; sangha in, 87; Thai monks in Britain, 169n26; Theravada Buddhism prevails, 8, 51, 159n27, 159n28; US funded Buddhist education in, 16; women called "nuns," 57

Thanh Từ, Thích, 150

Theravada Buddhism, 8, 51, 57, 61, 159n27, 159n28

Thích Bồ Đề. *See* Bồ Đề, Thích

Thích Đạo Quang. *See* Đạo Quang, Thích

Thích Mãn Giác. *See* Mãn Giác, Thích

Thích Nhất Hạnh. *See* Nhất Hạnh, Thích

Thích Thanh Từ. *See* Thanh Từ, Thích

Thích Thiên-Ân. *See* Thiên-Ân, Thích

Thích Tịnh Từ. *See* Tịnh Từ, Thích

Thích Trí Hiền. *See* Trí Hiền, Thích

Thích Viên Giác. *See* Viên Giác, Thích

Thiên-Ân, Thích, 3, 4, 31, 116

Three Jewels: bowing, 140; five precepts, 46, 168n6; initiation, 48; intention, 4, 66; taking refuge in, 7, 47, 62, 79, 140, 157n6

Tibetan Buddhism, 10, 69, 149, 150, 151

Tịnh Từ, Thích, 3–4, 31, 40, 154–55

Tran Van Khoat, 26

transpacific: connected to Gulf South, 25, 135, 153; crossings, 108, 123; lineage, 62; networks, 5, 23, 85, 123; Quán Thế Âm invokes, 107; ties, 147, 155

Trí Hiền, Thích, 31, 32

two-Buddhism model, 9–10

Tylor, Edward Burnett, 126

U

Ullambana, 101, 120. *See* Vu Lan

Unification of Buddhist Organizations, 16–17

universal love, 120

US naval ship, 107

V

Vạn Hạnh Buddhist Center, 38, 43

Vạn Minh Pagoda, 74, 91–92, 93, 94, 97

Vesak, 13*fig*, 43, 132, 161n68

Viên Giác, Thích, 144

Vietnam War, 5, 15. *See also* American War

Vietnamese American Young Leaders Association (VAYLA), 37

Vietnamese Buddhism: Buddhism as a global religion, 155; expressions of spirituality, 152; lack of global recognition, 150; modern roots, 8; place of heritage in, 115; pluralizing, 149; racialization of, 14, 18; regeneration of, 148, 149, 150; social body of, 87; struggles for control, autonomy, and visibility, 21; transmission to the Gulf South, 14; Zen-Pure Land union, 4, 7, 9

Vietnamese Buddhism in the Gulf South: made and unmade, 153; making, 155; plurality of, 112; politics of, 5; propelling, 8; shaping, 9; spread of, 34

Vietnamese Buddhist Congregation of Mississippi, 39

Vietnamese Catholics: Gulf South, 38, 44; home altars, 129; New Orleans, 30, 35; scholarly interest in, 6; spiritual center for, 26

Vietnamese Freedom and Heritage Flag, 11, 12, 67, 113, 120, 147

Vietnamese United Buddhist Churches of America, 73, 171n5

Vĩnh Minh Diên, 75.

violence of statelessness, 135

Vipassana, 10

Võ Tá Hân, 73

Võ Văn Tường, 14

Vu Huu Chuong, 29

Vu Lan: celebrated differently in Vietnam, 115; compatriot Buddhists, 113; conducted in Vietnamese, 116; conveys contradictory messages, 119; debt to their mothers, 104; expensive promotion of, 111; familistic traditioning, 148; few children attend, 121; and filial piety, 101, 116, 119, 121, 147; in the Gulf South, 111, 112, 115; laity presents monastics with gifts, 114; large numbers of participants, 13fig; legend of Mulian, 19, 104, 110, 147; meaning of, 115; mother figure, 102, 111, 113; navigate family obligations, 102; red rose, 116; solemn ceremony, 100; spiritual powers are at their peak, 103; Ullambana, 13fig, 101, 120, 173n3;

variations of, 149; Vietnamese Mother's Day, 101, 115, 120, 148; Vu Lan Sutra, 113; widening the audience, 11; worship hall offers refuge during, 81

W

West Bank. See New Orleans.

Western Paradise, 75. See also Pure Land

worship halls: building, 82–83, 86, 88, 89–90, 98–99; concrete foundation of, 95; emptiness, 81; prominence in, 85; raise the, 89; spaces of, 13; transpacific network, 85. See also temples

Z

Zen: blended with Tibetan Buddhism and Vipassana, 10; Bodhidharma, 78, 144; Buddhist center, 32; gray robes, 62; Japanese, 168n17, 178n23; masters, 3, 31, 75, 91, 149; meditation, 78–79, 157n1; practice, 154; and Pure Land are parallel practices, 75; Pure Land less authentic, 69; self-power, 7; sidelining Pure Land, 4; teachings, 51; traditions, 9; translator, 49

Zen–Pure Land union, 4, 7, 9, 75, 79, 150